Justice and
Consequences

Justice and Consequences

John P. Conrad
American Justice Institute

LexingtonBooks
D.C. Heath and Company
Lexington, Massachusetts
Toronto

Library of Congress Cataloging in Publication Data

Conrad, John Phillips, 1913-
  Justice and consequences.

  1. Criminal justice, Administration of—United States—Addresses,
essays, lectures. 2. Corrections—United States—Addresses, essays, lectures.
3. Prisons—United States—Addresses, essays, lectures.
I. Title.
HV8138.C644   346'.973   78-348
ISBN 0-669-02190-3

Published simultaneously in Canada

Printed in the United States of America

International Standard Book Number: 0-669-02190-3

Library of Congress Catalog Card Number: 78-348

*For my daughter
Louise Conrad Stout
who has used friendship
as the best penology of all*

Contents

Foreword

Judge David L. Bazelon

I first met John Conrad when he was preparing his international survey of corrections, *Crime and Its Correction*, which concludes: "[M]ore than most human institutions, corrections needs a vision to work toward. . . . The first step toward the attainment of that vision is to reopen the dialogue on the great issues."[1] This book helps make that dialogue possible by exposing the comfortable myths of corrections: the myth of purpose and the myth of criminal justice without social justice.

Perhaps the only enduring principle of corrections is the myth of purpose. Since the advent of nineteenth-century English utilitarianism, our society has evaluated correctional practices in terms of overarching social goals. But we live in the kingdom of shifting ends. The god of rehabilitation was overthrown by deterrence, whose reign is now threatened by the so-called new ideal—incapacitation.[2] The tragedy of this succession lies not only in the narrowing of our social vision but also in our inattention to the morality of our means.

Those of us who have visited prisons have encountered the abyss that divides practice from prescription. Our society has never made the necessary effort—the investment of energy and resources—to test the rehabilitative ideal. Nor is it likely that we will be willing or able to incapacitate enough of the population to guarantee public safety. We devise nibbling programs in tribute to each new correctional god, but to characterize programs as incomplete does not mean they are without pernicious effects. Longer sentences, for example, may not deter crime, but they will exacerbate overcrowding in prisons.

Conrad trains his focus on the human means of our shifting ends, on the ontology rather than the teleology of corrections. Once he dispels the myth of purpose, we are left with the harsh reality of prisons themselves. Correctional justice begins not with evanescent social goals but with humane treatment. The built-in brutality and dehumanizing nature of overcrowded, mammoth institutions must concern us not only because these conditions disserve the correctional gods but because they do not comport with human decency.

Assuming *arguendo* that incapacitation can lower recidivism rates, these statistics cannot be the sole measure of value in corrections. It is amoral, if not immoral, to make cost-benefit equations our lodestar. Neither the costs nor the benefits of providing or withholding vital human services can be objectified. Every human being is entitled to physical necessities, medical and mental-health services, and a measure of privacy.

David L. Bazelon is senior circuit judge of the U.S. Court of Appeals for the District of Columbia Circuit.

Beyond the elements of decency, prisoners should be given the opportunity to make their time in prison something other than dead time. They need programs to provide relief from boredom and idleness, which are surely among the greatest cruelties in our prisons. For those that are willing, there should be tools available for self-improvement—libraries, classes, physical and mental activities. Finally, decency and morality should inform structural considerations in the correctional system; decentralized, community-based programs offer promise for avoiding the inhumanity we expect from massive central prisons. As Conrad notes, morality must shape prison architecture as well.

This book serves a vital need. It helps return our focus from the passing gods of "purpose" to the futility and frustration of prison life. But there is an even more destructive myth that clouds corrections and criminal justice—the hidden assumption that criminal justice can be achieved without social justice. I agree with John Rawls that "justice is the first virtue of social institutions."[3] We will never achieve the goals of corrections or the criminal law in the absence of social justice. As long as we direct our attention and resources exclusively toward the criminal and correctional apparatus, we will be reacting to, and not acting on, our social problems. We cannot reasonably expect judges, correctional officers, or prison administrators—the janitors of our criminal-justice system—to cure our social ills.

Violent street crime, which causes the greatest alarm, is a fever that society cannot ignore. But the path of total reliance on incapacitation or punishment is a superhighway leading to a cow path. In a nutshell, these instruments of repression are doomed to failure if we refuse to deal with the conditions that breed crime.

There are those who say that we cannot list with certainty the causes of criminal conduct. I believe that this is both true and irrelevant. Crime is not a simple chemical reaction but a complex social phenomenon. We cannot expect to isolate and identify each factor in the social web that envelops crime. What we can and must do is acknowledge those social and economic conditions that accompany crime and that make criminal behavior more likely, if not certain.

One clue we have is that a viable family structure is crucial for social integration. A child's sense of roots and values begins with his family. We are learning that the childrearing practices of the poor do not differ markedly from those of the affluent. But poor parents have relatively less time for their families; they are overwhelmed with the struggle for survival. A parent who cannot put food on the table cannot convey to a child a sense of order, purpose, or self-esteem. The National Academy of Sciences Advisory Committee on Child Development found that "the degree and rate of family disruption increase[s] with the degree of economic deprivation and urbanization. . . . Concomitant and consistent with changes in the structure of the family are changes in . . . the well-being of children. Children growing up in low-income families are particularly susceptible to physical, intellectual, emotional and social damage."[4]

These problems are exacerbated in the streets. Overcrowded slums are not a place for a child to develop a sense of his own worth. Our experience with delinquents and criminals is that they feel cut off from society and insensitive to other human beings. In the boilerplate language of presentence reports, the slum dweller is labeled "street-wise." This means that he has the cunning and the emotional armor needed to stay alive in the streets. None of the providers of treatment services—psychiatrists, psychologists, or social workers—can strip this armor and implant middle-class sensibilities into those who have lived in the slums twenty-four hours a day. Sentencing schemes and correctional programs will hardly reverse this social process.

The child of social neglect will grow into an adult faced with economic hardship. The statistical correlation between crime and unemployment confirms what common sense tells us. Some years ago, Washington witnessed a huge surge in theft in the month of August. I asked the chief of the police robbery squad for his speculations about the reason for the crime increase. "I don't have to speculate," he said. "I know the cause. August was a wet month. The rain left great numbers of day laborers and construction workers jobless. Whenever it rains several days in a row, there's no work, no money, and we know we are in for a lot of trouble."

In 1967, the President's Commission on Law Enforcement and the Administration of Justice found that "the life histories of most offenders are case studies in the ways in which social and economic factors contribute to crime. . . . The task of corrections therefore includes . . . change of the community and its institutions."[5] But politicians, academics, the press, and the public have opted for the nostrum of repression rather than confronting poverty, discrimination, and ignorance. Our leaders pander to the public's demand for easy answers and call on the hired hands of the criminal-justice system to sweep the social debris under the rug.

In 1930, a young official in the Justice Department, testifying on the need for better crime statistics, told an appropriations subcommittee of the House of Representatives that one subject "that would be interesting in connection with crime statistics is the relation to crime of unemployment, of disease, and of the various items which make up the economic life of a country."[6] The official was J. Edgar Hoover. Today, fifty years later, it is time—long past time, in fact—to confront the relationship between crime and the accident of birth.

John Conrad has indeed made a significant contribution here to the "dialogue on the great issues." He makes it abundantly clear that it would be easy for us to concede the inevitability of social injustice and find the

serenity to accept it. The far harder task is to feel its intolerability and seek
the strength to change it.

Notes

1. J. Conrad, *Crime and Its Correction* 304 (1965).

2. See, for example, A. von Hirsch, *Doing Justice* (1976).

3. J. Rawls, *A Theory of Justice* 3 (1971).

4. National Research Council, *Toward a National Policy for Children
and Families* 38-39 (1976).

5. President's Commission on Law Enforcement and the Administration of Justice, *Task Force Report: Corrections* 2.7 (1967).

6. Quoted in S. Ungar, FBI 361 (1976).

Preface and
Acknowledgments

In the days when the San Quentin gas chamber was still in use, a curious deception was practiced. The procedures for execution provided for three levers in the mechanism that released cyanide into the vat of acid to initiate a chemical reaction that ended the life of the condemned prisoner. Only one of the levers controlled the sack of cyanide; the others had no sack attached. Three guards pulled the levers simultaneously at the warden's signal, none of them knowing which lever was the operant. A similar practice is often used by firing squads; some of the rifles issued to members of the team are loaded with blank cartridges.

It is easy to deride these subterfuges. The participants in an execution cannot so readily relieve themselves of responsibility for killing the prisoner. No stretch of the moral imagination is needed to prove that whenever a man is shot, gassed, burned in an electric chair, or hanged, the whole society shares the responsibility. For many, that responsibility is willingly accepted. It is hard to see how the unwilling can expiate whatever guilt they feel. Nevertheless, that guilt haunts those of us who have worked as close to the gas chamber as I have.

The days when my duties included the regular interviewing of murderers admitted to condemned row are now far in the past, but I still have to tour jail tanks and maximum-security cellblocks. The momentous collision between what is and what ought to be that preoccupies the moral philosopher still strikes home for me. Confronted with the debris of social injustice, some horrified witnesses decide that all this ought not to be, that no social end is worth all this misery, and that prisons must be abolished. That position is dismissed as foolish sentimentality by those who are convinced that what is wrong with criminal justice is that it is not administered with sufficient severity to enough offenders.

Readers of these essays will sense my ambivalence. I know enough about prisons to say that at best they are unhappy places where tragedies are enacted every day. At worst, they are horrifying reversions to callous barbarism. I also know enough about prisoners to say that whatever the causes of crime, many prisoners are terrible men and women who deserve punishment and restraint. I conclude uneasily that for the foreseeable future we must make the best of our ugliest public institution, so discordant with life, liberty, and the pursuit of happiness. The prison penalizes all of us for our tolerance of social injustice. We can relieve the shame to some extent by making prisons as decent and humane as we can. We all have a long way to go toward such an end.

The key is to rid ourselves of our heritage of utilitarianism. That philosophy has governed the theory, if not the practice, of American penologists for the last two centuries. The assumptions of the utilitarian deny the criminal his standing as a person endowed with free will. Rather, he is thought to be helpless to do other than he did; the task of the penologist is to change him. Along with most of my colleagues, I used to accept the notion that our work was "people-changing," a phrase that has gone out of fashion. The people changer went about his work convinced that the criminal could not change himself unaided by the ministrations of professionals of many stripes.

Within this professionalism is the determinist view of the human condition. In these chapters I have been explicit about my belief that for most of the criminals under the control of criminal justice the choices open to the will were few and unsatisfactory. Our only hope is to enlarge the range of choice for those who are the victims of social injustice. The penologist cannot possibly reduce the prevalence of social injustice in the larger society, but there is much more that he can and should do in the domain assigned to him. He must begin with the tasks before him; he must convert the experience of social control into a situation in which choice is enlarged. That this can be done is without question; we have only to contrast the prisons of Scandinavia and the Low Countries with the typical American state prison to know what can be done when care replaces indifference.

We have to begin with the concept that a prisoner is still a citizen, although under restraint. Despite all the influences that have damaged his humanity, he must be treated as a citizen, a being endowed with free will. He is not the robot of determinism to be manipulated in the processes of people-changing. Isaiah Berlin reported what should be the final word on determinism in his affectionate essay on the Oxford philosopher, J.L. Austin. In the course of a seminar on moral problems, Austin muttered, *sotto voce*, to Berlin, "They all *talk* about determinism and say they believe in it. I've never met a determinist in my life, I mean a man who really believes in it as you and I believe that men are mortal. Have you?"[1] I have not—not even on condemned row, not even in the "hole" at any of the maximum-security institutions I have visited. Men and women will continue to choose. When the choice ranges widely, few will choose to harm others. When the choice is narrow, rage and necessity will force the choice of evil actions. We have to make it possible for those who are so constricted to choose good things—even in prison.

Acknowledgments

My career has been spent on the margins of penology and of the academy. It has put me squarely in the middle, displeasing the penologists and the academicians. I have been fortunate to have had many opportunities to say what I think. I find myself so often in disagreement when listening to others saying what they think that I have decided to put some of my essays into a more permanent frame than in scattered journals and collections of readings. I hope that I am contributing to thought about an ugly and persistent problem. For much too long our decisions about criminal justice have been governed by tradition and by the revulsion we feel, either for the criminal himself or for the places in which we lock him up.

My appreciation must first go to Margaret Zusky and Carolyn Yoder of Lexington Books for making this book possible and for tactfully prodding me into the steps necessary for converting photocopies into a manuscript. This appreciation is much more than the customary grace note among the acknowledgments. Without them, this book would still be a project that I would get around to in a future cluttered with all my other procrastinations.

Acknowledgments to the editors and other sponsors of these chapters are sprinkled throughout this book. I am deeply appreciative, not only for the formal permission to reprint but also for the chance they gave me to speak my piece in the first place.

To Simon Dinitz, my colleague for many years, I offer my thanks for allowing me to publish our joint chapter, "The State's Strongest Medicine," and also for his unique kind of counsel, a blend of learning, common sense, and a vision of the future that might be.

Finally, the conventional words of appreciation will hardly suffice for my wife, Charlotte. She has tolerated my sequestration at the typewriter on too many occasions when we could have been enjoying life together.

Note
    1. Sir Isaiah Berlin, "Austin and the Early Beginnings of Oxford Philosophy," in Isaiah Berlin, ed., *Essays on J.L. Austin* (Oxford: Clarendon Press, 1973), p. 15.

1 To Lift the Utilitarian Fog

What is the word for that sound—a cry, a groan, a bellow? It comes from the middle of the Aged and Infirm Ward, loud and wordless. Seated in an old wheelchair, naked to the waist, diapered around his middle, the old man half-rises as he utters this terrible noise at intervals during my brief visit. There is a puddle of urine under the chair. A prisoner-orderly mops it up. It is a task he must perform many times a day.

The Aged and Infirm Ward is an annex to the main, maximum-security prison. It is crowded with old men serving out their lives for crimes that have long been forgotten. There are a few younger men; they are prisoners with chronic diseases or men who have been disabled by stabbing or gunshot. The eye perceives a vaguely hospital-like ambience. The beds are white enamel, and in the summer heat there are no blankets over the sheets. But there is a smell of stale urine, as though the whole building had been soaked in it for a long time. Flies and mosquitoes flit in through the open windows.

A group of prisoners crowded around me, a stranger. Perhaps I was an inspector who could do something for them. Perhaps I was a lawyer who might take up a cause. "This goes on all day and all night. He pisses and shits on the floor. He is not in this world. Why do we have to live with this? How would *you* like it? Can't you do something?"

There was nothing I could do, except to capture this scene in my memory for possible testimony in court many months in the future. I looked up the old man's file. Now approaching eighty, he had been committed to that prison in the late 1940s for murder in the first degree. No details of the offense. No relatives or friends; apparently no one had ever visited him. There had been some desultory correspondence a year or so before between a prison-department official and his opposite number in the department of mental health concerning the feasibility of removing the old man from prison to a state hospital. It led to agreement that he was probably as well off where he was as he would be in a hospital or in a nursing home.

There the matter stands. The old man has been in his present condition for many years; it is not clear from the files when he last functioned as an ambulatory prisoner. There is no reason to suppose that he will die soon from natural causes. Most of his fellow prisoners are old and inured to the indecencies of prison life. They are unlikely to harm him, much as they resent his presence among them. Perhaps some of them can foresee their own

1

decline into this helplessness. They blame the impersonal system, the system they know they cannot successfully attack. Sooner or later, most prisoners resign themselves to a situation they cannot hope to change.

Scenes of this kind come readily to mind as I review the thirty-five years that I have worked in and around prisons and jails. Worse tales can be told. Young men butchered in knife attacks over sex; young men shot to death as they clambered over concertina wire in desperation to escape. Murders, assaults, and rapes are frequent, and they remind the observer and the prisoner alike of the danger and fears that saturate the prison community. The consciousness of the prisoner—and of the guards, too—is lowered to an obsession with the physical self and the need for protection. To the apprehensions that haunt the prisoner throughout his waking hours, there is more to be added: the tedium of make-work and idleness, waiting for something to happen, the indifference of the officials, the filth that accumulates for daily removal. It is true that most prisoners can accommodate to all these ills and more. No one has proved that the harm done by a stretch in an American prison is irreversible. Nevertheless, this is a scene of misery, and the years wasted in it will not be restored.

No malign fate ordained this wretchedness, as might be said of life in the urban slums from which most of these prisoners have come. This system for the infliction of suffering has been deliberately created by the state. It is because of the calculated planning of the harm done in prisons that there is an increasing sense of outrage about what the state does on behalf of its citizens.

Every day the prison official must violate the basic precept of a good man's life: he must do to others as he would not be done by, he must preside over or participate in harming his fellows. Alone among the institutions of the state, the prison and the criminal-justice system of which it is a part must administer pain to citizens.

For the legislator, the judge, and the moral philosopher who offers them guidance, the harm can be abstracted from these dreary realities. Arguments can be couched in the brisk language of logical analysis. We can speak of the proportionality of sanctions to the act of the offender and its nature and quality. We can switch to the elegant Latin that still speckles legal discourse and distinguish between *mala in se* and *mala prohibita*. Risks and experiences can be calculated with all the appearances of science. Nice points can be made of the relative culpability of the offender and the extent to which it may be allowed to aggravate or mitigate the punishment to be imposed. The language is bloodless and odorless—so many years in an old and overcrowded prison for this offense, more for more serious crimes, less for an offense less serious.

At a particularly remote level of abstraction there runs a debate over the reasons for punishment, the justifications for administering it in the forms that we use, and the theories that lie behind these reasons and these justifications. For the practical administrator—including myself and the colleagues with whom I spent most of my working career—the debate between the retributivists and the utilitarians had an unreal quality, rather like the disputes between the Big-endians and the Little-endians in Jonathan Swift's Lilliput. It was—and still is—much more urgent to persuade the legislature to provide funds by which minimum standards of decency and safety can be maintained than it is to settle on the general justifying aim of punishment. Whatever the reason for establishing a prison, it exists as a reality that the official cannot fundamentally alter. Unlike the medical practitioner who is enjoined, ''in the first place, do no harm,'' the prison official knows that harm is what he must do. His best hope is that he shall do no unnecessary harm.

When I first signed on at San Quentin, we were all utilitarians, although not many of us—myself included—could have given a satisfactory definition of that term. Some of us believed that we were on the threshold of a new profession, a discipline derived from Freud, that could administer rehabilitation to criminal offenders. Others supposed that San Quentin was protecting the public by locking away hundreds of dangerous men. Less hopeful, still others reasoned that the experience of incarceration, fairly and rationally administered, would so intimidate the prisoners that they would refrain from crime for the rest of their lives. It was quite possible to combine all these views and speak of the multiple and conflicting purposes of corrections. In those now-distant days, not many of us would have accepted the idea that all these aims—if they were truly aims at all—were secondary to the grim process of retribution.

If this issue had been raised with me in those early and hopeful days at San Quentin, I think I would have seen the point, but I would have wondered why it mattered. Our assignment was to devise ways of rehabilitating these unfortunate men whose present circumstances were obviously and painfully the working of retributive justice. Thirty years later I see that all these abstractions matter a great deal. The criminal-justice system must administer suffering to criminals, some of it unavoidable, some of it needless. The rarefied dispute between the retributivists and the utilitarians winds through a conceptual labyrinth at the center of which we may find principles by which a prison can be managed without disgrace to the state.

Justice and Justification

The idea of justice is older than Hammurabi. Justice is easier to define in its breach than in its essence. We are quick to recognize injustice when we see it, either when it is a prevailing condition in society, as it was in Nazi Ger-

many, or when it is an action by a bigoted official or a bureaucrat misinter-
preting a regulation. When we conclude that a citizen did not get what he
deserved, we brush against the problems of deciding what is a citizen's due
and by what criteria we can settle this matter. Philosophers have wrestled
with these issues for thousands of years, and they are still unsettled. It is not
for me to rush into this thicket to clear it out. I shall limit this consideration
to the avoidance of injustice; I believe that the primacy given to the
utilitarian justification of punishment inevitably leads to serious individual
injustices. The maxim of the English courts, "justice must not only be done
but it must be seen to be done," is applicable. We can now see in the
statistics of penology that injustice is done when utilitarian decisions are
made, and much more injustice would be done if the criminal justice system
followed faithfully the doctrines of the utilitarians.

Because the processes of punishment are ugly and inconsistent with so
many of the values of our culture, we have welcomed the comforting alternative that utilitarianism offers. It suggests the antiseptic and impersonal
processes of quarantine and the cure of contagious disease. That set of
pretensions does not comfort the criminal nor does it delude his keepers,
but it resounds well in the disputations of philosophers and social scientists.

The claims of utilitarianism have become too eroded by statistics to help
manage the criminal-justice system. We do not know how to cure criminals.
The numerous efforts to discover programs that might have a predictable
rehabilitative effect have come to naught.[1] We know that a large number of
criminals can be successfully intimidated, but another very large number
cannot, and the latter includes some of the most vicious men with whom
criminal justice must deal. It is obvious that those who are confined in
prison are incapacitated from committing crimes against the general public.
But to incapacitate a number significant enough to reduce crime we must
predict future criminal behavior for many more offenders who would not in
fact continue their criminal careers. The net that we must spread to catch all
these offenders will be so wide as to expand the prison population beyond
all reason.[2] We still lack any but the most speculative evidence that potential
criminals are deterred from committing crimes by the spectacle of the
punishments administerd to actual offenders.[3] Not only are we aware from
gathering the data of criminal justice that we cannot achieve the goals of
utilitarian justice, but there is also reason to suppose that if we did we
would commit serious injustices. It is time that we acknowledged
retributivism for what it is, a necessary consequence of a criminal act.

The Primacy of Retributivism

Retributivism allows the offender his standing as a person capable of making choices between good and evil. He chose to commit a crime. He is then

punished without manipulation by those who would make his reform a precondition to his release. In a retributivist system, there is no need to predict his future behavior, which may or may not be criminal in the later course of his life. His punishment is determined by the seriousness of his crime and what is considered a just desert for those who commit it.

If he chooses, he may make the occasion of his punishment a framework for self-improvement. That is his affair, as it is for any citizen, but if the offender is in prison the state must make available to him what he cannot get for himself.

If his punishment is incarceration, he will be incapacitated from the commission of further crimes while he remains in custody. After his release, his identity will be known to the police, and many offenders find it too risky, too inconvenient to commit further crimes. Some criminals will be intimidated by the experience of imprisonment or even by the conviction of a crime with a lesser sentence, but society cannot count on this result, nor can the optimum extent of intimidation be gauged for any criminal.

But we cannot separate from the retributivist actions of the criminal-justice system all these secondary consequences, even if we wished to. Where benefits beyond the operation of retribution are gained, both society and the criminal are gainers. Society being what it is, and human nature being what it is—especially when subjected to the enormous stress of punishment—no one should count on the systematic achievement of these benefits.

In what I have proposed here, I have come close to the accommodation of retributivism with utilitarian aims that culminates H.L.A. Hart's lucid analysis in *Punishment and Responsibility*.[4] Hart arrived at a model of a retributivist theory of criminal justice that allowed a place for the utilitarian objective of crime prevention by recognizing that the processes of punishment can contribute toward that goal. I will argue that the administration of retributive justice cannot avoid preventing crime, although that should not be and is not its justifying aim. Because of the inefficiency of criminal justice, many criminals—perhaps most criminals—fail to receive a just desert for their offenses. Nevertheless, those who are punished as they deserve will be restrained and may be intimidated. Jeremy Bentham's famous "felicific calculus" will be applied so far as it can have any application to offenders under the control of the state. The intimidating sequence of arrest, trial, conviction, and penal control either in prison or in the community is inseparable from the punishment that the criminal must undergo. Some are intimidated for the rest of their lives, but others find that they can take whatever the state can impose on them and come back for more. Social institutions, like the human beings who design and manage them, do what they can. Uniform success is not within their conceivable grasp.

The Rewards of Punishment

Retributivism is expressed in a system that administers just deserts for the commission of crimes. It is necessary to trace the idea of desert to its source—the rules that make order possible in any society. Most citizens obey the rules, both written and unwritten, by which they live without thinking twice about the penalties for not obeying them. Those who disobey the rules must be penalized for two reasons. First, for those crimes that are universally condemned in every culture and throughout history—murder, rape, robbery, and theft—the community's sense of outrage must be expressed. Those who live by the law and rely on it for protection generally feel revulsion and hatred for these acts and those who commit them. Whether they can accept it or not, most prisoners sense the hatred that the public feels toward them. This hatred is lively enough to motivate the severe punishment of those who commit these ancient crimes of blood, lust, and rapine. It is notable that even in our well-informed society we do not hate the white-collar criminal sufficiently to send him to prison under any but the most exceptional circumstances, and then for short terms, despite the immense damage he usually does to the structure of trust on which we all rely. It is not always easy for a twentieth-century observer of the law to come to terms with Sir James Fitzjames Stephen, that implacable nineteenth-century judge, but I do not question the validity of his aphorism that "[t]he criminal law stands to the passion of revenge in much the same relation as marriage to the sexual appetite."[5] In spite of the disapproval that philosophers from the time of Plato express for revenge as a motivation, it is still an unabated justification for the criminal law. Those who commit infamous crimes deserve revenge, so far as the general public is concerned, and those who doubt the strength of this conviction must explain why undue leniency in sentencing is excoriated as a denial of the rights of the victim.

The second reason for retributive punishment is the general need to preserve the integrity of the law. No rule can survive if there is no penalty for not observing it. That penalty, when it is imposed, is the desert of the convicted offender. It is here that a good deal of heavy weather can be made in the definition and justification of a system of desert. Feinberg's interesting essay, "Justice and Personal Desert" explores all the ramifications and much of the relevant literature on this topic, and I follow his reasoning in most respects.[6] What justifies the attachment of a desert to a rule is the essential question. In his essay on the "new retributivism," Bedau asks if it is necessary to assign punishments for the violation of rules.[7] In the case of crimes, he asks, why would it not be enough to accuse, to denounce, to blame, or otherwise to cast public obloquy on the offender without going to the length of punishing him? Bedau asserts that the retibutivist cannot respond that punishment will prevent crime, because crime prevention is a goal for the future; the retributivist justifies punishment because of the crime, which is in the past. Crime prevention cannot be the justification of the punishment that is a good in itself, the sufficient consequence of a rule violation. So, why is denunciation not enough retribution?

The retributivist's reply must rest partly on the traditions of the system that has for centuries responded to crime by administering punishments of ferocious severity. That severity was partly revenge—as Sir James Stephen aptly put it—but it was also a strenuous denunciation of those who crack the public order. It is only during the last two centuries that the law has abstained from the death penalty for offenses now regarded as minor misdemeanors. And even during the last half-century we have seen a drift away from the use of incarceration for the lesser property offenses. When I was a functionary at San Quentin, it was common to encounter forgers whose offense was the signing of a bad check to pay for a Saturday-night bar bill or petty thieves who were serving a year or so for trivial shoplifting larcenies. Valuable as these men often were in providing cheap white-collar services to the prison administration, they are no longer to be encountered in most American penal facilities. Surely we are becoming less severe with criminals, but we have not yet gone so far as to agree that a ceremony of denunciation would be sufficient reinforcement of the rules or adequate reprobation. The decision to incarcerate is essential to the denunciation of a grave crime; the combination of denunciation and imprisonment is embedded in our traditions as a necessary consequence of wrongdoing. We shall not rid ourselves of our prisons by limiting retribution to verbal expressions of disapproval.

This is a society that has relied on the prison as the linchpin of the criminal-justice system for many generations. Before the modern prison came into being, justice was a monstrous exercise of cruelty, as Foucault has forcibly reminded us.[8] The break away from those cruelties was generally applauded; the work of Beccaria, Howard, and Bentham encountered surprisingly little dissent, except from a few worried judges who feared for the public safety if the death penalty for theft was removed from the law.

But the answer to Bedau must be more than an appeal to patience with the trends of history and the processes of social evolution. An ordered society must depend for social control on a system of rewards and punishments. It may be possible that some day citizens will work to produce goods and to achieve excellence without expectations of personal gain and improvement of status, but we have not yet seen a society in which such selflessness is a norm, in spite of the prophecies of Karl Marx and his followers. It may also be that peaceful and lawful conduct of all citizens can be assured without attaching consequences of a punitive nature for those who violate the criminal law. So far, not even the most-law-abiding nations, not even the enviable Dutch and Danes, have provided us with such an example. Certainly Americans are far from such an achievement.

We live in a society in which consequences set the limits on what may and may not be done. The models of which conventional moral philosophers, economists, jurists, and most common men and women approve call for a state in which merit is rewarded, effort and gain are closely related, and avenues are always open to those who wish to improve their circumstances. Such a society must provide adverse consequences for those who infringe on the rights of others. Any society in which a predictable pattern of such consequences did not exist would be an intolerable anarchy, nasty and brutish in the sense that we commonly refer to as Hobbesian. Order in this model of society depends on choice and free will. Citizens must have reasons to choose as they do if life is to be worth living.

That comfortable and just society, surely a utopia that never was, would not be crime-free, given the fallibility of mortal men and women and their passions and their weaknesses. However, the crimes committed in such a community could not be charged to social inequities. A walking tour of any state prison in America will remind the observant intruder of the immense distance this nation must transverse before it achieves such a just society. Perhaps as many as 80 percent of the people to be seen in these prisons come from the lowet socioeconomic status, a statistic that cannot be appreciated without quoting Hobbes on nastiness, brutishness, and anarchy. These prisoners are men and women who were born as losers to parents who were losers. Their choices have been restricted to passive acceptance of the miseries of poverty, with or without resort to narcotic anodynes or to engagement in the hustling life. From the loser's part of town, not many emerge into those sectors of society in which the range of choice widens. For the loser, one open path leads from the infant's crib to a cell in jail or prison. The adverse consequences that ensued from the crime he committed were inevitable; there was always trouble ahead. If it was not jail, it was the welfare with all its humiliations, or the life of meaningless loitering occasionally interrupted by bouts of casual employment.

"The System That Breeds These Crimes"

The critique by Marxist criminology, drawing on these tragic facts, is now obvious to the point of banality. Conventional criminologists have not always been able to accept the connections between the *lumpen* proletariat, from which Marx thought that thieves and cutthroats would be recruited, and our alarming experience with mounting crime rates.[9] It is this strange society of ours that is abnormal, not the people we send to prison. No other society in history has penalized failure so savagely, whether the failure was fault of the individual or ordained by the social structure.

In an article written for the *New York Tribune*, Marx made it clear that the punishment of criminals, as carried out in capitalist society, depended on the supposition that they enjoyed free will when their crimes were committed. That supposition was open to challenge. "Is there not a necessity," he wrote, "for deeply reflecting upon the alteration of a system that breeds these crimes, instead of glorifying the hangman who executes a lot of criminals to make room only for the supply of new ones?"[10]

To reflect on this spreading stain on American civilization with the perspective of 125 years is to confirm the validity of Marx's critique. After the Civil War a succession of economic miracles led Americans to conclude that we truly were a chosen people, destined to live in prosperity and harmony. Criminals were seldom the preoccupation of the comfortable classes. The issues that Marx raised in his *Tribune* column vanished from the public discourse. A century later, hard times, race conflict, and the increasingly rigid stratifiation of society have combined to transform Marx's mildly worded question into a strident polemic.

It does not follow that because Marx asked the right question that he had a solution that we can use. The inevitable revolution that Marx foresaw as the culmination of the historic struggle of the working masses is distant and dreaded by a people who have seen the terrible institutions that revolutionary movements have generated since Marx's time. Believers in a new dawn that will break at some foreseeable time as the inevitable result of the sufferings of the American working class and the contradictions of capitalism have an unrealistic perception of the political history of this country. Marx's critique was a necessary challenge to the established social order in every country. His solution and those of his followers cannot remedy our chronic social disarray.

The alternative answer is not for a criminologist to formulate. We can affirm that Marx was right, up to a point. Crime is overwhelmingly, although not exclusively,' the result of the contradictions inherent in a capitalist society beset with grave social and technological problems. We can and must say that the criminal-justice system is limited to moving criminals through a process that leads from crime to adjudication to punishment. It thereby asserts that wrong is wrong and must be punished. We cannot invest more meaning in this unwieldy but necessary process. It is evident that the deterrent effect is slight, that it reforms very few who are caught in it, and that it fails to intimidate many men and women who discover that the life of crime—even with the appalling conditions that prevail in our prisons—is preferable to the inanition of their neighbors.

What is to be done? The optimism that once infused American life with the faith that better things were always coming for everyone has faded. We have lost our way to that utopia in which conduct would be directed by social and economic rewards and punishments. The punishments are still there, although not as severe as they once were, but they are symbolically administered to only a fraction of all the citizens who violate the law. The rewards are out of sight for a very large class of society. A politics of bold rationality may yet return us to a course leading to true equality, with opportunity in sufficient supply to make a decent life possible for every citizen able to make an effort. Until that time comes, criminal justice has unfinished business from which its policy makers and practitioners have been distracted by their commitment to an impossible objective of crime prevention. Because we have all been utilitarians for so long, we suppose that there is a goal that we could reach if we were wise enough, well enough endowed with talent and resources, and well enough supported by an indifferent and often hostile public. We have accepted impossible responsibilities. Because we have been unable to accomplish these impossibilities, we have lost credit that we should never have sought. It is time to shed these absurd commitments.

The state must do what it can as well as it can. If the penal system has no goals, there are still duties that must be performed. Probation and other community controls of the offender must be carried out credibly and efficiently. The prisons and other incarcerative facilities must be managed in a lawful and safe manner. Failure in these respects is not permissible, and accountability for failures must be strict, a matter for executive and judicial intervention.

The direction of change in American society promises to make the discharge of these duties increasingly difficult. Twenty years ago, in an approximately full-employment economy, it was not unreasonable to assume that a prisoner minded to desist from crime could learn a trade while serving his term and expect to improve his circumstances to the extent that they would be preferable to a life of crime. It never was as simple as that, of course, but the investments that were made in vocational education, the efforts made to interest employers and unions in helping released prisoners find jobs, and the prevailing beliefs of penologists combined to attest to flickers of optimism about the reintegration of the offender in a community that had expelled him. There were enough tales of success to keep the optimism alive.

Realism will hardly allow us even those modest hopes. A very large proportion of the penal population comes now from the redundant underclass, men and women for whom our economy has no use. They could be kept safe and well fed, they could be schooled and put to work in the artificial world of the prison, but to give them hope would be to deny the hopeless prospects of the loser in the present economy. He may find casual work on the margins, but he will find no path leading to career employment. Retributivist justice will mean little to the loser; his liberty has been meaningless too. As for the aims of the utilitarians, although the loser will be incapacitated, it can hardly be expected that the permissible indignities and terrors of prison will intimidate him or that many of his friends and neighbors on the streets will find his predicament so intolerable as to be deterred from crime themselves.

What more instructive indicator of the pathology of our society can be found than the administration of criminal justice? The docile prisoner of earlier times, well aware that he was paying a debt to society, morosely certain of the hostility of the world outside, has been replaced. Conflict and rebellion permeate our penal systems. Black prisoners see that they are vastly overrepresented, and, whether the inference is correct or not, they attribute this state of affairs to a racist system of police and courts. Social invention fails us; we continue to attempt to manage the unmanageable; the methods that penologists thought were appropriate thirty years ago are still in use, not that anyone believes that they are effective or appropriate but because no one has thought of substantial improvements.

The truth is that the daily management of hundreds of men or women in the unnatural conditions of the prison will induce callousness and blind the keeper to the miseries that might be in his power to relieve. That old murderer in the Aged and Infirm Ward, incontinent of bowel and bladder, stretches the redundancy of his fellow prisoners to the ultimate absurdity. Redundant himself, his condition keeps an orderly busy feeding him and clearing away his excrement. His survival adds to the punishment of everyone around him. If we are advocates of retributivist justice, does retribution have to be so horrible?

The pluralistic maze of American society has conferred many benefits on all of us. It has also made the achievement of social justice difficult if not impossible, perhaps more difficult than in any other western nation. So long as the criminal-justice system operates as unsafely and callously as is now the case, it is a part of the mosaic of social injustice. So long as social injustice prevails, there will be criminals. If there is an inevitability about their crimes, we still have to treat them as though they freely chose crime when they could have refrained. We have yet to design a social order for determinists, and it is unlikely that we would like such a society if we could have it.

Reform of the criminal-justice system need not wait until the tides of social injustice recede. We have it in our power to correct the appalling imperfections that can be recognized by the eyes, ears, and nose. Looking farther, listening well, and pondering the human condition in these precarious times, many more of the remaining imperfections can be legislated and administerd out of existence. We have only to think and feel what we are doing as we manage this awful apparatus for the infliction of harm.

Notes

1. To support this point, it is customary to cite Douglas Lipton, Robert Martinson, and Judith Wilks, *The Effectiveness of Correctional*

Treatment (New York: Praeger, 1975), and Martinson's exegesis: "What Works? Questions and Answers about Prison Reform," *The Public Interest* 35 (Spring 1974):22-54. To these references there should be added the report by the National Academy of Sciences, *The Rehabilitation of Criminal Offenders: Problems and Prospects* (Washington, D.C., 1979). All these references rely on the assessment of rehabilitative programs in prisons and in the community by the criterion of recidivism. The crudity of this kind of evaluation should be obvious—although it is accepted by many social scientists—but there is no gainsaying the assertion that penologists have never been able to prove the effectivenes of any of the treatments they have administered. There are anecdotes that demonstrate that they can succeed in changing the lives of individuals, but these anecdotes do not generate hypotheses that can be translated into generalizations.

2. See Stephan Van Dine, John P. Conrad, and Simon Dinitz, *Restraining the Wicked* (Lexington, Mass.: Lexington Books, D.C. Heath, 1979), pp. 115-125.

3. Alfred Blumstein, Jacqueline Cohne, and Daniel Nagin, eds., *Deterrence and Incapacitation: Estimating the Effects of Criminal Sanctions on Crime Rates* (Washington, D.C.: National Academy of Sciences, 1979), pp. 19-63.

4. H.L.A. Hart, *Punishment and Responsibility: Essays in the Philosophy of Law* (Oxford: Clarendon Press, 1968), pp. 230-237.

5. James Fitzjames Stephen, *General View of the Criminal Law of England* (London: Macmillan, 1863), p. 99.

6. Joel Feinberg, *Doing and Deserving: Essays in the Theory of Responsibility* (Princeton, N.J.: Princeton University Press, 1974), pp. 55-94.

7. Hugo Adam Bedau, "Retributivism and the Theory of Punishment," *Journal of Philosophy* 75 (November 1978):601-620.

8. Michel Foucault, *Discipline and Punish: The Birth of the Prison* (New York: Pantheon Books, 1977), pp. 3-31.

9. Karl Marx, *Capital: A Critique of Political Economy*, trans. Eden Paul and Cedar Paul (London: J.M. Dent and Sons, 1930), p. 711.

10. Karl Marx, "Capital Punishment," *New York Daily Tribune*, 18 February 1853, quoted in Jeffrie G. Murphy, "Marxism and Retribution," *Philosophy and Public Affairs* 2 (Spring 1973):217-243.

2 Things Are Not What They Seem

The Ontology of Criminal Justice

What criminologist of my generation can forget the massive figure of Hans Mattick rising from his chair with a question to ask in that high rasping voice? The question would always be bluntly phrased, but it would always be relevant, if not always welcome to the person to whom it was addressed. His tragic death early in 1978 brought to an end a unique career. An authentic sociologist of the old Chicago school, he was profoundly concerned all his life with the collection of facts on the site, in the neighborhood, in the cellblocks so that he could better understand the meaning of things.

The 1979 winter issue of the University of Toledo Law Review *(vol. 10, no. 2) was dedicated to his memory. Readers who remember him as fondly as I do will be pleased with the oral-history interview conducted by John Laub, in which Hans's fresh and vigorous language resounds from each page. They will also appreciate Norval Morris's evocative recollections of the colleague with whom he worked for so long.*

Introduction

It was a sunny afternoon in New Orleans, and Hans Mattick and I were strolling through the French Quarter after lunch. We were attending a meeting of the American Sociological Association, and soon we would have to return to the windowless conference rooms for a few more hours of deep thinking. Now was the time for conversing about what each of us had been doing since our last encounter at some other assembly of the criminological clan. We passed a music store with a loudspeaker above its entrance pouring forth some fine old Dixieland jazz. Suddenly Hans stopped in midsentence: "Listen," he exclaimed. "In about eight bars, the trombone is going to go boomp . . . —boomp—it's a great moment." We listened. The trombone did indeed go boomp . . . boomp, and it was indeed a great moment. "Isn't it wonderful?" Hans asked with a beaming smile. There was a man who lived intensely, savoring moments most of us miss. Knowing him intermittently, as I did (we lived in different cities, and I never worked on a project

This chapter was my contribution to the celebration of Mattick's memory; it is reprinted with the permission of the editors of the *University of Toledo Law Review*.

with him), enhanced my career. Adventitious fortune brought us together often enough to remind me of how much can be done by a caring man with a good mind.

I admired the annual reports he wrote as the director of the Center for Research in Criminal Justice of the University of Illinois at Chicago Circle. With candor and panache they joyously celebrated the Center's accomplishments, exposed the frustrations of research administration in all the discomfort they imposed on the author, and fearlessly berated bureaucratic stupidity and inertia. Along the way, Hans would sprinkle comments on how things were going in the small world of criminological research, usually in language of ruthless specificity. Annual reports are ordinarily written for the reader to scan and put aside. Almost alone in this class of obligatory self-expression Hans Mattick's reports captured attention and called for response.

His fourth report, for 1976, was a good example.[1] After an account of the year's research and achievements, he moved to an essay on the state of criminal justice as seen by an old hand at its administration. What caught my eye was a paragraph in which he proclaimed the need to devote more thought to the "epistemological and ontological puzzles of criminal justice."

Epistemological mazes constitute my daily environment, as they must for any social scientist. Who does not mutter to himself as he tries to interpret his data, "how can I be sure I know what this stuff means?" But to borrow *ontology* as well as *epistemology* from the technical vocabulary of the philosopher was an unfamiliar approach to the riddles of criminal-justice research. So I wrote to Hans—as I usually did after reading his reports—applauding his concern for epistemology but curious to know what ontological puzzles he had in mind. This is the relevant paragraph of his reply, which I reproduce here because it is so characteristic of his creative skepticism:

> If I could sum up my entire education, experience and reflection in a single sentence, it would be: THINGS ARE NOT WHAT THEY SEEM. [Hans's capital letters] That is the ontological puzzle we have to face every day, and that is what I mean when I say: "The criminal justice system demands the re-examination of basic assumptions and the testing of rationalistic theories by empirical methods so that mythological appearances can be separated from existential realities," and I might have added, "if any."

Things are not what they seem. But what are they? The cops in the squad car seem to be vigilant and impersonally efficient, inured to, but unaffected by, the weaknesses of human nature. Under the scrutiny of social research, it turns out that the patrolling squad car makes little or no difference in deterring or apprehending criminals.[2] Formally photographed in the dignity of their robes, the justices of the Supreme Court seem learned, disinterested and prescient; epitomes of all that their colleagues in inferior courts should be. But a casual observer wandering into a dingy municipal courtroom will find harried judges in robes identical with those worn in higher courts processing a blur of defendants, hardly knowing whether it is justice or its miscarriage that they are dispensing. And glimpsed in the distance from the highway, the maximum-security prison seems impregnable, a reminder to the public of what is in store for the wicked and foolish. Inspection of the statistics of crime discloses, however, that of the wicked and foolish, only the unluckiest few will find their way into prisons, where their treatment will seldom reform them but often will shame us all.

It is not my purpose to trace the influences that have opened our eyes to the disparity between appearance and reality in criminal justice—between things as they seem and things as they are. The ontological puzzle that preoccupied Hans Mattick was partly exposed by the efforts of the research community of which he was for many years so eminent a member. In this contribution to the celebration of Hans's memory, I will confine my reach to one corner of the ramshackle system of criminal justice—the punishment of the malefactor.

We are heirs to a firmly entrenched, though never realized, expectation that a carefully designed set of principles of sentencing, thoughtfully enacted by the legislature and wisely administered by the judiciary and the penal authorities, can and will reduce crime to a tolerable level and convert criminals into law-abiding citizens. It *seems* that it should be possible to create such a system, and many earnest people, including myself, have devoted their careers to its design. I urge here that this vision is irreconcilable with the reality of what is possible; that one of the most ominous delusions in contemporary life in this country is the belief that criminal justice can do much more for us than it is now doing. I intend to show that the imposition of a teleology on criminal justice—a goal for its accomplishment—obstructs its humane administration and distracts us from the real business of correcting the social injustice with which crime is so intricately associated. The punishment of criminals, to which this chapter now turns, is perhaps the most tragic example of the teleologically induced delusion under which we labor, for while punishment is by no means a useless function of criminal justice, it is one from which unattainable benefits are expected.

The Retributivist Position

From the earliest times of which we have records, the belief has been fixed that criminals must be punished. The reasons can be classed under two headings: retributivist and preventive. In their considerations of things as they ought to be, philosophers have attempted to reconcile these reasons, but only in the last two centuries have these reconciliations had serious practical effect. Before the Enlightenment, moralists could propound theories of punishment in any form they pleased, but the judges and the executioners paid no heed. The gallows, the hulks, and transportation to penal colonies were the responses to crime in those days; such punitive measures exceeded by far the rigors of the Mosaic law. The thousands of corpses swinging from crossroad gibbets in the reign of Henry VIII were those of men and women punished for crimes far less significant than murder.[3] But the moralists eventually found their way to influence. Undeniably, one result of the ascendancy of the moralists has been an amelioration of the conduct of the state toward offenders, but a confusion of thought about punishment has been its further consequence. It is with the confusion that I am primarily concerned now, and I want to find a way through the labyrinth of ideas and rationales to the present state of our thought about punishment.

The lines of reasoning that justify retribution extend from Moses through Saint Augustine and the theologians of the Roman Catholic Church and find a common ground in the idea of natural law and the belief that man as an actor is endowed with free will. Retribution is, therefore, a moral necessity, the consequence entailed by a wrongful act. Arguments for retributivism have mounted in complexity from the time of Moses, who found no need to formulate a justification for punishment.

Without detailing the development of retributivist doctrines in minds as diverse as Saint Augustine and Immanuel Kant, what the doctrines of these men have in common, despite immense differences in approach, is the position that guilt must be matched with punishment. Discussion of this principle has tended to bring out three pronouncements in elaboration: the matching of guilt with penalty will "annul" the wrong done by the criminal; the punishment must "fit" the crime so as to constitute the annulment; and offenders have a "right" to punishment so as to be treated as moral agents, not as means to an end apart from themselves.[4]

But how is punishment to be determined? The question still perplexes those who must concern themselves with putting principles into practice. Clearly modern man cannot tolerate the indiscriminate brutality that our ancestors found unobjectionable. In his attempt to determine what constitutes a *just desert*, a term commonly used with reference to the retributivist principle of matching guilt with punishment, the retributivist must consider how he can specify, by some additional principle of proportionality, a schedule of punishments that provides for the nature of the punishment itself, its severity, the terms that may mitigate or aggravate it, and the reasoning that might settle these issues. But the intricacies and nice points that come so easily to retributivist philosophers' minds when they stake out a justification for their general position are seldom matched in any consideration of how much punishment is required for a particular just desert. Hegel's approach to this problem recognizes the difficulty and then dismisses it:

> [W]e are faced with the insuperable difficulty of fixing punishments (especially if psychology adduces in addition the strength of sensual impulses and consequentially either the greater strength of the evil will or the greater weakness, or the restricted freedom, of the will as such—we may choose which we please). . . . It is easy enough from this point of view to exhibit the retributive character of punishment as an absurdity (theft for theft, robbery for robbery, an eye for an eye, a tooth for a tooth, and then you can go on to suppose that the criminal has only one eye or no teeth). But the concept has nothing to do with this absurdity, for which . . . the introduction of this specific equality is solely to blame.[5]

The difficulty of fixing punishments by any reasoned proportionality is recognized as a Gordian Knot, to be cut by the common sense of the judge. The impossibility of arriving at a basis for proportionality between crime and punishment does not in the least affect the validity of the concept. The strands of the knot are to be turned over to the judge to do as he pleases with them. For Hegel, the reasoning is simple:

> Reason cannot determine, nor can the concept provide any principle whose application could decide whether justice requires for an offense (1) a corporal punishment of forty lashes or thirty-nine, or (2) a fine of five dollars or four dollars and ninety-three, four, &c., cents, or (3) imprisonment of a year or three hundred and sixty-four, three, &c., days or a year and one, two or three days. And yet injustice is done at once if there is one lash too many, or one dollar or one cent, one week in prison or one day, too many or too few.

> Reason requires us to recognize that contingency, contradiction and show have a sphere and a right of their own . . . and it is irrational to strive to resolve . . . contradictions within that sphere. Here the only interest present is that something actually be done, that the matter be settled and decided somehow, no matter how (within a certain limit).[6]

Hegel's attribution of primacy to the state's interest over those of any individual is characteristic of his thought.[7] For him, the prime interest was that of the king of Prussia, and what the judge, appointed by the king, decided was a just punishment was a just punishment—"within certain limits."[8]

Hegel wrote in 1821, and it cannot be said that much progress has been made toward a less forced resolution of this paradox since that time. The retributivist of 160 years later firmly believes that the state has a responsibility to the criminal and to society to alllocate a just desert for the crime committed.

The most recent attempt to "operationalize" the concept that Hegel so fiercely defended is to be found in *Doing Justice*, von Hirsch's Report of the Committee for the Study of Incarceration.[9] Von Hirsch and his colleagues created a scale by which the penalty imposed upon any criminal would be fixed according to the seriousness of his crime and the seriousness of his prior record, the latter to be measured by the number and gravity of his previous offenses.[10] The Committee worried about the magnitude of the penalties to be built into this scale and decided on a principle of parsimony: sentences are to be as brief as possible unless a case for more severity can be made.[11] But although the orientation of the Committee seems to have been a principled retributivism, the interest of prevention could not be suppressed. Thus, the concern about deterrence that characterizes much contemporary thought about punishment receives recognition in the committee's "hypothesis" of diminishing returns: "once penalties reach modest levels of severity, further increases are unlikely to have much added deterrent usefulness."[12] Based on this reasoning and without other justification, the Committee recommends the adoption of five years as the maximum penalty for any offense other than murder. Incarceration is to be reserved for serious offenses causing grave bodily injury, with lesser crimes to be punishable by intermittent incarceration or warnings and reprimands from the bench.[13]

Although von Hirsch constructed an elaborate apparatus to settle the justice of desert, the issue remains where Hegel left it—a concept to be applied as the legislature and the courts see fit—"within certain limits." The matter is to be resolved within limits determined by parsimony and a supposition about the effectiveness of punishment as a deterrent. For this modern retributivist justice is still as rough as it was in the hands of Hegel, and it is also settled in about the same way.[14]

Prevention

If retributivism can be reduced to a logical term after all the winds of disputation have subsided, the moral arguments that can be summoned in support of the utilitarian position on punishment stand in stark contrast, for they are complex and difficult, indeed, to resolve. Although, as I have suggested above, the preventive objectives of criminal justice had little or no effect on practice until the great reform wave that swept over Europe in the course of the Enlightenment, the position itself has a history that goes at least as far back as Plato.[15] Because the utilitarian position gained full sway in the moral doctrines of the nineteenth and twentieth centuries, it is important to trace the development of these doctrines and consider the kind of support they presently enjoy.

Antecedents: Plato

Plato's views on the subject of punishment shifted with the years and with his increasing pessimism about the future of his city. In *Protagoras*,[16] a relatively early dialogue, the visiting philosopher whose name is used for the title, expounds the preventive goals of justice with seeming clarity:

> Just consider the function of punishment, Socrates, in relation to the wrongdoer. That will be enough to show you that men believe it possible to impart goodness. In punishing wrongdoers, no one concentrates on the fact that a man has done wrong in the past, or punishes him on that account, unless taking blind vengeance like a beast. No, punishment is not inflicted by a rational man for the sake of the crime that has been committed—*after all one cannot undo what is past*—but for the sake of the future, to prevent either the same man or, by the spectacle of his punishment, someone else, from doing wrong again. But to hold such a view amounts to holding that virtue can be instilled by education; at all events the punishment is inflicted as a deterrent. . . . [Y]our fellow countrymen, the Athenians, certainly do inflict punishment and correction on supposed wrongdoers, as do others also. This argument therefore shows that they too think it possible to impart and teach goodness.[17]

There is a vein of optimism about about human nature in Protagoras's argument that seems to have been partly acceptable to Plato, whose views were expressed through the person of Socrates. Plato was not to be convinced that goodness was a subject that could be taught, but in the dialogue, Socrates did not dispute Protagoras's explication of the purposes of punishment, nor did he argue that punishment should be "blind vengeance."

In a later dialogue, *Gorgias*, Plato, through Socrates, accepts the views put forth by Protagoras and then goes on to suggest a rationale for punishment that seems to prefigure the "medical model" of correction. Speaking through Socrates, but without the usual indirection of the "socratic" method, Plato conveys the thought that punishment is good for the wrongdoer:

> *Socrates*: Where and to whom do we take the sick in body?
> *Polus*: To the doctors, Socrates.
> *Socrates*: And the unjust and intemperate?
> *Polus*: To the judges, do you mean?
> *Socrates*: To suffer punishment?
> *Polus*: Yes.
> *Socrates*: Then money-making rids us of poverty, medicine of sickness, and justice of intemperance and injustice. . . . [O]f two who suffer evil either in body or in soul, which is the more wretched, the man who submits to treatment and gets rid of the evil, or he who is not treated but still retains it?

Polus: Evidently the man who was not treated.
Socrates: And was not punishment admitted to be a release from the greatest of evils, namely wickedness?
Polus: It was.
Socrates: Yes, because a just penalty disciplines us and makes us more just and cures us of evil.[18]

So far, in the earlier phases of his thought, Plato has adopted the position that to punish the criminal for the harm he has done is a useless concession to the anger that prompts "blind vengeance." He considers that punishment can have only one useful purpose, to "treat" the wrongdoer and rid him of his wickedness. How this is to be done is left uncertain; in view of the propoals later advanced by Plato in the *Laws*, written in his old age and in dire pessimism about the future of Athens, it is unfortunate for us that we do not have the benefit of his advice about the proper administration of punishment as he might have given it in his earlier dialogue with Polus and the other young men clustered around Socrates. But geniality had long since left him when he wrote the *Laws*. In accents reminiscent of Leviticus, he wrote:

> Whosoever shall be taken in sacrilege, shall, if slave or alien, have his misfortune branded on hands and forehead, be scourged with such number of stripes as the court shall think proper, and be cast forth naked beyond the borders. For if he suffer that judgment, he may perchance be made a better man by his correction. For truly judgment by sentence of law is never inflicted for harm's sake. Its normal effect is one of two; it makes him that suffers it a better man, or, failing this, less of a wretch. If ever a citizen [*as distinguished from a slave or an alien who, in Plato's view, might have more cause to commit a crime*] be detected . . . in gross and horrible crime against gods, parents, or society, the judge shall treat hm as one whose case is already desperate, in view of the education and nurture he has enjoyed from a child and the depth of shame to which he has sunk. Whence his sentence shall be death, the lightest of ills for him, and he shall serve as an example for the profit of others. . . .[19]

In this pronouncement to a group of foreigners inquiring about the superior laws of Athens, Plato has added the concept of deterrence, which now seems almost to outweigh the benefits of punishment to the offender. Clinias, the respectful Cretan in colloquy with the august "Athenian" who propounds the principles of the *Laws*, is not so bold as to ask how a man can become better for being branded, sourged, and cast forth naked, nor does the Athenian elaborate.[20] Nevertheless, we can infer that once one has committed evil one's own good requires that he be purged by punishment. Like the retributivists, Plato does not trouble much over relating the precise level of sanction to the nature of the evil committed, but he allows a wide range: death, branding, scourging, fines, restitution, and imprisonment. In the *Laws*, where he has the most to say on the topic, he is not rigorous in formulating a rationale for the proportionality of punishment. In most cases, the judges are to be allowed discretion once a finding of guilt has been reached.

For a city in decline and disorder, much afflicted by crime, Plato prescribes a severe order. Imprisonment is frequently mentioned as a proper and available penalty, but in only one places does he specify what is to happen to those who are incarcerated. The following regime is laid out for those who violate the laws on "impiety," a category of infraction that Plato regards as very grave, although the reader is left uncertain about its scope:

> In the case of conviction [*for an act of impiety*] . . . [i]mprisonment shall form part of the penalty in all cases. . . . [T]here are three prisons in the state, a *common jail* in the market place for the majority of cases, for safe custody of the persons of the commonalty, a second attached to the noc-turnal council[21] and known as the *house of correction and a third in the heart of the country in the most solitary and wildest situation available, and called by some designation suggestive of punishment*. . . . [T]he law shall direct the judge to commit those whose fault is due to folly apart from viciousness of temper or disposition to the house of correction for a term of not less than five years. Throughout this period they shall have no com-munication with any citizen except the members of the nocturnal council, who shall visit them with a view to admonition and their souls' salvation. When the term of confinement has expired, if the prisoner is deemed to have returned to his right mind, he shall dwell with the right-minded, but if not, and he be condemned a second time on the same charge, he shall suffer the penalty of death. As for those who add the character of a beast of prey to their atheism . . . and thus do their best for lucre to ruin individuals, whole families, and communities, the law shall direct the court to sentence a culprit convicted of belonging to this class to incarceration in the central prison, where no free citizen whatsoever shall have access to him, and where he shall receive from the turnkeys the strict rations prescribed by the curators of the laws. At death he shall be cast out beyond the borders without burial.[22]

Plato's powerful mind was at work on the ills of Athenian society, which were worsening toward the end of his long life. Looking back into a past that was for him partly legend and partly history, he thought he saw an age of demigods and heroes, a world in which laws must have been redun-dant and the inner goodness of man was all the control that society re-quired. Looking around him, he saw a society that was tenuously controlled and in need of strong measures if order was to be maintained. His *Laws* reflect the firm belief that the guilty must be punished for their own good and for the protection of society as well. Here is Plato's prefiguration of the utilitarian justification of punishment. Though the almost ferocious severity he would visit on some offenders may shock some readers into supposing that he was a closet retributivist, a fair reading of his thought on this subject must lead to the conclusion that for him punishment could only be justified by some gain to be expected for the offender himself and for the society he had offended. His disavowal of vengeance in *Protagoras* is confirmed in the *Laws*. Even the unfortunates who were to be relegated to the central prison in the wilderness were to suffer for the good of their souls, not as society's revenge for the horrible wrongs they had done. Neither Plato nor the hundreds of commentators on the criminal law who considered the principles of punishment after him questioned the need for a punitive response by society to the actions of the criminal until the gradual coalescence of the positivist criminology in the nineteenth and twentieth centuries.[23]

I have dwelt on Plato's thought about the uses of punishment at such length because of the enormous influence he has exercised throughout the history of western philosophy—no subsequent philosopher can escape him. It is far too much to attribute our approach to crime and punishment to his ideas, but in this thought there are embedded two themes that have persisted in criminal jurisprudence throughout its agonized and bloody history. First, Plato and most of his successors endorsed the simple principle that the state is responsible for determining through orderly procedures who must bear the guilt for violations of the law.[24] And second, Plato knew that punishment had to be not only justified but also specified. In spite of his vagueness about reasons for the kinds of sanctions he proposed, he was clear that different categories of crime required different levels of "treatment," to use his word, and that the level should correspond to the seriousness of the offender's condition. Unfortunately, the impression is conveyed that in the prescription of the penalties, it hardly mattered what was done to the convicted offender so long as the penalty was harsh. Plato's model code was indeed harsh, but that was not the point he wished to convey; offenders were to be punished to restore them to their "right minds," not for some vague objective like annulling the wrong they had done.[25]

Eighteenth-Century Thought: The Dilemmas
of Judicial Terror

Over the two millennia following the death of Plato, little thought was given to the nature of the penalty from which a prisoner might benefit. The stress was on a sanguinary version of deterrence.[26] The ghastly tortures that accompanied the public execution of some criminals in France and other continental countries were so extreme that they transcend modern understanding, but these absurd severities had their apologists. Radzinowicz recapitulates a massive literature favoring capital punishment for relatively minor transgressors.[27] One prominent contribution to the theory of deterrence cited by Radzinowicz was a pamphlet published in 1785, by one Reverend Martin Madan.[28] In this tract, Madan reasoned that punishments ought to be administered with a view to preventing crime. Prevention is "the great end of all legal severity: nay, the exerting that severity, by making examples of the *guilty*, has no other intention but to deter others. . . . If this were not the case, all punishment would be nugatory, and therefore cruel."[29] Madan's logic led him to conclude that, since the value of punishment depends on the fear inspired in potential wrongdoers, capital punishment must be superior to any other penal measure. "The terror of the example . . . is the only thing proposed, and one man is sacrificed to the preservation of thousands."[30]

Madan was aware of the paradox that in his times the number of capital crimes was very great, and the rate at which they were being committed was increasing in spite of the frequency of executions. He thought he understood the reason: the law was not being properly enforced. If the judges would carry out the intent of the law, capital laws would prevent offenses, but if they made the execution of the laws unpredictable, the law would lose its deterrent value. Madan concluded on a smug note: "How monstrous it is to take men's lives away under pretence of example . . . and yet do this with such a partiality, as to destroy the very end of their sufferings, by so far weakening the force of that example, as to render it void and of none effect!"[31]

Radzinowicz reports that although Madan's tract had wide circulation, the statistics of capital punishment of the time show that the majority of judges did not agree with him. Reprieves were numerous, and royal pardons were granted frequently, usually upon the recommendation of the judge who had pronounced the death sentence.[32]

Much more influential than Madan was the Reverend William Paley, whose quite different reasoning was set forth in his *Principles of Moral and Political Philosophy*, which received wide and lasting circulation in both England and the United States.[33] Published in the same year as Madan's pamphlet, 1785, it influenced the draftsmen of the Reform Act of 1836 and survived as an active element in the literature of political philosophy until late in the nineteenth century. Like Madan and most of his contemporaries, Paley considered the purpose of punishment to be the setting of examples to the public. He approved of capital punishment for a variety of offenses, to include sheep-stealing and those frauds, such as counterfeiting and the forgery of notes, that reduce the public confidence in the integrity of commerce. Unlike Madan, however, he thought that strict administration of the penalty was neither necessary nor just. His analysis of the issue is worthy of review today: *mutatis mutandis*, it states an important argument frequently heard in contemporary discourse about penal policy:

There are two methods of administering penal justice.

The first method assigns capital punishments to few offences, and inflicts it invariably.

The second method assigns capital punishments to many kinds of offences, but inflicts it only upon a few examples of each kind.

The latter of which two methods has long been adopted in this country, where of those who receive the sentence of death, scarcely one in ten is executed. And the preference of this to the former method seems to be founded in the consideration, that the selection of proper objects for capital punishment principally depends upon circumstances, which, however easy to perceive in each particular case after the crime has been committed, it is impossible to enumerate or define beforehand; or to ascertain however with that exactness, which is requisite in legal descriptions. Hence, although it be necessary to fix by rules of law the boundary on one side, that is, the limit to which the punishment may be extended; and also that nothing less than the authority of the whole legislature be suffered to determine that boundary, and assign those rules; yet the mitigation of punishment, the exercise of lenity, may without danger be entrusted to the executive magistrate, whose discretion will operate upon those numerous unforseen, mutable and indefinite circumstances, both of the crime and the criminal, which constitute or qualify the malignity of each offence. Without the power of relaxation lodged in a living authority, either some offenders would escape capital punishment, whom the public safety required to suffer, or some would undergo this punishment, where it was neither deserved nor necessary.[34]

No one can consider the magnitude and frequency of the hideous atrocities committed by the state in the name of justice during those centuries without wondering how it was that God-fearing and civilized men (both Madan and Paley were clergymen) could give countenance to them. Paley was concerned about this question and commented in a perceptive explication: "The frequency of capital executions in this country owes its necessity to three causes:—much liberty, great cities, and the want of a punishment short of death possessing a sufficient degree of terror."[35] He noted that the English were an enviably free people, so free that they would not tolerate a police force with powers of discretionary arrest or restraints that were common in the autocratic governments of the continent. Further, the eighteenth century was a period of great upheaval in which men and women migrated from the countryside, creating great and unmanageable cities, which multiplied crimes and provided incentives to "libertinism."[36] "[T]hieves and robbers [collected] in the same neighbourhood, which [enabled] them to form communications and confederacies that [increased] their art and courage as well as strength and wickedness. . . . These temptations [could] only be counteracted by adding to the number of capital punishments."[37] Finally, he observed that the law simply did not provide for a lesser punishment than death that would be "sufficiently terrible to keep offenders in awe.''[38] Later in this chapter I shall argue that the chasm between the full penalty of the law and the lesser punishments still exists and still affects whatever deterrent effect the criminal code may be able to exert.[39]

To Paley's enumeration of the reasons for the severity of the English law, there should be added the general apprehension and dread instilled in the governing classes by the French Revolution and, later, the Napoleonic wars. Riots and popular uprisings much like those that preceded the fall of the Bourbons were occurring in the English countryside and even in London. It was no time to change the nature and assumptions of the criminal law. Indeed, reliance on traditional institutions, the apparent foundation of national stability, was generally approved by those whose prosperity and survival depended on that stability.

The primacy of the deterrent effect of the criminal law was unquestioned by these eighteenth-century writers. Control of an increasingly restless population, undergoing a massive social change, poorly policed and possessed of obvious grievances, required that precedence be given to using the law as an instrument of terror. It is noteworthy that the mainstream of thought about punishment was in apparent accord that symbolic punishment of a few might be deterrence enough. I shall reserve until a later section of this chapter a comparison of this quite explicit rationalization of severity to the situation at present in this country.[40]

The New Vision: Intimidation,
Incapacitation, Reform

Up to the nineteenth century and well into it, the severity of the written law was maintained on the understanding that only its terrors would preserve the control of the criminal classes. For at least two centuries, a generous strain in English culture had argued otherwise, though to little practical effect. Radzinowicz cites Sir Thomas Moore, Francis Bacon, Sir Edward Coke, George Fox (the founder of the Society of Friends), and Bishop Jeremy Taylor, among many others, as eloquent in decrying the ferocity of the written law and the caprice of its execution.[41] Their views did not prevail until the beginning of the nineteenth century when, through the influence of John Howard and Jeremy Bentham in England, Charles Louis de Montesquieu in France, and Cesare Beccaria in Italy, a new vision of punishment and its limits began to gain authority.

The new vision was a principled blend of intimidation, incapacitation, and reform. It was not without its rigors; terror was implicit in these visionaries' thinking, and sometimes it was boldly explicit—particularly in the case of Bentham. But it was a successful, ideological leap forward from the mixture of terror and mercy that had characterized the criminal law up to that time. Slowly, the new ideology became dominant. Each of these remarkable men mentioned above played a part in bringing it about, and it is tempting to recount the contribution each made. Because the persistence and the ingenuity of Jeremy Bentham accounted for the transformation of ideology into legislation and policy, I shall limit this discussion to his astonishing contributions.[42]

To undertand Bentham, it is necessary to keep in mind that he defined himself as a censor of the law, a critic whose function it was to say what the law ought to be. Only a specialist far more versed than I in the history of the English common law could do justice to a description of the condition of jurisprudence that Bentham learned as a precocious young man in the Inns of Court and spent the rest of a long life trying to change. The jumble of statutes, precedents and pleas that had accumulated without repeal over the centuries was beyond the mastery of any single lawyer and beyond any conceivable justification. Added to the confusion of written and unwritten laws, there was a labyrinth of independent courts with separate enough histories but overlapping jurisdictions. The legal professions had learned to be comfortable with this bewildering state of affairs, and there was no disposition to change. The English, after all, enjoyed the envy of their continental neighbors for the liberties that were enjoyed by all ordinary subjects of the crown. Such critics of the law as there could be told off with references to the much worse state of affairs that prevailed everywhere else.

The great Blackstone *Commentaries* not only described this condition of the law with evident satisfaction but also provided a perspective of pride in England as an abode of freedom protected by an ancient structure of law, to be disturbed only at the peril of losing the liberties of the British subject.[43] Blackstone, as an expositor of the law, performed a service of great moment in the development of jurisprudence, but he is important here for an entirely different reason. His complacency about the English law created a focus for the role that Bentham chose for himself. Blackstone might be an expositor of the law, but Bentham would be its censor. If Blackstone described the law and said what it was and how it came to be, Bentham would say how it *ought* to be. Bentham's orderly mind guided him to a long and industrious career that led into many investigations of needed change for the better, not only for the law itself, but in public administration, state control of services, and, most important for my subject, the humanization of systems of government.

A long and illustrious line of English philosophers, beginning with Bacon but most notable for the contributions of Hobbes, Locke, and Hume, had established a tradition of the liberal study of politics in which the principles of constitutional government were formulated on a grand and enduring scale. None of these magnificent thinkers had thought it necessary to enter into the details of administration and jurisprudence that would support the social goals they had identified as proper for the English culture. It fell to Bentham to design the practical application of the great doctrines of his predecessors. He saw it as his task to define what had to be done if the law was not to become more oppressive than it was protective. He combined logic with an empirical appetite uncommon for his time; he was never content with explanations that depended on history and tradition alone.[44]

His importance to thought about penology can be found in the pedigree traced from him through the Mills and the other utilitarians down to the Fabians and the contemporary British Labour Party. The continuity is a theme that has passed through the generations stressing the responsibility of governments to solve social problems as they arise. The solution to problems must be based on empiricism and embedded in a meliorist context.[45]

His approach to social problem solving was specially evident in the strange and comic history of Bentham's *Panopticon*.[46] Because the *Panopticon* makes one of the most important points that I want to stress, it will be useful to recapitulate the idea and its origin. Bentham's younger brother, Samuel, while working with Russian mill-owners eager to take advantage of progressive English ideas about industrialization, had proposed the design of a model workshop.[47]

> An inspector, stationed in a central lodge, could observe any given workman without that workman knowing whether or not he, in fact, was being watched. The idea was that the capacity of one inspector would be greatly increased. Each workman, believing that he might be seen at any time, would be more inclined to stick to his work and the consequence would be a considerable increase in productivity.[48]

While visiting his brother in 1786, Bentham became fascinated with the idea. He saw that the design was adaptable to the construction of a model prison. With his penchant for neologisms, he gave it the name of Panopticon, "from the two Greek words—one of which signified everything, the other a place of sight."[49] He described its application as follows:

> Taking in hand this idea, I made application of it for the purpose of the case in which the persons subjected to inspection were placed in that situation, not only for the purpose of being subjected to direction, but also for the purpose of punishment: in a word, as a place of labour and confinement for convicts.

> To the carrying of this design into effect, two requisites were necessary: The first and appropriate form of architecture, . . . and an appropriate plan of management. . . . In the course of my reflections on this latter subject, I came to my conclusion that the customary plan pursued in works instituted by Government and carried on, on account of Government, was,

in an eminent degree, ill adapted to the purpose: though to this general rule, particular exception there might be; but to the particular purpose in hand, they had no application. Accordingly, management by contract, I became convinced, was the only plan that afforded a good probability of success.[50]

Undaunted by his complete lack of experience in managing anything, or by his total unfamiliarity with the criminal classes, Bentham seriously intended to become the manager of a pilot Panopticon. The success of such a venture would justify its adaptation for hospitals, orphanages, poor-houses, and schools, as well as for the correction of criminals. For more than twenty years he struggled with the ministers of George III in a vain effort to persuade them to let him proceed with the social invention that, he was certain, would revolutionize the administration of justice. So confident was he of the merit of his plan that he invested large sums of his own money in the purchase of a site for the construction of the first Panopticon. The government, hard pressed by the cost of the Napoleonic wars, absent-mindedly gave him some encouragement, but in the end decided against the plan.[51]

The idea of the Panopticon has a significance for the administration of justice that has generally escaped notice.[52] The contrast between the Panopticons and the hulks, or between the Panopticons and transportation to Botany Bay, the other alternative to hanging, reminds the twentieth-century reader that Bentham's social invention was an enormous advance toward the introduction of humane values in the administration of criminal justice.[53] Unlike the philosophers of jurisprudence from whom he drew some of his ideas, Bentham saw that only generous thoughts unaccompanied by action would flow from the abstractions of even the most severe censors of the law. If the criminal law were ever to move away from its contemporary brutality, there had to be a specific plan. Good intentions in themselves are ornaments to the indolent; their realization rqeuires the imagination and skill of a social engineer. Surely Bentham was more than a benevolent censor of the law. He was one of the first social engineers in history.

His abortive attempt at the design of a prison was remarkable because it was the first attempt by any reformer to deal with the practical details of the humane management of offenders. Instead of inveighing against the indecency of criminal justice, as so many of his contemporaries had done so eloquently, and instead of documenting further the horrors of the state's retaliation against wrongdoers, he considered what alternatives could be devised to replace the existing evils.[54]

What is important for us to recognize in the plan for the Panopticon is Bentham's concept that prisoners would actually be the better for the experience of their confinement.[55] No one before Bentham had tired to design a prison with such an objective; indeed, it must be said that very few since Plato had thought that reform was a proper objective for a penal term. Somehow, out of the welter of optimism that emanated from the Enlightenment, Bentham had conceived the notion that it was a function of the criminal-justice system to change prisoners into citizens. Aside from the vague suggestions laid down by Plato to the effect that the members of the Athenian nocturnal council should act as counselors to prisoners in the house of correction, Bentham has a right to stand nearly alone as the first proponent of rehabilitation as an objective of criminal justice.[56] He has an exclusive claim to have been the first to outline a detailed program for its administration.

The transatlantic traffic in ideas during the early years of the nineteenth century is difficult to retrace, and although we know that Bentham's work was familiar to American intellectuals of the time, we cannot be sure that the designers of the Pennsylvania or the Auburn prisons had any knowledge of the concepts he had advanced. But optimism was in the air; the Enlightenment, the American and the French Revolutions had brought an end to old regimes and old ideas as well. If it was true that man was naturally good, as the philosophers claimed, then the effort to make good men out of bad might be worth making, after all. In any event, a change was imperative. The revelations of John Howard required governments to make basic reforms in the administration of prisons.[57]

It is beyond the scope of this disquisition to review the history of English utilitarianism, that powerful strain of thought that still permeates the outlook of the English-speaking people on morals, justice, and politics. Bentham's name is inextinguishably identified with the movement as its founding thinker, but in the course of two centuries many of his ideas have undergone major changes. That would not have surprised him; he firmly believed in the application of the experimental method to politics and administration and expected that evidence drawn from examined experience would modify both principles and practice. He would not, however, have expected that any influence would change his commitment to the greatest-happiness principle, a term that he always capitalized. It was, for him, nothing less than the *raison d'etre* of the state; it was the government's responsibility to do all things possible to achieve the greatest happiness of the greatest number. To accomplish this great end, Bentham prescribed attention to four principles of utility: subsistence, abundance, security, and equality. If each of these principles was maximized (one of Bentham's more successful neologisms) then the greatest happiness would be achieved.

Concern about criminal justice, therefore, arose from the requirement that the state should maximize *security*, a term that Bentham carefully defined in a series of axioms establishing that a citizen's security applied to his person, reputation, property, and "condition of life." The object of the penal law was to prevent offenses that might reduce the citizen's security. This was to be achieved through the use of the "felicific calculus," (another neologism, regularly revived in evocation of a fancied quaintness in Bentham's thought), by which he meant that the pain of punishment must exceed the pleasure of the illegal act sufficiently to deter the offender and all those minded to commit an offense.[58]

It followed that because crimes were interferences with the security of the citizen, it was the responsibility of the state to prevent them, not merely to indulge the citizens' desire for vengeance. His reasoning was clear and explicit:

> General prevention ought to be the chief end of punishment, as it is its real justification. If we could consider an offence which has been committed as an isolated fact, the like of which would never recur, punishment would be useless. It would only be adding one evil to another. But when we consider that an unpunished crime leaves the path of crime open, not only to the same delinquent but to all those who may have the same motives and opportunities . . . we perceive that punishment inflicted on the individual becomes a source of security to all. That punishment . . . which appeared base and repugnant to all generous sentiments, is elevated to the first rank of benefits, when it is regarded not as an act of . . . vengeance . . . but as an indispensable sacrifice to the common safety.[59]

At this distance in time it is hardly possible to recapture the impressive leap of imagination that this passage represents.[60] For Bentham to take the position that general prevention is the object of punishment was a bold and courageous act for a censor of the law.[61] Even more remarkable was the corollary of this position:

> With respect to any particular delinquent, we have seen that punishment has three objects: incapacitation, reformation, and intimidation. If the crime he has committed is of a kind calculated to inspire great alarm, as manifesting a very mischievous disposition, it becomes necessary to take from him the power of committing it again. But if the crime, being less dangerous, only justifies a transient punishment, and it is possible for the delinquent to return to society, it is proper that the punishment should possess qualities calculated to reform or intimidate him.[62]

So far as I know, this paragraph contains the first explicit reference in the literature of criminology to the familiar objectives of restraint, rehabilitation, and special deterrence. It is a measure of the great influence that Bantham has exercised on our thought that an intellectual commitment to these objectives has permeated our thought about punishment ever since.

The Panopticon idea follows inevitably from the paragraph just quoted. If punishment was for the purpose of incapacitation, reform, and intimidation, thee aims certainly could not be accomplished in the horrifying conditions that prevailed in England's jails and hulks, and banishment to Australia was a cruel evasion of the problem. What was needed was something new under the sun, a place of confinement that was not a prison, not a human rubbish heap, but a place that could hold the offender and reform him—or if that were not possible, at least it might intimidate him. Unlike his contemporary, William Paley, Bentham saw that it was essential to innovate a new kind of institution in which the experimental method could be brought to bear on the problems presented by the common criminal of his time. As a life-long disciple of Francis Bacon, Bentham firmly believed that the experimental method, which had succeeded so well in the natural sciences, could be just as effectively applied to human affairs. The Panopticon was to be a laboratory for the conduct of experiments, first with convicts, then with paupers, the mentally ill, orphans, and any other problem people for whose welfare the state had to accept responsibility. It was a commitment that honored Bentham's humanity and scientific integrity, if not his common sense.

Our Teleological Inheritance: Mattick's Ontological Puzzle

It was Bentham, then, who imposed teleology on criminal justice. Following utilitarian principles, criminals are not to be merely punished; they are to be punished for a trinity of purposes: incapacitation, reformation, and intimidation. Achievement of these purposes is success; failure to achieve them is failure. Bentham was spared what would have surely been the inevitable failure of the Panopticon had the ministers of George III been so foolish as to contract with him for the management of such a facility. His successors have not been so fortunate. Teleology has called on them to succeed, but success has eluded them. The charges of failure have become increasingly credible as means have been found to measure the results of later attempts to achieve these utilitarian goals.

Choice of priorities among the Benthamite goals has varied among his successors. The penologists of antebellum nineteenth-century America were mostly convinced that intimidation was all that was needed. For them, to break the prisoner's will by forcing him to conform to a regime of stringency was to reform him. On that point, the once-famous Elam Lynds of Auburn and Sing Sing was eloquent and explicit.[63] There was no question in his mind that he had the grim responsibility of reforming criminals by subjugating them to a rule so severe that no man, once released, would run the risk of returning to it. I doubt that Lynds and his peers had read Bentham or were even aware of utilitarian doctrines, but they accepted his ideology.

So did the religious enthusiasts who convened the first congress of the National Prison Association in 1870. Bentham, the rationalist, would have disapproved of their fervor as firmly as he would have condemned the miseries that the conventional penologists of the times administered to their prisoners. But the first National Prison Congress was a rare event that precisely dates the foundation of a new ideology. Assembled by a group of clergymen and pedagogues at a time when the nation was reconsidering its values in the light of the recent Civil War, the new National Prison Association formulated and adopted a Declaration of Principles that was to govern the aspirations of penology—but not its practice—from that time forward.[64]

The Declaration consists of thirty-seven precepts, beginning with the first principle that "Reformation, not vindictive suffering, should be the purpose of penal treatment of prisoners." Specific and uncompromising mandates for education, religious instruction, medical care, and vocational training follow. It is a positivist manifesto. The assumption is firm: criminals commit crimes because of identifiable and remediable faults, and it is the obligation of the state to identify these faults and remedy them. It follows that once this is done, the criminal can leave prison and return to society as a useful citizen. The indeterminate sentence, eventually to prevail throughout the nation, obviously receives its justification from these principles. The length of the criminal's sentence should be fixed by the time required to reform him.

The adoption of the Declaration of Principles was an astonishing reversal of a durable tradition in American criminal justice. A historian of the event has written:

> The convention was in the hands of reformers who had arrived with prepared speeches while the traditions had no spokesmen. Overwhelmed with inspired addresses, with prayer and song and much exhortation, even the hard-headed wardens were carried up for a mountain-top experience. In their enthusiasm for the ideal they rose above the monotony of four gray walls, men in stripes shuffling in lock-step, sullen faces staring through the bars, coarse mush and coffee made of bread crusts, armed sentries stalking the walls. They forgot it all and voted for their remarkable Declaration of Principles.[65]

From that time to the present, there has been little doubt about the legitimacy of "rehabilitation" as a proper goal of punishment. Though prayer and song swayed the wardens and keepers in 1870, far more substantive considerations supported the Declaration of Principles in the decades that followed. America was entering an era of boundless optimism. All human problems seemed capable of solution. The spread of education and belief in its value led to the conviction that criminals had to be afforded its benefits if they were to be reformed. The immense success of medicine in eliminating many of the scourges of disease suggested to many that the cure of the diseases that criminals suffered from—especially syphilis and tuberculosis—might enable many to be reformed. As time went on, the new science of psychology was put into the service of the rehabilitative ideology and so was the practice of social casework.

There was an historical convergence at work. The Declaration of Principles was followed, as though it had been a prophecy, by the efflorescence of educational, medical, and psychological services that promised reform through treatment of the criminal as a man with problems to be solved. In this benign new ideology, the goal of intimidation seemed sure to be obsolete and inconsistent with the remaking of criminal man. It was not surprising that some penologists began to speak of transforming prisons into hospitals.

The authors of the most influential textbook of criminology now in use summed up all these high hopes as follows:

> The history of imprisonment in the United States reveals a trend toward emphasis on treatment and away from punishment. The view which is now formally expressed by most prison leaders is that the prison should make every possible effort to treat prisoners, within the framework of a system of security. It is observed that practically all prisoners return to free society sooner or later and that use of punitive methods alone does not produce the desired reformation of these prisoners.[66]

These authors carefully added that although the verbal commitment to treatment was unqualified, the execution was far from matching the rhetoric.

In this gap between precept and reality, Hans Mattick's ontological puzzle can be found, like an inscription underlying a palimpsest. For nearly a century the public and its legislative representatives took for reality the availability of means to reform criminals through remedial treatment in prison and professional guidance in the community by probation and parole officers. If rehabilitation seemed to fall short of success it could be maintained that more and better personnel were needed. There was a consensus that the overriding purpose of the correction of offenders was—or should be—their rehabilitation.

This objective took on a reality in public disclosures that never corresponded to the realities of daily prison routines. Up to the present, and in spite of the Declaration of Principles and all subsequent pronouncements, few decisions to commit criminals to prison or to release them on parole have been governed by the offender's need for treatment or his later progress toward rehabilitation. As they did in the past, within the constraints of the law, judges commit men to prison because they believe the crime committed was of a gravity that warranted that degree of severity. Parole boards release prisoners because they believe that on a scale of proportionality enough time has been served.[67] It has never been shown that rehabilitative progress has ever played a significant part in parole decision making. The authenticity of a policy is tested by the decisions it ratifies. It is beyond question that there never has been a policy that controlled the disposition and management of adult criminals by reference to a goal of rehabilitation.

Criminological thought has emerged from the era in which it was generally held that the rehabilitation of convicts can be a prime goal of punishment. That belief was the foundation of the Declaration of Principles. Incantations of that manifesto were followed by innumerable publications in which different paradigms of rehabilitation were advanced.[68] The recent, well-known work of Martinson and his associates, however, has deflated claims and expectations. Perhaps it has done so more than was warranted by the nature of the studies this group conducted, for the demonstration that the administration of such programs has not resulted in a reduction of recidivism is not a proof that convicts cannot be helped on an individual basis, nor is it an acceptable basis for arguing that the effort to help them should be discontinued.[69] Nevertheless, few penologists now claim that treatment is the service a prison must provide so that the goal of reducing recidivism may be achieved. The utilitarian teleology has failed at this point, and there is no reason to believe that it can succeed, in spite of Bentham's hopes. The prison is not and never can be a hospital.

The same collapse of teleology must be pronounced for the goal of incapacitation. Until very recently not much systematic thought had been given to the degree to which crime could be reduced by incarcerating persistent criminals. Habitual-criminal laws had long been, and still are, in force in most states, though in irregular use.[70] But it was not until the publication of the landmark study of Wolfgang and his associates that serious attention was given to the possibility that long terms of confinement for certain classes of criminals might have a salutary effect on the rates of crime.[71] One of the most cited conclusions of that complex research was that a very small group of chronic recidivists—no more than 18 percent of the nearly four thousand delinquents studied—were responsible for about two-thirds of the serious crime. This clue was seized upon by commentators who argued that if the criminal-justice system could not reduce crime by reforming criminals, it could surely incapacitate them by appropriately long prison sentences for persistent offenders. Since then, an impresive array of statisticians and operations-research analysts have engaged in studies intended to assess the value of various sentencing policies in reducing crime by incarcerating those most inclined to commit it. Expectations have faded. Any policy intended to reduce violent crime by as much as 25 percent, it has been found, will require the accumulation of huge numbers of convicts in prison. Unless the country is willing to accept increases in prison population amounting to 400 to 500 percent, even this relatively modest goal is beyond achievement.[72] Other studies provide no shred of hope that crime can be significantly reduced by a policy of systematic incapacitation of chronic offenders without a radical reconstruction of the criminal-justice system, to say nothing of an enormous investment in prison construction.

There remains, of Bentham's trinity of purposes, the goal of intimidation. There can be little doubt that this, too, "works" on an individual basis. The rates of recidivism for persons incarcerated in prisons are variously estimated. Data from the California system, carefully collected for many years, indicate that the overall recidivism rate fluctuates around 45 percent, with considerable variance among crime categories.[73] That figure suggests that about 55 percent of prisoners are either intimidated or reformed or both. But the precise meaning of the data is unclear. Some first offenders are certainly impressed with the rigors of their experience and do not recidivate, but at the other end of a continuum of which we know little, there are men who have come to the end of their criminal careers and are to be counted as nonrecidivists, though probably not really intimidated.

Does it matter? At present we are probably holding about 250,000 men and women in prison at any time, most of them for periods of considerably more than a year. The number of felonies committed in any year amounts to about 11 million.[74] The paltry number of felons who are incarcerated can be increased, if we wish, but hardly by enough so that their postrelease behavior will seriously affect the crime rates.

There can be no question that all three of Bentham's purposes of punishment can be accomplished, as to some prisoners, with individual effects that bear on known risks from specific criminals. Some will be intimidated, though we can never be sure how much punishment will intimidate any particular criminal, and we can be sure that no punishment we can administer will intimidate some career offenders. Some will be reformed, but this result is unpredictable. All will be incapacitated, though we cannot be sure what length sentence is enough incapacitation. And it is the penologist's duty to do anything he can that will prevent his prisoners from committing more crimes, whether that goal is achieved by incapacitating them, reforming them, or intimidating them. But he and we must not suppose that anything he does in prison will have any marked effect on the crime rate.

We expect too much from a system that has the same chasm between severity for a few and leniency for most that dismayed the Reverend William Paley and Sir James Fitzjames Stephen. Between the crushing experience of imprisonment and the nominal experience of probation, society has provided little reality to the consequences of wrongdoing. Threatening potential criminals with hanging and actually hanging some has been replaced by threatening them with prison but confining only a symbolic few. The punishment is more humane, perhaps, but the method hardly more effective. We can, if we please, rationalize the system by acknowledging that, at least, we are accomplishing limited goals with some of those we confine. We must not suppose, however, that the criminal-justice system as it now stands or as it might be improved will seriously affect the incidence of crime.

Reality and Appearance in Criminal Justice

I think the nature of the ontological puzzle is now clear. In Plato's parable of the cave, an audience of fettered men were compelled to fix their attention on a puppet show, which, never having seen the real world, they came to regard as the only reality.[75] When unfettered so that they could turn their heads and see the world about them, only the show they had seen seemed real. Like these unfortunates, the general public has for a long time watched a show mounted by theorists and public officials, a show that, because of faulty assumptions, does not correspond to the realities of criminal justice. Those who watch the show learn that criminal justice has many purposes and that a system exists to carry them out. Its failures, they have come to believe, are those of execution, not of design, and one day the system will be so efficiently managed that crime will be reduced to a negligible level. If the public can be freed of its platonic fetters, it will discover a reality that must be explored with vastly different assumptions in mind.

The truth is that criminal justice depends on a principle of symbolic punishment, which is inherently unjust. In a contentious essay, Caleb Foote demonstrated this proposition as trenchantly as I have ever seen it done. Proceeding from the statistic that, in California, only 10 to 15 percent of felons convicted in the superior courts are sent to prison, he arrives at the following position:

> If the masks of individualization and rehabilitation are stripped away, the basic function of discretion in paroling and sentencing is revealed: to adjust an impossible penal code to the reality of severe limitations in punishment resources. By an impossible penal code, I refer to the fact that given economic constraints, full or equal enforcement is . . . out of the question. . . . From the masses of convicted persons legislatively declared to be eligible for imprisonment, most must be diverted and only a small proportion winnowed out for actual imprisonment. What we have is a system of symbolic punishment in which each San Quentin inmate stands for half a dozen or a dozen other convicted felons who are by any standard equally eligible to be there but for whom there are no beds.[76]

Foote considers this system profoundly unjust and immoral. He holds that the state of California has three choices: a vast expansion of the system to assure the punishment of all who are guilty; an adjustment of penalties to fit the limited punishment resources; or a continuation of the present unjust system of symbolic punishment.

Foote has been unfettered. He has turned his head from the puppet show and stared at the reality of the penal system—one in which legislation and administration have created appearances of purposeful action toward the goal of crime reduction that are at a great remove from the reality of symbolic punishment randomly administered. As the years go by, the abyss between appearance and reality widens. In similar fashion, the traditional adversary system of criminal trials has degenerated into a symbol that distracts the public from the reality of the daily negotiations in the prosecutor's office. At another level of the system, the new police technology seems to offer the public increased safety from the criminal but really distracts us from the exceedingy low rate of crime clearance in the larger cities in the country. Appearances conceal the increasingly nominal performance of the system.

The Task Ahead

Little is left of the utilitarian model of criminal justice from which Bentham hoped for so much—except his indispensable notion that a system was needed and that, if it was conscientiously administered, the primitive horrors that accompanied the traditional dispositions of criminals would come to an end. The system must be reconstructed to correspond with the capabilities of a community to maintain both the necessary social control and the democratic institutions that are threatened by the excesses of control.

It is in the writing of Emile Durkheim that I find the beginning of the thread that will lead us out of the labyrinth of confusion that the criminal-justice system has become. It will be recalled that Durkheim shocked his contemporaries and puzzled many later students with the assertion that crime is normal. He held that it was inconceivable that any society could be exempt from crime. Man is by nature normative; he judges his fellows as he perceives their conformance with the socially established norms. It follows that man punishes to maintain social cohesion; if he does not enforce consequences on those who deviate from norms, the community loses its solidarity.[77]

Opinions will differ as to how much solidarity has been lost in American society and to what extent that loss is attributable to the decline in the efficiency of the criminal-justice system. But when merit goes unrewarded and crime goes unpunished, as they have in this country, the citizen learns that norms and standards of conduct are meaningless and every man might as well be for himself alone. Durkheim had a word for this state of affairs:

anomie. And when anomie takes over, it feeds into anarchy such as can already be seen today in some American cities and in some corners of our culture.

If we accept Durkheim's analysis, in any society the nature and extent of crime provide clues to what is wrong, just as a fever signals an illness. Durkheim thought that, in a society of saints, there would be minor deviance from the norm of saintliness that would have to be classified as criminal; from these acts of deviance the saints would infer what would have to be done so that the imperfect might achieve perfection.[78]

Somewhat more obvious clues to what is wrong can be found in our high-crime areas. Chronic unemployment of any class of people, poor public services, the invisibility of opportunity, all contribute to the anomie that makes criminal behavior natural. This is not a new revelation; American sociologists from Merton and Mills have argued to this effect for many years.[79] In spite of these clues, however, the notion persists that the adoption of a hard line, a tough new realism in the administration of justice, will prevent crime.[80]

A tough approach to crime might work in a system that, as to all, freely and fairly rewarded for good deeds done and penalized for wrongdoing. But, for large sections of our society, hard work and good service are futile and unrewarded. And to an alarming extent, it makes little difference in these same sections that wrong is done; the wrongdoer will not be punished nor will his victim be protected or compensated. Social justice depends on rewards and penalties; it does not exist where either is absent. Criminal justice is meaningless, if not oppressive, where social justice fails.

Lawyers and judges have much at stake in solving Hans Mattick's puzzle. Theirs is the formal responsibility for the administration of justice; where justice fails, censors of the law are urgently needed. Complacency about a system in which justice is not being done is a failure of professional responsibility that lawyers cannot evade. The example of Bentham calls for the censor's discriminating perception of error and the social engineer's ability to design a needed innovation.

The most unsparing reconstruction of criminal justice cannot solve the problem of crime, but that does not excuse the lawyer and the social scientist from the tasks of reconstruction. The rot of American cities, the decay of our institutions, and the inefficient performance of our economy are maladies of which crime is only one symptom. But crime as we know it today destroys the cohesion that the country must have if we are to cure the underlying pathology. It will not save us to abandon the pretense that police, prosecutors, judges, and wardens somehow can remedy the affliction of crime, but those who must dispose of the social debris can set the example of honest attention to reality by stating their limitations and those of the system and, at the same time, call for similar reconsiderations by other elements of the social, economic, and political system.

Kant said, "If legal justice perishes, then it is no longer worth while for men to remain alive on this earth."[81] The survival of legal justice depends on action to achieve social justice. Those concerned with either must act to improve the condition of both.

Notes

1. Center for Research in Criminal Justice, *Fourth Annual Report* (1976).

2. G. Kelling, T. Pate, D. Dieckman, and C.E. Brown, *Kansas City Preventive Patrol Experiment* (1974).

3. G. Rusche and O. Kirchheimer, *Punishment and Social Structure* 19 (1968).

4. Much of this argument is derived from Kant, but it is elegantly disposed of by Quinton, who dismisses these doctrinal pronouncements as confusions which obscure the true nature of punishment as a *logical* necessity, not a term in a moral argument. Quinton, "On Punishment," in *The Philosophy of Punishment* 55-64 (H.B. Action, ed., 1969). For Quinton, the conflict between the retributivist and the utilitarian aims can be clarified by noting that punishment can only be administered to the guilty; it is possible to inflict suffering on the innocent, but that is not punishment which, by any definition, must be a consequence of a wrongful act, defined either in the law or in a set of accepted moral values. Thus, a thief is to be punished by the court according to the law if he is found guilty; but the punishment a habitual liar faces may be ostracism, loss of credit, or other social consequences. The point for Quinton is that "if a man is guilty he is to be punished."

5. G.W.F. Hegel, *The Philosophy of Right* sec. 101, at 72 (T.M. Knox trans. 1957).

6. *Id.*

7. This position influenced the ideas of Marx and his followers on the formulation of socialist law. Although, as I have suggested, Hegel's chief interest was that of the king, not that of the proletariat, the attraction of this kind of reasoning for Marx was irresistible, even if the king's interest was precisely the interest that Marx wished to overthrow.

8. I have not been able to discover just what limits Hegel had in mind.

9. A. von Hirsch, *Doing Justice* 132-40 (1976).

10. *Id.* at 133.

11. *Id.* at 136.

12. *Id.*

13. *Id*. at 136-39.

14. With pleased confidence in its handiwork, the Committee notes that if its scheme is adopted, "[n]o longer will it be possible for one offender to be sent to prison for years, while another convicted of a similar crime walks out the courtroom door on probation." *Id*. at 139. It is not clear how the Committee hopes to rid criminal justice of plea bargaining, nor does this conclusion reconcile the disparity between the years in prison for the recidivist and the grant of probation for the first offender within a framework of retribution.

15. See text accompanying note 3 *supra*.

16. E. Hamilton and H. Cairns, "Protagoras," in *The Collected Dialogues of Plato* 308-52 (1961) [hereinafter cited as Hamilton-Cairns]. All further references to Plato are taken from this edition. For the convenience of readers using other editions, the conventional pagination of the 1578 Estienne edition is given. In this case "Protagoras," 324b.

17. Hamilton-Cairns, *supra* note 16, at 321 (emphasis added).

18. *Gorgias*, 478a-d; Hamilton-Cairns, *supra* note 16, at 261-62.

19. *Laws*, 854d; Hamilton-Cairns, *supra* note 16, at 1415-16. Plato is terrifyingly severe in this section, but the existence of lesser crimes is acknowledged: some may be expiated by a fine, for nonpayment of which the alternative would be "long terms of prison, pillorying, and marks of degradation."

20. Plato no longer relies on Socrates to express his views, but designates an Athenian who must be no other than the philosopher himself.

21. Plato's plan for the nocturnal council was that it should consist of ten senior magistrates "and the whole body of persons who had won supreme distinction." They were to meet before daybreak, "the time, above all others, when a man is always freest from all other business." See *Laws*, 961b; Hamilton-Cairns, *supra* note 16, at 1505 (footnote this author's).

22. *Laws*, 908-09; Hamilton-Cairns, *supra* note 16, at 1463-64 (emphasis Plato's).

23. For a brief review of the positivist movement, see Y. Rennie, *The Search for Criminal Man* 67-78 (1978). Probably the full efflorescence of criminological positivism can be best appreciated in K. Menninger, *The Crime of Punishment* (1968), wherein the position is held that punishment is an anachronism in the light of the achievements of modern psychiatry and that detention of the criminal should be reserved for the incorrigible because they are incorrigibly dangerous—not because they are to be punished or should be punished.

24. The ethical and juridical problems contained in assigning this responsibility are intricate and deserve the profound reflection that has been given them, far more profound, I think, than the quirky views expressed in the *Dialogues*. Plato made the remarkable leap away from simple

retributivism—or "blind vengeance"—to an early utilitarianism, but evidently he did not consider it worth his while to develop full rationales for the kinds of sanctions he proposed.

25. Throughout Plato's thought about the *polis* there runs the theme of control. There was no question in his mind but that the city had to protect itself from those who would weaken its cohesion or damage its institutions. The criminal law had to be used to win the conflict between the Athenian establishment and those elements that would displace it or shake its firm control. Socrates had to die on that account, but the stability of the state took precedence over Plato's reverence for his master.

26. A vivid description is found in M. Foucault, *Discipline and Punish, the Birth of the Prison* (1977). For an account of the peculiarly ingenious forms of brutality visited on persons to be executed in eighteenth-century France, see *id*. at 3-69.

27. I.L. Radzinowicz, *A History of the English Criminal Law* 231-68 (1948).

28. "Thoughts on Executive Justice, with Respect to Our Criminal Laws, Particularly on the Circuits. Dedicated to the Judges of Assize; and recommended to the Perusal of All Magistrates; and to All Persons who are liable to serve on Crown Juries; by a sincere Well-wisher to the Public." *Id*. at 240.

29. *Id*. at 240.

30. *Id*. at 241.

31. *Id*. at 242.

32. *Id*. at 245.

33. W. Paley, *The Principles of Moral and Political Philosophy* (11th Am. ed. Boston 1827).

34. *Id*. at 374-75. Writing from the perspective of a century later than Paley, Sir James Fitzjames Stephen, the nineteenth-century judge and historian of the criminal law, confirmed Paley's account of the flexibility of the law of punishment:

> It was never intended that capital punishment should be inflicted whenever sentence of death was passed. Even when the criminal law was most severe, the power of pardon was always regarded as supplementary to it, and as supplying that power of mitigating sentences of death which the words of the law refused. . . . Down to the end of the Reign of William IV, [what was known as the Recorder's Report] was made after sitting at the Old Bailey to the King in council, the King being always personally present. The list of persons capitally convicted was on those occasions carefully gone through, and the question who was and who was not to be executed was considered and decided.

> This practice was discontinued at the beginning of the present reign, partly because the number of capital offenses was so much reduced that there was no longer any occasion for it, partly because it would have been indecent

and practically impossible to discuss with a woman the details of many
crimes then capital. [3 J.F. Stephen, *A History of the Criminal Law of
England* 92 (1883).]

In this vein, an English High Court justice once remarked to me that
in his experience he found himself often wishing that he could pronounce
sentences of the most awful severity in public and on the next day quietly
commute these sentences to the utmost lenience; he believed that the British
public needed to be forcefully reminded of the requirement of law observance in maintaining a civilized society, but he had no confidence that offenders respond favorably to long sentences in prison. Today, Paley's argument in favor of a standardized sentence subject to executive revision is
often advanced as an argument in favor of sentencing by parole boards. As
good a statement as I have ever seen of this position is to be found in Professor Caleb Foote's brief essay, "Deceptive Determinate Sentencing," in
Determinate Sentencing: Reform or Regression? 133-40 (1977). Professor
Foote recounts his extensive observations of the California Adult Authority, formerly the parole board in that state, and then discusses in great concern the role the Adult Authority played in reducing outrageous sentences
imposed by heavy-handed judges. He laments the increased rigidity that will
result from the enactment of determinate-sentence legislation.

    35. W. Paley, *supra* note 33, 381.

    36. *Id.*

    37. *Id.* at 382,

    38. *Id.* at 383. Sir James also added his practical confirmation of
Paley's hypothesis:

[T]he means now available for disposing of criminals, otherwise than by
putting them to death, are both more available and more effectual than
they formerly were. In the days of Coke it would have been impossible
practically to set up convict establishments like Dartmoor or Portland, and
the expense of establishing either police or prisons adequate to the wants of
the country would have been regarded as exceedingly burdensome, besides
which the management of prisons was not understood. Hence, unless a
criminal was hanged, there was no way of disposing of him. Large numbers
of criminals accordingly were hanged whose offences indicated no great
moral depravity. The disgust excited by this indiscriminate cruelty ought
not to blind us to the fact that there is a kind and degree of wickedness
which ought to be regarded as unpardonable. [3 J.F. Stephen, *supra* note
34, at 92.]

    39. Paley thought that the purpose of punishment embraced both the
reformation of the criminal and the deterrence of the public. He had no
confidence in the capability of prisons, as then administered, to reform
anyone, but he thought that with the introduction of solitary confinement,

prisons would be rid of the corrupting influence of one prisoner on another, and he added that the terror of the experience would deter many from the commission of crimes. He went on with a proposal for change that might give him a claim to be the first author to conceive a basis for indeterminacy in sentencing. Not only would prisoners be required to work in solitude—and to support themselves from their earnings—but,

> I would go further; I would measure the confinement, not by the duration of time, but by the quantity of work, in order both to excite industry, and to render it more voluntary. But the principal difficulty remains still; namely, how to dispose of criminals after their enlargement. By a rule of life, which is perhaps too invariably and indiscriminately adhered to, no one will receive a man or a woman out of gaol into any service or employment whatsoever. This is the common misfortune of public punishments, that they preclude the offender from all honest means of support. (W. Paley, *supra* note 33.)

Paley is deprecated by Radzinowicz as "not an original thinker," despite the immense influence he exercised on political philosophy in his time and for many decades after his death. I., Radzinowicz, *supra* note 27, at 249. Yet the passage quoted has no precedent in English penal thought before his time and certainly entitles him to consideration as an original and innovating commentator. Undoubtedly his views on capital punishment, which were much debated, obscured the more interesting suggestion that release might be linked to industrious performance in prison.

40. See notes 76-80 *infra* and accompanying text.

41. Radzinowicz, *supra* note 27, at 259-67.

42. Readers interested in pursuing the interaction among them and their disciples and with other figures in the years of the Enlightenment should begin by consulting Radzinowicz's magisterial history, not only for its coherent narrative but also for its exhaustive compilation of the references.

43. See, generally, W. Blackstone, *Commentaries.*

44. Graham Wallas, a twentieth-century admirer, commented that, "he was a born psychologist—born unfortunately before the discovery of modern psychology." He might also have been counted as a born sociologist; his mind had a proclivity for organizing the facts and reasoning from them to generalizations. Even his turgid prose and his unfortunate predilection for neologisms qualify him as a rightful ancestor to a long line of unreadable and unread sociologists. See G. Wallas, *Men and Ideas* 19-48 (1940).

45. As contrasted with the revolutionary vision of Karl Marx (who formed a special antipathy for Bentham in particular and for all utilitarians in general). See 2 K. Marx, *Capital* 671 (Everyman ed. n.d.). (This is an *ad hominem* denunciation of Bentham's person and characteristics, ironically

ignoring the similarities between Marx's description of Bentham and his own removal from the world and industrious literary fecundity.) Revolution was not for Bentham, who correctly perceived that the utilitarians' gradualism in reform was fatally inconsistent with any view of history as a record of class conflict. It is instructive that Marx had little time for, and less interest in, the administration of criminal justice; apparently there is only one brief discussion of the topic in the entire corpus of his work. [K. Marx, *On Capital Punishment* 485-89 (L.S. Feuer ed. 1959)] (This note argues that there are regularities in the incidence of crime in all capitalist countries, which must be attributable to the fundamental conditions of modern bourgeois society. Marx adds in passing that "punishment is nothing but a means of society to defend itself against the infractions of its vital conditions, whatever may be its character. Now what a state of society is that which knows no better instrument for its own defense than the hangman?") Bentham, however, with all his radical programs for change had no more specific objective than the creation of a society that would achieve the greatest-happiness principle in the daily lives of ordinary men and women. To Bentham, the statutory and administrative measures that the state would have to take to correct abuse and inefficiency would lead eventually to a closer approximation of the greatest happiness of the greatest numbers in society.

46. The episode is often dismissed by even the most admiring commentators as the eccentricity of a brilliant but impractical theorist, cooped up all his life apart from the realities of crime and the daily business of administering justice. His biographers usually concede that he was incapable of prescribing realistically for the harsh and disorderly world from which he had always been protected. That assessment is probably true enough, although I cannot resist the comment that the more popular solutions to the problem of prison design—the internationally accepted Pennsylvania system of solitary confinement, and the Auburn silent system, standard for America—were at least as foolish in principle as the Panopticon, and certainly much less generous in concept.

47. Samuel Bentham, an engineer and something of an architect, too, had emigrated to Russia, where the seemingly liberal regime of Catherine II had attracted many adventurous young professionals and intellectuals from all over the world.

48. J. Steintrager, *Bentham* 79 (1977).

49. *Id.*

50. *Id.* at 79-80, quoting 11 J. Bentham *Works* (Bowring ed. 1962).

51. A final settlement of £ 23,000 was made to compensate Bentham for his investment in visionary penology. None of his biographers have reckoned the actual amount of that investment, but it is clear that he learned a great deal about the machinery of administration from the twenty years of effort he devoted to the Panopticon.

52. His contemporaries, when sympathetic to his ideas, told Bentham that he was far ahead of his time. One disciple, Sir Samuel Romilly, himself a penal reformer of stature, explained to Bentham that, after all, "the public does not care tuppence for prisons and prisoners at any time, but . . . during the French Wars, they care nothing at all." *A Bentham Reader* 192 (M.P. Mack ed. 1969) [hereinafter cited as Mack]. Late commentators impatiently dismiss Bentham as an inconvenient eccentric who was unfortunately taken seriously enough to justify the construction of four monstrously inefficient Panopticons at Stateville, Illinois. One respected text summarily rejects both the architecture and the theory: "That such a theory was without either practical or scientific validity hardly requires further discussion, now, two centuries later." R.M. Carter, R.A. McGee, and E.K. Nelson, *Corrections in America* 159 (1975).

53. Although the absurdity of the Panopticon is obvious to Bentham's most uncritical admirers now, the context of the times places the humane intentions in a light that reflects the impressive powers of Bentham's imagination. Mary Peter Mack, his most industrious biographer, remarks that:

> Taken by themselves his reforms do not perhaps seem so advanced, but measured . . . against the brutality, the bestiality rampant in the hulks and prisons of eighteenth century England, they were amazingly progressive. The fundamental injunction in those days was, let the men rot! They were pitched into fetid hulks, three or four to a berth; left often to starve unless they could pay for food; left shivering in the dark, without medical care, left defenseless among every kind of malefactor. . . . These conditions had been exposed all over England and Europe by Bentham's favorite reformer, John Howard. . . . Bentham hoped to take up where he left off, and actually to transform the entire institutional structure by setting up Panopticons all over England. (Mack, *supra* note 52, at 192.)

54. Michel Foucault correctly observes that the Panopticon should be seen as a machine for amplifying power. The prisoner is seen but does not see; the keepers collect information about him, but he has no way of communicating with the ominiscient keepers or learning what they think about him or plan for his fate. Under the circumstances in which he is being kept, there is no need for communication; the keeper's power is economical and impersonal and efficient beyond the power that could be exercised by one human being over another in any other circumstances prevailing at that time. Foucault, *supra* note 26, at 195-228. Foucault attaches a significance to the Panopticon that would probably have surprised Bentham. In his view, it is symbolic of the state's use of knowledge to increase its power over the individual. That it came into being in the eighteenth century was to be expected: "The 'Enlightenment,' which discovered the liberties, also invented the disciplines." These methods for administering "the accumulation of men" made possible the substitution of a calculated technology of subjection—which Foucault designates as "Panopticism" for the traditional

violent forms of power. I doubt that Bentham would have objected to this analysis, but it is improbable that he would have put it in quite that way.

Although I must agree that Bentham's social engineering might have amplified power in the way that Foucault supposes, no one has been able to take advantage of that opportunity. Few Panopticons have been built, and the results obtained have varied from disappointing to disastrous.

55. It is impressive to read his argument, not merely for its confident exuberance but also for the objectives he sought: "Morals reformed—health preserved—industry invigorated—instruction diffused—public burthens lightened—economy seated, as it were, on a rock—all by a simple idea in architecture!" 4 J. Bentham, *supra* note 50, at 39.

56. See note 21 *supra*.

57. J. Howard, *The State of the Prisons* (Everyman ed. 1929).

58. Mack, *supra* note 52, at 243-47: "Pannomial Fragments." The famous opacity of Bentham's style is nowhere so evident as in these "fragments." Augustune Birrell, a writer now hardly remembered, remarked that reading Bentham was like "masticating an ichthyosaurus." Even the most respectful reader will find it difficult to convert this ichthyosaurus into intellectually digestible nourishment.

59. 1 J. Bentham, *supra* note 50, at 396.

60. Compare, for example, the remarks on the same subject uttered by Bentham's eminent contemporary, Immanuel Kant:

> Judicial punishment can never be used merely as a means to promote some other good for the criminal himself or for civil society, but instead it must in all cases be imposed on him only on the ground that he has committed a crime; for a human being can never be manipulated merely as a means to the purposes of someone else and can never be confused with the objects of the Law of Things [*i.e.*, goods or property]. His innate personality [*i.e.*], (his right as a *person*) protects him against such treatment, even though he may be condemned to lose his civil personality. He must first be found to be deserving of punishment before any consideration is given to the utility of this punishment for himself or his fellow citizens. The law concerning punishment is a categorical imperative, and woe to him who rummages around in the winding paths of a theory of happiness looking for some advantage to be gained by releasing the criminal from punishment or by reducing the amount of it. . . . If legal justice perishes, then it is no longer worth while for men to remain alive on this earth. [A. Ross, *On Guilt, Responsibility and Punishment* 54-55 (1975), quoting I. Kant, *The Metaphysical Elements of Justice, the Metaphysics of Morals*, pt. 1, at 100 (T. Ladd trans. 1965).]

Kant's position as here set forth, and in many other passages like it, has always been regarded as purely retributive, an allegiance to the *lex talionis* that had prevailed for so long in discourse about the criminal law. We cannot be sure that he had Bentham in mind in his reference to "the winding paths of a theory of happiness," but the shoe fits. Reverence for Kant has not prevented philosophers of succeeding generations from disassociating themselves from these views; so respectful a writer as Alf Ross condemns his position as "barbaric and antiquated." *Id.* at 57.

Note the escape clause in Kant's declamation of woe; he is concerned that justice be first focused on guilt and desert, and only then may it consider the usefulness of punishment for other ends. Repelled by Kant's apparently uncompromising severity, most contemporary writers gingerly consider and reject this passage as unadulterated and traditional vindictiveness. Read literally, the only way to read Kant, it is clear that he was fully aware that punishment does serve subsidiary purposes, but the obligation to punish must be limited to the guilty, and the court has no business considering anything else before it makes that judgment of fact.

Kant was a man of his times, fully cognizant of the fraility of human nature and the callousness of judges and officials. If justice is categorical imperative, as he was convinced it is, it cannot be trifled with by bringing in other considerations to confuse those who administered it. It was a reasonable position for an eighteenth-century philosopher.

61. In the preface to his recent collection of essays, Thomas Kuhn remarks that for a twentieth-century scientist to understand the work of a predecessor as ancient as Aristotle requires him to understand how and with what conditions Aristotle saw the physical world. He concludes: "When reading the works of an important thinker, look first for the apparent absurdities in the text and ask yourself how a sensible person could have written them. When you find an answer, I continue, when those passages make sense, then you may find that more central passages, ones you previously thought you understood, have changed their meaning." [T.S. Kuhn, Preface to *The Essential Tension: Selected Studies in Scientific Tradition and Change* at xii (1977)]. So let it be with Bentham. In his exhausting effort to address the complexities of what had previously been thought to be a realtively simple subject, he found that the existing language did not possess resources to make the distinctions he needed to make, so he invented new words. The logic of his demonstrations was equally complex, and his notes to himself, probably not meant for publication, are couched in a grammar so tortuous as to be virtually unintelligible to the modern reader.

62. 1 J. Bentham, *supra* note 50, at 396.

63. The literature concerning this fascinating character begins with the interviews conducted by Gustave de Beaumont and Alexis de Tocqueville. G. de Beaumont and A. de Tocqueville, *On the Penitentiary System in the United States and Its Application in France* 161-65 (1964). See also W.D. Lewis, *From Newgate to Dannemora: The Rise of the Penitentiary in New York*, 1796-1848, at 84-91 (1965).

64. The full text of the Declaration of Principles is contained in the republished Proceedings of the First National Prison Congress and available from the American Correctional Association, College Park Maryland.

65. B. McKelvey, *American Prisons: A History of Good Intentions* (Montclair, N.J.: Patterson Smith, 1977), pp. 91-92. Reprinted with permission.

66. E.H. Sutherland and D.R. Cressey, *Principles of Criminology* (New York: J.B. Lippincott Company, 1960), p. 460. Reprinted by permission of Harper and Row, Publishers, Inc.

67. See D. Gottfredson, L. Wilkins, and P. Hoffman, *Guidelines for Parole and Sentencing* (1978). This book is based on a massive study of parole decisions by the United States Board of Parole (now the United States Parole Commission), in which a statistical effort was made to model the parole decision-making process. It transpired that parole decisions were entirely governed by the criteria of severity of the crime and the estimated risk of further crime, the "salient factors," which could be scored to establish guidelines. The guidelines make no provision at all for progress toward rehabilitation or other clinical estimates. Although allowance is made for aggravation or mitigation of the guideline sentences (which might to some extent allow for success or failure in rehabilitative programs), only 8.7 percent of the decisions were below guidelines in 1975, whereas 7.5 percent were above.

68. This literature is indeed vast, and a footnote attempting to be representative would be hopelessly disproportionate to this chapter. I think it can be fairly said that a typical representation of the faith in the "rehabilitative ideal" is contained in R. Clark, *Crime in America* (1970).

69. D. Lipton, R. Martinson, and J. Wilks, *The Effectiveness of Correctional Treatment* (1975). See also Martinson, "What Works?—Questions and Answers about Penal Reform," *Pub. Interest*, Spring 1974, at 22-54, for a much more readable version of this position.

70. L. Sleffel, *The Law and the Dangerous Criminal* (1977). This volume is a detailed account of legislation enacted to control criminals considered to be dangerous.

71. M. Wolfgang, R. Giglio, and T. Sellin. *Delinquent in a Birth Cohort* (1972).

72. Van Dine, Dinitz and Conrad, "The Incapacitation of the Chronic Thug," *J. Crim. L. & Criminology* (1979). A fuller report of this research will be found in S. van Dine, S. Dinitz, and J. Conrad, *Restraining the Wicked* (1979).

73. See California Department of Corrections, *California Prisoners* (1974). This is an annual compilation of prison statistics. The most recent

issue is for the year 1974, but the data I refer to have been stable for many years.

74. M. Gottfredson, M. Hindelang, and N. Parisi, *Sourcebook of Criminal Justice Statistics*—1977, at 397, 628 (Feb. 1978).

75. 7 *Republic*, 514b-517d: Hamilton-Cairns, *supra* note 16, at 747-50.

76. Foote, *supra* note 34, at 138 n. 19.

77. E. Durkheim, *The Division of Labor in Society* 108 (Simpson trans. 1933).

78. E. Durkheim, *The Rules of Sociological Method* 69 (Solovay-Mueller trans. 1938).

79. R. Merton, *Social Theory and Social Structure* (1957). See also C.W. Mills, *The Sociological Imagination* (1959).

80. E. van den Haag, *Punishing Criminals: Concerning a Very Old and Painful Question* 184-88 (1975).

81. I. Kant, *supra* note 60.

3 The State's Strongest Medicine

The Indiana Lawyers' Commission expresses the concern of Indiana lawyers about the condition of the law and the institutions that administer it. So far as I know, it is a unique organization enlisting the talents and the resources of the profession to improve the quality of justice. For several years the commission has interested itself in the quality of criminal justice, taking a hand in a complete overhaul of the criminal law. That done, the commission convened a symposium on the entire criminal-justice system, seeking guidance on the measures that should be taken by Indiana to bring the administration of justice to a peak of effectiveness. The entire proceedings have been published under the title An Anatomy of Criminal Justice, *edited by Cleon H. Foust and D. Robert Webster (Lexington Books, 1980).*

My colleague, Simon Dinitz, and I were invited to present a paper on the future of the prison. We had been fortified by a visit to the Indiana State Penitentiary at Michigan City two years before; based on that observation and a surprising profusion of data on Indiana criminal justice that was made available to us, we produced this paper. We had been asked to conclude with a series of ukases embodying the commands that we would give to the State of Indiana for the improvement of its system if we were endowed with absolute power in that normally democratic state. For the benefit of those readers unfamiliar with prerevolutionary Russian administrative law, an ukase *was an edict issued by the Tsar having the full force of law. There are times when both Dinitz and I wish that we could enjoy such a prerogative over criminal justice with the accompanying authority to enforce such ukases to the limit.*

Introduction

We begin where our colleagues leave off—at a point generally considered to be at the end of the line. For all the reasons generally cited in support of alternatives to incarceration, we share the prevailing belief that any overhaul of any state's criminal-justice system should concentrate on the creation of an effective array of community-based correctional services, beginning with a realistic administration of probation and parole, but going far beyond these traditional services to include innovations that will be discussed by our associates in this colloquium. We confidently forecast that this shift to community corrections can and will succeed; in this cause the interests of public economy, good sense, increasing knowledge about human nature, and ordinary decency all converge.

Standing in the way is the ancient resistance to change of any kind in any public institution, in this case reinforced by the community's natural anger against the criminal. Throughout history, that anger has called for vengeance, for casting him out, not for reconciliation. The measure of our civilization is to be found in our power to convert unreasoning anger into intelligent concern. As we contemplate the shifting responses to the criminal throughout our history, we can see that perceptible movement toward that intelligent concern has been made in the countries of the West. It is for the Russians, heirs to centuries of incompetent and brutal tyranny, to sentence their citizens to long years of incarceration under conditions that for generations have been outlawed in Western penology. We have a long way to go before we match our practice with our aspirations, but there is a distance between the present conditions of our prisons and those prevailing in this country a century ago, or those prevailing now in the infamous Gulag Archipelago.

There is much to denounce in the American practice of corrections. We have begun this chapter in an apparently self-congratulatory vein because we want to deal with a defeatist theme that prevails in contemporary comment about criminal justice. To sum up that theme in its simplest form, the argument runs that prisons are no good, never have been any good, never can be any good, harm everyone involved in them, and ought to be abolished. Not many advocates carry the argument to this extreme; the prevailing modulation is that prisons are no good, never have been any good, never can be any good, and only the most dangerous offenders should be confined to them. It follows from this position that no more prisons should be built, that those now standing are perfectly adequate to the needs of the foreseeable future, and that the state should use the money now spent on building and maintaining prisons for more socially constructive purposes.

This generous position rests on several perceptions of the state of criminal justice with which informed observers must agree. We do indeed confine many people in prison who could be punished just as effectively and at far less social cost in other ways. Many American prisons are terrible in the most literal sense of that adjective, physically dangerous to guards and prisoners alike. Finally, so long as we rely on prisons to dispose of offenders, they will be used for the punishment of men and women who could be sentenced to a more constructive penalty. Alternatives to incarceration are more plentiful than these advocates suppose, but there is still far too much use of prison cells for offenders who might just as well remain on the streets.

Our contention is that the advocates of deprisonization exaggerate, and to the extent that their exaggerations are taken seriously by the prison-reform movement, prisons will deteriorate, to the great disadvantage of the prisoners who have to be confined in them, the guards who have to control them, and the general public that relies on them—probably far more than it should—for protection. It is not true that prisons are no good, nor that they cannot be made better. It is not true that confinement in prison is irremediably destructive. The sweeping assumption that there is no important difference between an overcrowded, vermin-infested, "big house" of violence and a competently managed, clean, and safe prison supports an argument for the falsest kind of economy. It is an obstruction of humane change in criminal justice. By lending their voices to this argument, people with unimpeachable credentials for high-minded motives lend their standing to the ignoble position that nothing should be done to improve our prisons because nothing can be done and nothing is worth doing.

The evidence that this is the consequence of the prison-moratorium movement is to be seen throughout the nation. With a very few distinguished exceptions, state correctional departments are drifting. The will to improve is corroded by the notion that nothing works, so why should any effort to improve be made? The best that can be done for criminals confined in prison is to keep them separated from the rest of society because, in the famous conclusion of Professor James Q. Wilson, we must recognize that "wicked people exist. Nothing avails except to set them apart from innocent people."[1]

That argument leads to the human rubbish heap, to the maintenance of human hells of abandoned hopes. That argument runs counter to the dominant theme of optimism that has always distinguished American culture from all others. We have been committed as a nation to the proposition that although man may not be perfectible he is certainly improvable. Once we decide that "nothing avails" for any class, group, or person we deny the validity of that proposition and erode its meaning for everyone living in a country that has always nurtured hopes instead of denying them. Let those who consider this language to be rhetoric inappropriate for a colloquium for logical disputation of the issues consider the contrast between the prospects of ordinary people in the rigidly determinist society of the Soviet Union and the hopes and aspirations still entertained by ordinary people in this country.

We hold that prisons can and should be improved and that the state can and should make strenuous efforts to improve them. Their changed role in the criminal-justice system calls for the reformulation of the principles governing their use and operation. A transformation is under way, whether we like what we see or not. It is urgent that thoughtful and informed leaders exert themselves to assure that these changes are reasoned, purposeful, humane, and carefully watched. If such an influence on change does not ensue from this colloquium, the changes in Indiana prisons will be the product of drift rather than intent. New York drifted into the disaster we remember as Attica. It is too soon to identify the forces that brought about the recent calamities at Pontiac State Prison in Illinois or at Reidsville Prison in Georgia, but certainly the state's inability to provide in advance for the cooling of hostilities was the product of drifting administration.

The changes in prospect must be recognized in advance. The good news is that there is reason to expect that some of the economic burden of incarceration can be relieved without increasing avoidable dangers to citizens from predatory criminals. We do not know how much the population can be reduced, and this is not the place to attempt an estimate. The fundamental principle is that the prison must be reserved as a last resort of the criminal-justice system, to contain only those scoundrels for whom no other sanction will do. It is for the people to say what categories of scoundrels are to be contained. It does not seem that there is a consensus on this matter.

As informed advocates, we are certain that the numbers should be fewer than those now confined in Indiana. This opinion is based partly on the data furnished by our hosts, which tell us that Indiana locks up a lot of felons who are not violent or dangerous by any definition of those loose terms. Over two-thirds of the prisoners admitted to Indiana prisons in 1976-1977 had been convicted of nonviolent or victimless crimes.[2] It is difficult to believe that none of those thieves, burglars, drug addicts, and con artists could have been managed in the community had there been an adequate array of community correctional services.

We also base this opinion on the demographic statistics, which indicate that the boom times for crime are nearly ended. The babies born in the fifties are outgrowing their foolish and headstrong ways. The babies born in the subsequent decades were fewer in number, even if they have not grown up to be wiser or more restrained.

There is good reason to expect that prison populations will subside from their present swollen dimensions. The subsidence will be less noticeable in Indiana than in her neighbors to the north and east. This is a state that has somehow avoided the worst of the penal avalanche of the middle seventies. Even now the prison population is less than the capacity of the prisons, a condition that is beyond rational aspiration in Michigan or Ohio. Consistently the rates of incarceration for 100,000 inhabitants in Indiana have been well below the national average. In 1971, the earliest year for which the figures are readily accessibly, Indiana confined 85 persons for each 100,000 of population; in 1975, this rate was 73. By contrast the same rates for Ohio were 85 in 1971 and 107 in 1975. The national average in 1971 was 96; in

1975 it was 113.[3] Indiana's prison population can be significantly reduced, but we must keep in mind that Indiana is penologically trim.

The transformation of the prison will not be easy to accomplish. Its present mission is to restrain a general population of predominantly non-violent felons. In the future, it will exclude the class whenever possible. The prison we foresee will house a much more specialized class, predominantly violent, somewhat younger than is now the case, and for the most part serving longer terms. Already we see in other states more advanced in this metamorphosis that a volatile, riotous, and intractable population is accumulating. One of us began work at San Quentin in the late forties. That prison, then the second largest in the land with a population exceeding 5,000, was the classic "big house" of conniving, thievery, intimidation, snitching, and easygoing bumbledom. Nobody worked hard—staff or prisoners—and if nothing good ever happened, little that was very bad happened, either. The evolution of the San Quentin climate of the forties to the present community of murder, rape, gangster intimidation, and extortion shocks those who can remember gentler days. It is easy to attribute the change to the prevalence of bad-check writers and thieves in the old prison, whereas in these more violent times the population is dominated by cutthroats and robbers. The statistics bear out this contention, but it is fair to say that the times are also different. The world of the late forties now seems to us like a period of halcyon placidity compared to the turbulence that we have lived through since. We have drawn on San Quentin for this comparison, but we have no doubt that the old-timers at Michigan City and Pendleton could make the same contrasts. Even as they are now, still diluted with nonviolent men, the prisons are more difficult to manage than they were; as the solution becomes more concentrated, the chemistry of the prison community will be potentially more explosive and dangerous.

As we consider the prospects for future prisons, we have to accept the likelihood that, although less space will be needed for fewer prisoners, they will be more difficult to govern. We shall consider the principles for their governance in the context of a society with commitments to the present and expectations of the future that differ radically from those that prevailed as recently as twenty or thirty years ago. Our two essential concerns are easy to state: Whatever the numbers of men and women to be confined, what should be the conditions of their confinement, and what should we expect of the processes to which we subject them? Ultimately our answers to that pair of questions will lead to a series of resounding ukases, the sense of which we can sum up in one commodious sentence: Prisons must be lawful, safe, industrious, and hopeful. The rest of this chapter will outline the means toward these four desirable, essential, and elusive ends.

The Lawful Prison

Above all, prisons must be lawful. The *lawful prison* is one in which it is the first goal of policy to prevent unlawful actions and conduct. Where violations of the law occur, they are punished appropriately under conditions in which the due process of the law prevails. If the prison is unlawfully administered or tolerates unlawful conduct by staff or prisoners, everything else that it attempts will be compromised.

Lawful control must be achieved. That objective requires a reconstruction of the model. For the old prison of the lockstep and silence, any size would do. Enough strong-arm guards had to be on hand to keep the convicts in line and to punish those who got out of it, but not much training and less skill was needed. Where there were not enough guards, convicts could be found to help maintain control. The atomized prison of the snitch, the stoolie, and the omniscient captain called for more managerial skill, but not necessarily more uniformed manpower. A prison housing thousands could be and was managed on these principles. But this prison achieved order through the application of methods considered intolerable in a free community. The prevention of free associations, the permeation of the entire population with distrust, and all the other devices of the autocrat were inescapably at variance with the freedom on which Americans place great value. Due process was ignored, quality before the law was irrelevant, and officials often and openly asserted that justice could not be administered in prison on the terms that are expected in the free community.

Everyone has a general appreciation that prisons can no longer be allowed to function as they did. The evolution has been swift and is continuing. We think the best statement of the principle that required the change is contained in the eloquent decision in *Morales* v. *Schmidt*: "[If] one of these rules of institutional survival affects significantly a liberty which is clearly protected among the general population, and its only justification is that the prison could not survive without it, then it may well be that the Constitution requires that the prison be modified."[4]

The modifications that the court had in mind do not allow the prison to be a lawless community in paradoxical surface compliance with society's requirement of lawfulness. The prison's disciplinary courts must not only administer due process, they must also assure that the laws and rules are enforced. Custodial officials must investigate crimes and must take the steps necessary to prevent them. This is not the place to discuss the deployment of patrols, the proper methods for the interrogation of witnesses, the prevention of the introduction of contraband weapons and drugs, and the myriad other tasks that have to be done every day to maintain prison discipline by lawful means. However, two organizational innovations should ease some of the burdens of compliance with the demands of due process.

First, disciplinary proceedings will be more credible if they are administered by an official who is external to the prison. Ideally, this official should not be responsible to the system itself, but at least he should be independent of the warden. The administration of discipline in Minnesota seems to approach the objective of independence. There, all disciplinary proceedings are adjudicated by a hearing officer appointed by the commissioner of corrections. His decisions may be appealed by the prisoner but not by the warden. The commissioner may reduce the punishment but he cannot increase it. Provision is made for the introduction and cross-examination of witnesses. It is understood that proceedings, will be expedited, especially in cases when the prisoner is in detention awaiting his hearing.

This system is not without problems. The prison community is not the free community, and investigations cannot be carried out with the same approaches or confidence. The rules of due process that prevail in adversary proceedings in free society must be significantly modified. Nevertheless, it is a huge improvement over the typical disciplinary committee that achieves a pale simulacrum of due process by administering *Miranda* warnings but combines the functions of policy, prosecutor, judge, and jury in a panel dominated by custodial officials and accountable only to the warden as the appellate functionary.

The second innovative support for the lawful administration of the prison is properly designed and administered grievance procedure. Such a system might take many different forms; experience is insufficient to specify the minimum essentials for achieving a fair and free ventilation of grievances with assurance that steps will be taken to remedy them when they are verified without detriment to the complainant. Such a system should begin with the prisoner's complaint to the grievance officer, followed by a remedy where indicated or an explanation where no remedy is possible or appropriate. Appeals to a departmental chief grievance officer should always be available, and provision should be allowed for external review of rejected appeals and also of the entire system. In some state departments the whole system is external; the ombudsman concept is based on complete independence of operations, with the ombudsman reporting directly to the governor.

We prefer the combination of internal grievance resolution at the initial stages with external intervention as the final step for one compelling reason. The submission and resolution of complaints provides the warden and his supervisory staff with a gauge of the extent to which the prison is in compliance with regulations and expectations. It affords the warden an occasion to be seen acting positively to improve the conditions in his domain. Further, the review of grievances provides the warden with a guide to the trouble spots, the points within his organization where timely action may avert serious trouble. Nevertheless, it will be an unusual prison in which the warden enjoys the confidence of the prisoners to the extent that a grievance system will be credible without external audit. A committee of informed and disinterested citizens should be available to look over the shoulders of the grievance officers and assure that their actions are more than the window-dressing that many convicts consider them.

To sum up the requirements of the lawful prison, there must be a commitment to undeviating law enforcement supported by adequate patrol and inspection. The adequacy of these functions is readily determined. If contraband is coming in, if violence is occurring anywhere in the prison, neither inspection nor patrol is adequate. Either more diligence by the staff on duty or more staff is needed. When felonies are committed, the responsible prisoner must be prosecuted, and a new and consecutive sentence must be added to his term. Rule infractions must be heard by an impartial and independent officer, whose decisions must be open to appellate review within the department. There must be an effective and credible grievance system to assure that as much trouble as possible can be forestalled by the redress of valid complaints.

Finally, something must be said about the administration of good time, or as the Indiana statute has it, credit time. Any administration of determinate sentencing must come to terms with the use of good time as an incentive for rule compliance and, perhaps, for other ends to be achieved in prison, such as, for example, program participation and completion. The Indiana law provides for three classes of good time. Class 1 allows one day of credit time for each day served. If a rule infraction is committed, a class 1 prisoner may be reduced to class 2, in which he earns a day for each two days served. A class-2 prisoner may be reduced to class 3, in which condition he will earn no credit time at all. Prisoners may be deprived of all or part of the credit time earned after a hearing of the charges against them, and, at the discretion of the commissioner, credit time lost may be restored.[5]

There can be no doubt that a well-managed system of remission of time to be served is the most powerful incentive to order in the prison that can be made available to the authorities. It is an ancient practice going far back into the nineteenth century but falling into disuse with the advent of the indeterminate sentence. So far as we can tell, and information is sketchy and mostly oral, good time as administered in the old days was a complicated game of cat-and-mouse in which the role of prisoner-clerks to make calculations was a dubious wild card. There is not much to be learned from long-past experience, but in states such as Texas that make substantial use of the practice of remission, the managers believe its use does indeed influence the conduct of prisoners.

We believe that much more study should be given to the adminstration of credit time in the interest of developing a model for its application. We believe that credit time should be vested, as provided for in the California law, to increase the incentive for compliance.[6] What can be taken away is not nearly so valuable in the earning as that which can be kept for certain. Other sanctions available for misconduct can be and usually are sufficiently severe to deter infractions, and the loss of credit time for the period in which the infraction occurred is one of the most powerful of such sanctions.

But even more important is the limit on the use of discretion. We are not informed on the rules that flesh out the application of the Criminal Code sections on credit time, but the law itself allows great discretion to the commissioner. A system of sanctions must be predictable if it is to be effective. The introduction of as much discretion as is provided in the Indiana law can only serve to reduce its reliability in the maintenance of discipline.

No one familiar with prison administration will claim that lawfulness is easily achieved either by the methods that we have proposed or by any others that are compatible with the laws of this democratic land. Order can be maintained by the imposition of official terror, and that was common in the bad old days. It is unacceptable now.

The Safe Prison

In the old days, prisons relied on unlawful procedures, but they were fairly safe. Riots occurred. Most of them resulted in a great deal of property damage and considerable rough handling of prisoners in retaliation but infrequent personal injury to the staff. A veteran of those times once explained it to us in this way: "Convicts wouldn't lay a hand on you. They didn't dare. They knew that if they did they'd be taken to a quiet place and beaten half to death. That's why we were safe then; we can't do those things any more and that's why conditions are so dangerous now." We do not assert that murders and assaults were unknown, but their incidence was certainly no more than in the slums from which most prisoners came, and it was probably less.

The increase in prison violence has been most spectacular in New York, Illinois, and California. The murderous obbligato of maximum-security life in those states may not be matched in Indiana, but we were reminded of the potential a couple of years ago when Warden Jenkins was taken hostage at Michigan City. Indiana is not immune to the viciously circular fury that infests so many prisons elsewhere.

The increasing hazards of prison life have coincided with the increasing concern over due process and observance of prisoner rights. That coincidence leads to a common and serious misinterpretation. The recognition of the prisoner's rights to fair and humane treatment is thought by some to have caused the violence. There is a connection. The intervention by the courts required innovation at a time when young men with an unprecedented addiction to violence as a way of getting what they wanted were pouring into the prisons. Unskilled and untrained staff who often regarded the changes they had to administer as unwise and inappropriate were confronted with disciplinary problems that would have been hard to resolve in the old regime. These new prisoners were bringing from the inner-city streets the experience of gang organization, the mechanics of narcotics distribution, and an acceptance of violence at a level hitherto unknown in prisons. The new approach to discipline was designed to cope with old problems. Many adjustments must be made before the state's obligation to maintain safety in the cellblocks is satisfied.

That obligation is unquestionable. In any situation the state must maintain its monopoly on the right to inflict violence and the means to inflict it. To yield that right to convicts in prison is a concession to anarchy. Further, the prisoner has a right to expect that if he conforms to laws and regulations he will survive the unpleasant experience of incarceration. We have now to consider what the state must do to achieve the objective of safety.

First, we must recognize that we are changing the prison regime without changing the prison premises. The Indiana State Prison was built in 1859 during the age of the lockstep, the unskilled prison industry of hard labor, and the autarchic control that prevailed in prisons everywhere. The management was expected to do little more than prevent escapes and subdue the occasional mutinies. With a present capacity of eighteen hundred and a population that approaches it, this is the mid-nineteenth-century prison to be found in nearly every state in the nation: obsolete, decrepit, oversized, dangerous. It is unsuited to its function, and its replacement should be an item of urgent business.

Let us be specific about our reasons for this drastic prescription. What is needed is a small prison for a small population consisting mostly of violent men serving terms somewhat longer than the present average. They should be working hard in a prison industry—a topic that we will come to presently—but they will need close observation and control. The methods of the nineteenth century are no longer available. The solution is a reconstruction of the experience of incarceration that will depend on a social structure encouraging and requiring interaction between prisoners and staff. In the old prison these interactions were deemed unnecesary and were discouraged on both sides of the invisible boundary between guards and convicts. In the new prison, interaction is the means of building trust and assuring the circulation of information with which control can be maintained without recourse to the surreptitious tidbits supplied by the unreliable and despised prison "rat."

That is the concept; how is it to be operationalized? We will accept the prevailing view of most authorities that prison populations should be held to a maximum of four hundred, divided into living units of no more than twenty. The design of the prison and its program should allow sufficient staff coverage during the day watches to assure that guards can be in daily close contact with groups in living quarters and at work assignments. The technology of television monitoring and turnstile counting should be strictly avoided; such devices are inefficient and contrary to the absolute necessity of human interaction. We do not mean that guards should think of themselves as therapists in any sense of that term. They are there to see and hear, to be seen and heard. The interests of order and predictability are served by the process of prisoners knowing the staff well enough to achieve an easygoing trust. Information is to change hands without fear that it will be misused, without expectation of special favor, and under conditions of respect and responsibility. Those who believe that staff-prisoner interactions cannot be of this character are limiting their vision by reference to popular and untrue stereotypes.

What we have now in the typical large prison is the worst of both worlds. Because the traditional methods of control are impossible, guards have to double up on patrol in the large cellblocks and around the yards in the interest of personal safety. Two guards working together all day will talk a great deal to each other and seldom to prisoners. Without that informal "rapping" no one really knows what is going on on the other side of that invisible boundary. Because no one knows, fear increases, and fear reduces the interactions even further. Demands for admission to protective custody increase and cannot be responsibly denied. Guards are too preoccupied with their own security to know convicts well enough to separate them from hostile and vicious stereotypes. The same is true of the convicts themselves, except that in these large communities of fear, the convict cannot be sure which of his peers he can trust and which he must regard as a dangerous enemy. The safety of the prison depends on converting this anonymous mass of humanity, of which the individual guard or prisoner can know so little, into neighborhoods in which everyone knows everyone else. Human beings were not meant to live in swarms or anthills, and in no situation except the prison and the mental hospital does this condition occur.

More is required than a reduction of the size of the prison to human scale. There are small prisons in America that are gruesome in the violence that staff and prisoners inflict on each other. Brute force survives wherever skill in human relations is lacking. There was a time when all a guard needed was a ladder to climb to the tower and a rifle to fire at mutineers and escapers. No training was needed beyond qualification on a rifle range, and often not even that was available. We are now entering a period in which the guard not only must be confident of himself in the martial arts but also must be easy and competent in human relations. Skill of the level required calls for extensive training in the vestibule, followed by regular and continuing training throughout the entire career. What is needed from the guard is a quality of service the intensity of which will put a heavy strain on his emotional stability. He will need the kind of refreshment that comes from regular exchange of experiences with others in similar situations. It is strange that in this country, where guards need this kind of support more than in prisons elsewhere, it is generally unavailable, whereas in the relatively peaceful prisons of northern Europe and Japan months of preparatory training are allocated to the recruit, followed by refresher courses along the way. It is no wonder that in so many maximum-security prisons many employees dread going to work in the morning and reach the end of the working day with relief that they have survived. In situations at that level of tension the staff is understandably violent, because they know of no other response in confrontations.

The Industrious Prison

Neither organization nor training will be of much use in reducing the violence of prison life if idleness prevails. It is a staple in the agenda of traditional prison reform that prison industries must be expanded to a level at which there is enough work for everyone to be fully and actively employed. Evidently no one listens to us. With rare exceptions (we know of no more than two in this country) the goal of the industrious prison is as distant as ever.

The result is that idleness is the normal state of affairs. The work to be done is spread so thin that it is no longer work. Prisoners are assigned to school, where they doze through classes in which nothing more is expected of them. Inescapably the yards and cellblocks are populated through the day with prisoners trying to cope with their ennui. Some play games, some lift weights, but all too many are scheming. It may be an avenue for escape, but more likely it is a deal for contraband or a gambling hustle. The vacancy of the day has to be filled somehow, and the satisfactions of outwitting the warden and the guards will fill it very well indeed.

None of this is news. The idleness of our prisons contrasts with the industry of prisons in other countries to our embarrassment. Our problem is partly political: the prison industry is an unwelcome competitor in any market and can be eliminated by legislation and administrative directive. Too often this result has been achieved by interests that begrudge prison industries the tiny share of the market they can hope to occupy. We have even seen the one industry on which prisons could count—the manufacture of license plates—severely curtailed by industrial invaders who have substituted stickers for annual replacement of metal plates. The economy of this innovation cannot be doubted, but the loss of work has been a severe blow to useful employment.

It is customary to deride such employment as license-plate manufacture as useless and inappropriate because no similar work exists outside the prison. That is not true. Punch-presses, metal fabrication, and industrial-painting processes are common in private industry. But even if it were true, work that fills the day usefully and at a fair rate of pay is preferable to the demeaning inactivity of the prison in which there is nothing to do but serve time.

Inveighing against the problem has not solved it and never will. Some states have succeeded in working out contract arrangements with private industries. Other states have aggressively and successfully carved off a large share of the state-use market. No doubt other arrangements have been negotiated; we do not pretend to an encyclopaedic knowledge of the state of prison industries. We have a modest proposal that has not, so far as we know, seen the light of day elsewhere.

We note the prosperity of the Federal Prison Industries, which not only keeps federal prisoners fully employed at much better wages than prevail in state prisons but also manages to make a substantial profit on its operations. The base of the federal industrial operations is access to the entire market of the federal government for the production of goods and services. We suggest that it should be possible for Federal Prison Industries to contract with state prisons for production for the federal market. In this way some stability could be provided for the state prison's industrial base, and administrators would be relieved of the need for an incessant search for employment suitable for convict labor. No doubt formidable difficulties lie in wait for this solution, but it seems to us that the effort to surmount them will be worth the while of those who will have to be mobilized to make it.

To keep prisoners busy is an achievement of great value, but still not enough. Men and women in custody can be and are employed without pay other than in the coinage of credit time. Such arrangements are hardly consistent with the assumptions of the market in which prison products are to be sold. In our culture, we cannot expect that a man will learn to gain satisfactions from his labor when it is not paid for, as is the case in some prison systems, or is paid for at the minute rates that are allowed in most systems. This basis for prison labor assures its inefficiency, justifies the resentment of competitors, and unfairly denies the worker the value of his labor. It is unlikely that the objective of wages paid at the rates prevailing in the free market will soon be realized; even the Federal prisons have not managed to achieve parity. But surely progress toward this goal will produce benefits more than commensurate with the effort of making it. The incentives that motivate free labor to produce will operate in the captive society, too. Prisoners who earn can support their families, keep them together and waiting for the day of release, and save toward a less precarious situation than they now face in the first weeks after their return to the community. Prisoners who are fully occupied at serious employment and paid accordingly will have less time and energy to devote to the hustling and scheming that goes on so incessantly now. There can be little question of the transformation that would be achieved in prisons by the adoption of a policy of full employment, fully paid. The wonder is that the effort to reach this goal is so lackadaisical, so defeatist. Eventually the transformation will have to occur if the conditions of prison life are not to get even worse than they are now. The prospects are not going to improve with time nor are the obstacles likely to diminish. This is a cause in which concerted action will be rewarded by early and tangible benefits. It cannot succeed without a major commitment to planning, negotiation, and appropriate legislation and administrative activity. That commitment cannot come too soon.

The Hopeful Prison

A criminal career is a desperate career, a career in which hope must be satisfied by transient "scores," ultimately and inescapably terminated by the successive disasters of apprehension, prosecution, conviction, and incarceration. Anyone experiencing this sequence may well abandon hope of rejoining the conventional society, if he ever had any such aspiration. Most prisons do little to turn the convict from desperation to hope. What has been done has been in the name of the amorphous word *rehabilitation*. Much has been said about the rise and decline of the rehabilitative ideal in recent years, and we do not propose to recapitulate a stale and meaningless argument based on almost completely false premises.

The point is that the commitment to the goal of rehabilitation in prison has been verbal, not substantial. Because prisoners could not be kept busy at work, they were sent to school, whether they liked it, whether they learned anything, and whether competent teachers were available. The most that can be said for correctional rehabilitation is that, more by accident than by design, some good programs are offered and some prisoners, not many, benefit from them. The notion is false that has been noised about so frequently in critiques of our penology, that prisoners have been regularly detained for failure to become rehabilitated. Those who make decisions about release on parole enjoy hearing from a convict about the progress he thinks he has made toward self-improvement; this subject matter has endless posibilities for dialogue at a parole hearing. But decisions about release turn on a simple question: has the man done about enough time? If he has not, no amount of demonstrated self-improvement will induce a parole board to release him. If he has done about the usual amount of time for the offense he has committed, he will be released regardless of whether he has profited from the meager opportunities available for bettering himself.

Much has been made of Martinson's widely heralded findings to the effect that, "with few and isolated exceptions, the rehabilitative efforts that have been reported so far have had no appreciable effect on recidivism."[7] This cautious conclusion was widely translated into the firm proposition that no rehabilitative method works. Although Martinson specifically rejected the imputation, it has worked its way into the general body of assumptions about penology. No one has calculated the damage that has been done by this oversimplification of a complicated and not well understood situation, but it must have been considerable. Prison staff have never been very confident of the value of what they were doing in the name of rehabilitation, nor have probation and parole officers. They got no reassurance from the news that rehabilitation does not work. Neither did prisoners and parolees. The motions are still gone through—what else is there to do? But we hear little of an innovating nature on the administration of services. The priorities in prison management go to meeting the exigencies of lawful control. We hasten to add that efforts in this direction are necessary and overdue. What we lack are the ideas and practice that afford the prisoner the reason to believe that there is hope for him in his desperate situation.

The point is that we cannot afford to convert our prisons into the kind of inferno that Dante conceived when he inscribed over its gate: "Abandon all hope, ye who enter here." The words are carelessly quoted by many, but their meaning seldom sinks in. For what is hell but a place in which there is no hope? And what more cruel punishment can we devise than to deprive a prisoner of hope that through his efforts or those of someone else his condition may be better in the future than it is at present?

Hope for a reasoning man must have a basis—for most prisoners there is at least the prospect of release. But release without reliable employment, without qualifications for steady and attractive work, and without the possibility of getting these qualifications will leave a man with a criminal record with only the hope that he may get lucky. And for most, getting lucky is going to mean getting away with a crime.

We believe we know that we cannot coerce people into self-improvement. What we know little about is the process by which self-improvement is initiated and proceeds, especially in the unpromising milieu of the prison. Here we can only suggest some principles that at least have the merit of general plausibility. First, there must be resources to choose from. From remedial elementary education to vocational training to group psychotherapy, believable programs offered by competent people have to be available at the option of the prisoner. In a full-employment prison, there is no reason why the prisoner should not contribute toward the cost of the program. Until that goal is achieved, such an expectation is unrealistic.

Second, there must be some incentive to engage in the program. For educational and vocational training programs, the inducement of good time allowed for program completion may get many started who would not otherwise take an initiative, but the real incentive should be demonstrably increased employability. Much depends on the support of vocational training by employers and unions. Where this support is visible in frequent inspections by industrial and union personnel, where it is followed by placement on desirable jobs after release, no other incentive will be needed. We grant that the difficulties to be encountered in realizing this prospect are formidable in today's economic climate, but experience indicates that a persevering effort will be well worth making.

Third, there must be no penalty for failure to engage in a program other than not earning good time for participation. In the past, wherever the indeterminate sentence prevailed, the penalty was seemingly formidable; not to be involved might be an embarrassment at a parole hearing. We have indicated our opinion that program participation had little to do with the length of incarceration, but the consideration that it might was certainly influential. In the new dispensation that we are now considering, we will do well to maintain the reality of choice.

But hope is not merely a matter of offering programs for prisoners to engage in as they please. The real hope for any prisoner should be an accepted place in the community. The reality of this acceptance has to be expressed in the interest and sustained involvement of the community. The activity of prison visitors, the participation of leaders in advisory committees, the presence of the community at religious and social events, all make connections that are essential to the maintenance of hope. Without these connections the only reality around the prisoner is what he sees of the cellblocks, the yard, and the industrial plant where he passed the time. A prison in which outsiders do not venture is a prison with good reason to suppose that the outside world is indifferent at best and probably hostile.

In his recent and deeply provocative book, *Discipline and Punish*, the French historian and philosopher Michel Foucault suggests that the effect of imprisonment is to convert a man into a case, thereby depriving him of the animating relations with others that sustain us, enrich our lives with meaning, and make life worth living.[8] The intuitive nature of this contention makes it difficult for a reader to estimate its value in understanding the true impact of the prison experience. We may allow that conclusion to pend, but there can be no doubt that in this age of systems, systems analyses, and systems planning and management, the tendency to convert prisoners into items to be processed according to the rules of systems cycles, with inputs, outputs, and feedback (instead of arrivals, departures, and consequences) have unreal and inhuman qualities inappropriate to social institutions. In the real world nobody lives like that so long as he avoids becoming a case, which most of us manage to do. Once the direction of a life is governed by standard decision-points at which judgments are made within guidelines based on an empirically derived theory, we become cases and irregularities of human existence are smoothed into data for a system. The student rebellions of the sixties made much of the unnatural effects of the computer on the nature of university life. Even more ominous for both the prison and the prisoner is the conversion of criminals into items for processing. A computer cannot allow for good luck, the interest of an altruistic counselor, the fortunate marriage to a supportive spouse, or the trust of an understanding employer. It can only make what it can of the masses of systematically coded data, very little of which offers hope to the prisoner of becoming anything better than he was.

Neither prisons nor prisoners can escape information technology. Unless the community can copiously add to it, the realistic hope for any prisoner's future is that it will be no worse than the dreary and unpromising past. Hope must be made of better stuff than flow charts and experience tables.

Conclusions

We are emerging from an era in which prisons were expected to be good for the prisoner and the staff was supposed to be expert in providing whatever the prisoner needed. It is a nice historical debate as to whether the Society of Friends, with the famous Pennsylvania System, or the English legal philosopher Jeremy Bentham, with the Panopticon, has the best claim as originator of the "treatment" prison, and we do not pretend to the historical erudition necessary to settle the question. But if is important to bear in mind that both the Quaker and Bentham were sure that what we now call a *total institution*—that is, an institution that totally occupies its resident's lives for months or years at a time—is good for people with social problems. In his important book *The Discovery of the Asylum*, the historian David Rothman documents the belief on the part of our nineteenth-century forebears that not only were prisons good for prisoners but also mental hospitals were good for the insane, orphanages were good for orphans, and poorhouses were good for paupers.[9] They even knew why: to separate the person in trouble from the influences on the streets that caused the trouble was a necessary step to his regeneration as a citizen. Bentham was enthusiastic: he began with a design for a circular prison for English criminals to replace the practice of confining them in rotting old hulks of ships in the Thames. The circular prison was never adopted by the English, wo considered the expense far too great for the treatment of undeserving malefactors, but it was adopted a century later by the state of Illinois, to the subsequent regret of all recent correctional administrators in that state. But Jeremy Bentham was convinced that institutions are necessary if the way of life of the criminal, the psychotic, the pauper, or the orphan is to be changed. He was convinced that education, work, and good medical care, administered in such a setting, would transform the occupants of these truly utopian facilities.

Later authorities took a different approach. Typical was the progenitor of the famous Auburn Silent System, Warden Elam Lynds, who was convinced that to reform a criminal his spirit had to be broken. The great French observer of early nineteenth-century American institutions, Alexis de Tocqueville, interviewed Lynds during his tour of this country and learned that "it was necessary to begin by curbing the spirit of the prisoner, and convincing him of his weakness. This point attained, everything becomes easy."[10] In a very different sense than Bentham or the Quakers had in mind—or contemporary prison reformers—Lynds believed that it was the task of the prison staff to change the prisoner, whether he wanted to change or not.

Two centuries of experience have lowered our expectations of the prison. No one would suppose that a spell in prison would be beneficial to a person in difficulty unless he had been convicted of a crime; most would suppose that commitment to a prison would be a serious misfortune, a crippling experience from which full recovery, let alone rehabilitation, would be at best unlikely. The damage wrought by prisons on prisoners is probably overestimated. In a recent review of the evidence, Hawkins concluded that: "the belief that all who enter prison are ineluctably doomed to deterioration proves, on examination, to rest on no more rational basis than the antithetical idea that, if only we knew how, panacean programs could be devised which would transform all offenders into model citizens."[11] Nevertheless the belief in doom persists. Sensitive men and women like the Quakers or the English Fabians in contemplating the modern prison are deeply disturbed at what their forefathers wrought two centuries ago. They now firmly contend that the prison can be no more than a necessary evil, to be used as little as possible. Their response to what they see is eloquent testimony to the indelible influence of the golden rule on our national conscience. Few can see a man sitting in a cell behind bars without empathy for him and without reflecting that the state is doing to him as we would not wish to be done to us. It does not relieve the conscience to hear that probably the convict will recover from his misery and in the mean time he receives his just desert.

The golden rule collides with the *lex talionis,* whose actual severity will not be literally revived, but whose underlying philosophy is just as indelibly inscribed on our cultural consciousness. The vigorously punitive notions of Warden Lynds would find a receptive public today if he would omit the explicit references to the whip and the curbing of the prisoner's will.

It is here that the smelly, unsightly, dangerous, and ugly world of the contemporary prison must be understood for what it is and for what it certainly will continue to be if the curious alliance persists between those who would abolish it and those who conceive it to be the only proper punishment for wrongdoers. At both ends of this continuum of opinion there is indifference about what prison is to be like. We can be sure that that indifference, if it prevails, will lead to prison conditions that no civilized society can knowingly tolerate.

It is therefore essential to set out a course for a reasonable and hopeful society to follow. The ukases that we would issue will lead to the lawful, safe, industrious, and hopeful prison as the only kind of incarceration that the American culture can indefinitely tolerate. Never having enjoyed the privilege, usually reserved for nineteenth-century tsars, of promulgating ukases, we cannot be sure of their proper form, but we insist on the following substance:

1. Because the prison is reserved for the custody of serious violators of the law, it is essential that all persons abide by the letter and the spirit of all laws, rules, and regulations. Violations of the law will be prevented by all reasonable means, prosecuted when they occur, and punished when a conviction is obtained.

2. Because the prison is governed by bureaucrats and other fallible mortals, it is essential that all prisoners have redress of their legitimate grievances. The warden will institute a grievance system, taking care to assure that its actions are independently reviewed by disinterested persons.

3. Because the prison is a community of persons in involuntary and close proximity with each other, it is essential that it should be small. Therefore, all possible steps will be taken to build prisons of a size not exceeding four-hundred prisoners and to demolish the existing facilities at Michigan City and Pendleton with all deliberate speed.

4. Because the state has direct and continuing responsibility for the safety of the prison community, sufficient personnel will be provided and trained to assure regular and systematic control through observation of and personal understanding of all prisoners therein confined.

5. Because citizens in prison are restrained against their will, the right of the citizen to work at wages consistent with those prevailing in the free community will be recognized, and industrial employment will be provided for those whose services are not required for maintenance of the facility.

6. Because prisoners will eventually be released to free conditions, it is essential that provision be made for their survival in the conditions of freedom. It is therefore required that appropriate educational, training,

and medical services be provided so that each prisoner can reasonably expect that his condition after release will be better than before incarceration.

7. The prison being a repository for temporary detention of citizens, all measures possible will be adopted to assure their return to lawful civic life, including the encouragement of contacts with organizations and individuals in the outside world, furloughs for those who have earned trust, and programs of community education or service when opportunity exists.

So be it in Indiana!

Notes

1. James Q. Wilson, *Thinking about Crime* (New York: Basic Books, 1975), p. 209.

2. Indiana's Criminal Justice System (reference materials supplied by the Indiana Lawyers' Commission), p. v-13.

3. Michael R. Gottfredson, Michael J. Hindelang, and Nicolette Parisi, eds., *Sourcebook of Criminal Justice Statistics, 1977* (Washington, D.C.: U.S. Department of Justice, February 1978), pp. 630-631.

4. Morales v. Schmidt, 340 F. Supp. 443.

5. *Indiana Criminal Code,* secs. 134-136.

6. See California State Senate, Senate Bill 42, Section 2931 (c) (1970).

7. Robert Martinson, "What Works? Questions and Answers about Prison Reform" *The Public Interest,* no. 35 (Spring 1974): 22-54.

8. Michel Foucault, *Discipline and Punish* (New York: Pantheon, 1978).

9. David J. Rothman, *The Discovery of the Asylum* (Boston and Toronto, Little, Brown, 1971).

10. Gustave de Beaumont and Alexis de Tocqueville, *On the Penitentiary System in the United States and Its Application to France* (Carbondale and Edwardsville, Ill.: Southern Illinois University Press, 1964), p. 165. For more about Warden Lynds, see also W. David Lewis, *From Newgate to Dannemora: the Rise of the Penitentiary in New York, 1796-1848* (Ithaca, N.Y.: Cornell University Press, 1965), pp. 86-89.

11. Gordon Hawkins, *The Prison, Policy and Practice* (Chicago and London: University of Chicago Press, 1976), p. 80.

4

Doing Good with a Hard Nose

The Achievement of Credibility in Criminal Justice

Throughout the sixties and seventies, the annual meetings of the National Institute on Crime and Delinquency (NICD) provided a forum for long-range thinking about the present and the future of criminal justice. I was asked to deliver a paper on the achievement of credibility in criminal justice for the NICD gathering in 1976. For a long time I had been impressed with the chasm between the lofty claims of altruism, professionalism, and enlightenment and the modest achievements about which we could hardly boast. As Hans Mattick might have put it, this chapter is a contribution to laying out our ontological puzzle. That puzzle's solution is a long way off.

On Broken Locks and the Chastity of Jane Doe

One of the incidental benefits of an occasional consultant stint is the perspective it affords on the problems to be encountered in accomplishing anything at all in the criminal-justice system. Let me offer a couple of recent examples to begin what I hope will be an orderly process from the particular in the real world to some general principles that I would like to propose for the improvement of the credibility of animal justice.

To prepare for a modest contribution of testimony in the landmark case of *James* v. *Wallace*, last year, I visited the Alabama Correctional Reception Center at Mount Meigs.[1] It is not my purpose here to describe what I saw; I have done that elsewhere, and so have many others. But I had an exchange with an inmate that sticks in my mind because it illustrates so vividly one of the fundamental issues in the achievement of accountability in the criminal-justice system. In the course of my tour of a brutally overcrowded cellblock, a small, frail young man approached me to ask if I could help him. His question was simple: the locks on most of the cells didn't work, and he couldn't protect himself at night. Could anything be done? I asked my escort, a gloomy sergeant who obviously did not relish his assignment, if it were true that the locks on these cells were inoperative. Yes, he said, that

I am grateful to the editors of *Crime and Delinquency* for their permission to reprint an article that originally appeared in their pages in October 1977.

was one of the problems in running a place like this. The inmates broke the locks faster than the staff could fix them. That was the kind of people they had to deal with. They were irresponsible, shiftless, and destructive. I gathered that there was no point in trying to keep the locks in repair, so attempts to maintain them had been abandoned.

I now switch to a sophisticated probation department in a northern city in which my views were sought about strategies of program development. One of the strategies to be implemented was a program of measured change in probation casework. So as to assess the effectiveness of probation service and supervision, a system of setting case goals was to be put into effect. No doubt the concept and the practice will be familiar to some of my readers. The personal situation of the probationer was to be carefully analyzed with a view to determining in what respects improvement was needed. An estimate would be made by the case supervisor and the probation officer, working together, of the requirements of an acceptable level of improvement within the expected term of probation supervision. There would also be an estimate of the "ideal" level of change, to provide a perspective on the degree to which the acceptable level might be surpassed. So far so good, I suppose. The people consulting me then went on to provide an example. We were to consider the case of Jane Doe, a sex delinquent whose problem was indiscriminate promiscuity with evey young man who came along. Her presenting situation was that she slept with a different boy every night. An acceptable improvement would be a state of affairs in which she slept with only two or three boys whom she really liked. An ideal state of affairs would be a sexual commitment to one boy only. Nothing was said about Jane saving herself for Mr. Right.

So I was asked what I thought of this sytem. There are a number of easy answers, of course. How are these changes going to be verified? What makes us so sure that a numerical reduction in the rate of promiscuity represents an acceptable improvement? If the probation officer's reputation is at stake on such a numbers game, what is going to prevent her from manipulating the numbers? I am afraid my reply was incredulous and dismissive.

What can we make of these two preposterous situations, drawn from the opposite ends of the correctional continuum? Opposite ends in more ways than one, we must note. We move from the prison to the probation department, from callous incompetence to open-minded eagerness to improve service, from indifference to accountability to an obsessive concern with it.

Let us consider the prison locks first. I do not have to labor the point that in any prison locks are vulnerable. Inmates can jam them, break them, pick them, and improvise keys for them. Without constant surveillance and regular inspection they will all break down with serious consequences for the security of the prison and everybody in it. A minimally competent prison administration will have a continuous program of checking and repairing locks. Without resort to the tedious vocabulary of management by objectives, procedures will be established for assuring their security. In a well-regulated prison, heads would roll if conditions deteriorated to the level admitted to me that morning in Alabama. The concern would not be motivated by a desire to protect vulnerable young men from sexual molestation but rather to assure control over unpredictable prisoners requiring maximum security. Here was a low-level objective having nothing to do with the goals of rehabilitation or the reduction of recidivism so frequently invoked by correctional hierarchs. Here was a well-understood duty to be performed, and it was not being done. At a later point in this disquisition I want to discuss the reasons for this appalling nonfeasance.

As for the program of measured change in probation, the obvious reservations that I cautiously recited do not go to the heart of the matter. The essential objection to this notion, which surfaces every now and then in the minds of insufficiently trained probation officers who have been overexposed to the ideologies of management by objectives and social casework, is that goals are established which we do not know how to attain. Let us agree that in principle it would be a good thing for Miss Doe to reduce the number of her sexual contacts. We might even go on to recognize that her behavior is symptomatic of much more fundamental disorders. Probably if we engaged a psychiatric consultant we could get a fascinating insight into the nature of her psychodynamics. But then what? Do we have the means for helping Miss Doe, especially if she sees no need to be helped? Does our psychiatric consultant have such a method? Can we really institutionalize a system of program measurement when we do not have a reliable program to measure? My experience and observation leads me to a negative answer to those questions.

Two principles emerge from our review of these two vignettes from contemporary corrections. First, we must see to it that those tasks are performed that are essential to our assignment. We must do what we know how to do and what we are expected to do. Second, we must avoid setting goals for ourselves without first assuring ourselves that there are ways of accomplishing them. To commit ourselves in broad daylight to the transformation of Miss Doe into a model of propriety, if not of absolute chastity, assures our eventual disappointment and, perhaps, some embarrassment if our commitment to this goal has been made before witnesses.

I cannot claim either originality or profundity in enunciating these elementary precepts. They are so obvious that the restless reader may be forgiven for wondering when the platitudes will cease and discourse will begin. And this is precisely the point at which I want to investigate the reasons why qualified commissioners, directors, wardens, and clinicians violate elementary rules so obviously derived from ordinary common sense. Let us try to identify these reasons and then let us consider what can be done to improve a management style so manifestly contrary to the best interests of the public and of management itself.

A Typology of Ineffectuals

My first level of analysis is addressed to the administrator and his ability to do his job. A sort of typology emerges when we study criminal-justice inadequacies in terms of the ineffectual decision maker and the way he makes decisions. The types I have to describe are surely well known, at least by reputation. Until we do something about them, the criminal-justice system has a hopeless task in trying to convert itself into a truly accountable element of the social system.

The first class in my typology is the administrator who does not care. He is easily found in the prisons and probation departments, but we can also find him dozing through a disgracefully short day on the bench in many a courtroom or on the take in a corrupt police department. We cannot account for those inoperative locks at Mount Meigs in any other way. The truth is that in the late twentieth century in this advanced and well-informed country, we still have people in charge of prisons who do not care what happens within the walls for which they are responsible so long as their bottoms are covered. Administrators of this stripe are at work, if you can call it that, in every section of the land; Alabama has been notorious because of a vigilant and courageous judge, but there are other states in other parts of the country in which prison conditions are just as bad. Every now and then a place like Attica or Columbus or Walpole erupts to cast a harsh light on the indifference and incompetence that have led to conditions beyond endurance. The hue and cry can be relied on to subside, and outside agitators will be identified as scapegoats who caused all the trouble in the first place. How do people become such monsters of indifference? It is tempting to oversimplify and bandy cliches about sadism and bigotry, but I suspect that the answer is simpler but more sinister. In the minds of these cynics, the people in those cells are the enemy, and the correctional staff is a thin red line of outnumbered men in precarious control. To help the enemy by making his life more comfortable is a foolish expenditure of effort. These enemies would not be where they are if they were not a worthless, shiftless, and bad lot. A variation on this theme is the view that everything has been done for these people and nothing works, so why try to do anything at all? A lot of probation departments are run on this principle. The dozing judge and the corrupt cop are likewise convinced of the uselessness of effort in criminal justice. They might be said to be terminal cases of trained incapacity; too old and too useless to make a living anywhere else but senior enough in criminal justice to be impregnable to ordinary disciplinary procedures.

My second class is typified by the man who does not know what is going on in his own domain. In Columbus we have had such a situation in a mild way in our municipal courts. These tribunals are presided over by thirteen overworked judges who seem to be conscientious men dispensing justice on a treadmill with small thanks from the community and working under conditions that seem intolerable beyond belief. A couple of years ago, a group of concerned citizens initiated a court-watching project to see how justice was done in the courtrooms in which most of it is dispensed in our city.[2] Enough money and people were mobilized to make a systematic study of the arraignment procedures and then to publish an elegant report on what they found out. What was most striking to me in their data was the contrast to be found when the distribution of responses to guilty pleas was examined. Each of the thirteen judges sat in rotation in the arraignment court, and evidently each had internalized his own guidelines. Just looking at the sentencing patterns for the three most common offenses (petty theft, assault, and bad checks), the study found that some judges were most severe on assault, and others were so lenient that none of the defendants convicted on such charges were sent to jail. No two judges had sentencing patterns in close correspondence. The report has been a special wonder around town. The project director has spoken often and well to numerous community groups of every description about these and other disturbing results.

So, not long ago I discussed the report with one of the most senior judges on the bench, a hard-working man who puts in long hours in an effort to keep an unmanageable workload in motion. He told me that he was sure that the findings were accurate. No one who knew the court and its problems should be surprised. After all, a judge hearing arraignments was dealing with a blur of faces and charges, each passing before him for a few minutes at most. He had to improvise a personal sentencing policy; he never had time to sit at length with his brother judges to discover what they did. Here was a conscientious public servant in a situation in which he had to admit that he really did not know what was going on.

This kind of ignorance is so easy to justify. Consider the warden at his desk, coping with correspondence, newspapermen, directives from the central office in the state capital—and researchers who want to know what he thinks and does about dangerous offendes. How can he find time to reconnoiter his prison in person, seeing for himself whether the reports he is receiving from his subordinates truly reflect the situation? It is easier and more pleasant to delegate not only authority but also the responsibility for review.

The consequences begin with the comforting belief that the process of intelligent delegation is working well and that trusted subordinates will not be
the target of second guesses. So the warden stays off the yard and out of the
security area except when conducting tours for unusually important guests.
Gradually he becomes a stranger in his own institution, seeing little and
hearing nothing except what he gets out of staff conferences and problem-
solving sessions. The situation that is deteriorating because of a lack of
competence, a misunderstanding of his wishes, or some serious lack of
resources will come to him too late to forestall the most serious kinds of
trouble. I know of prisons where the warden did not set foot in the hospital
or the segregation unit from one end of the month to the other. The consequences for the warden and for his institution in each case were disastrous.
No malevolence, and probably no indolence either; the warden simply had
not organized his work in such a way that he could know what was going on.

The third class in this typological analysis of administrative distress is
surely familiar to us all in some degrees. The administrator does know what
is going on, and cares enough to do something about it, but finds that the
resources for doing it cannot be found. Let me go back to Alabama for a
moment. The director who had the responsibility for remedying the truly
awful situation in the prisons of that state was, by all accounts, a decent and
well-meaning man, as troubled as anyone else about the conditions for
which he had to bear some responsibility. I am told that he made a personal
campaign out of appearances before community groups, service clubs, and
legislative committees seeking support for the facilities and staffs that he
knew he needed but did not have. The hard fact was that he did not get
them. What he got was a swelling intake of new prisoners and a declining
number of prisoners being released. Too late to save his reputation, he
resigned.

His was an extreme case and a sad one. It characterizes all too many
situations in our field especially during these years in which the volume of
work to be done has distorted the quality of performance beyond reason.
Our problem is one of changing roles and, in doing so, changing expectations of ourselves. After all, the administrator is trained as a bureaucrat,
not an advocate. As he reaches higher levels of responsiblity he can hardly
avoid the advocate role, and many distinguish themselves by their
resourcefulness. Others do not, and occasionally we find one who frankly
says that he does not think it is his place to tell the public what kind of
criminal-justice programs it should support. I heard that humble acceptance
of personal insignificance from a strategically placed administrator in a
nonsouthern state not so long ago, and I was as shocked as I hope you are.
For who is going to tell the people what has to be done to avoid the worst if
not the advocate-bureaucrat? Who is going to administer the reforms that
must be instituted if not the advocate-administrator? The self-abnegation

of the administrator who keeps to his paper shuffling and his inhouse directives is not commendable humility; it is an abdication of fundamental
responsibility, a recipe for the creation of the stagnant conditions too often
to be seen in our troubled domain.

The fourth and final figure in our typology is the administrator who
cannot move. He knows what should be done, he can define an objective,
but for the lack of planning experience and capability in himself and in his
staff, nothing happens the way he wants it to happen. Bold changes are proposed, imposing outlines of a better future are presented to an approving—
or at least interested—public, but politics frustrate him, the details of the
plans are never credibly developed, and nothing gets into motion but the
rhetoric of hope and the language of recrimination and excuse. I have no
horrible examples to present to you. I suppose that if we examine our collec-
tive experience we can populate this class sufficiently to discuss the problem. The root of the trouble in these situations is not so much the resistance
to change of which we are so often accused as the lack of resources for making orderly changes. Most correctional departments are understaffed in
planning talent, and that is natural enough. The bureaucrat who can run the
daily business of his department has usually been rather carefully budgeted
to do exactly that; nothing is left over for the excitement of drafting a
detailed plan of innovative action. It is one thing to say that at the beginning
of the next fiscal year we are going to introduce a plan of team policing, or a
new and streamlined system of docketing cases appearing in our court, or of
tearing down and replacing a maximum-security fortress with small
community-based prisons and other facilities. It is quite another to draw up
plans to put these ideas into practical form for a budget request and then to
get the money to carry them out and to train and develop personnel to make
the changes work.

It has been the conventional wisdom that these kinds of changes occur
only when there are enough resources to permit the administrator to take
large risks or when there are grossly insufficient resources but the organization is in so much trouble that something has to be done. This is an interesting
formulation, and it may very well be true in part—the part about the well-
provided agency. But one of the legacies of the Law Enforcement Assistance
Administration is the accumulation of a considerable expertise in correctional
planning. There is no excuse for any correctional agency that does not work
with disciplined plans and projections. Planning need no longer be a bag full
of wishful promises laid on in the roundest of numbers.

Impossible Ends and Possible Means

For the last fifteen years, public administrators have been exhorted to
reform their ways by adopting the practice of management by objectives

supported by the technology of systems analysis. It was not so long ago that management savants were telling us that the stonemason who thought he was building a cathedral was somehow more productive than the stonemason who was merely fitting one stone to another with mortar. Somehow that difference was related to advanced management concepts that could be translated into performance budgeting and the planned-programming budgeting systems (PPBS). I turn to this set of ideas now because, in spite of the storybook banality of the comparison of stonemasons, and in spite of the subsidence of performance budgeting, management by objectives, and other administrative concepts of the sixties, there remain some usable residues.

My own early adventures with this constellation of related concepts began in California, where the logic of performance budgeting seemed to promise a way out of the underbrush and a clear view of the forest. We learned that the keystone of performance budgeting was the objective of the agency and our goal in public service. This goal had to be measurable, and the measure of its achievement was the sum of the measures of our achievement of subsidiary goals, which had to be arranged in hierarchical fashion. The California Department of Corrections in those days had a lot of people who could be turned on by such an exercise. I was one of a number who worked in hours and after hours on the ideas of performance budgeting with approbation from higher authority and no little annoyance from the cooler heads among our colleagues.

We were working in the heyday of the medical model of corrections and were not at all queasy about the use of recidivism as a measure of our achievement of the goal of changing offenders into citizens. Surely if we developed enough of the right programs we would end up changing our inmates into people who would not recidivate. Our task thus was the generation of the right combination of vocational, adult educational, industrial, counseling, and religious programs to meet the varied needs of the people in our control. There were other goals: the maintenance of control and the achievement of profitability in prison industry, but we agreed that the reduction of recidivism was one of the most critical measures.

All that enthusiasm and hard work may or may not have gone for naught. I do not believe it was entirely wasted, but the legislative-analyst and the legislative-budget committees were used to the traditional budgeting format and saw no good reason to change. If we thought our efficiency would be increased by persisting in this new-fangled budget system, we could persevere, but we were to submit a conventional budget for their review.

About that time, I moved to Washington and the Bureau of Prisons, which was in the process of indoctrination in PPBS, which Congress did not like any better than the California legislature liked performance budgeting. As I look back now, we had made a serious error in our conceptualization, and it is a good thing for all concerned that our legislative masters did not allow us to proceed as we had planned.

It was a hopeless task to set goals for ourselves in the reduction of recidivism. If that were the measurement of our goal achievement, we would be seen by ourselves, the legislature, and the general public as far more unsuccessful than we really were. The truth is that our objective cannot be rehabilitation without a proven method of achieving such an elusive goal. We do know that recidivism rates fluctuate, but we have little or no empirical reason to believe that these fluctuations are in any way related to what we do in corrections. The more likely case is that recidivism is principally influenced by the rates of crime and the level of unemployment. However that theoretical position comes out, we have no reason to suppose that what we do in prison has more than a casual, almost random effect on recidivism. This is the important element in what we have come to think of as the message of Martinson.[3]

So what is the objective of corrections? How shall we establish our goals so that we can achieve accountability? I suggest that in the conventional sense neither corrections nor any other element of the criminal-justice system has an objective. The police neither prevent nor reduce crime; the correctional system must not be expected to change criminals for the better. The justification for what we do is not the achievement of an objective; we have no place to go like the National Aeronautical and Space Administration reaching for the moon before the end of the sixties.

What we do is a process, maintaining the custody or supervision of offenders in corrections. The police have another process to administer, the detection of crime and the apprehension of criminals. Processes go on and on without reference to the achievement of ultimate goals. What the police do has little or nothing to do with the crime rate. What correctional staffs do have little or nothing to do with the rates of recidivism.

So we justify our work in the criminal-justice system by doing it as well as we can. We have to meet our obligations. The locks on the cell doors have to work every day and every night, and that is one of the hundreds of objectives a prison warden for which must be held responsible. The probation officer who is attempting to set limits on Miss Doe's sexuality may or may not be wasting her time, but her obligation is the less ambitious duty of helping Miss Doe find an honest job, a decent place to live, and to facilitate the delivery of such services as Miss Doe may want of those to which she is entitled.

It is the task of our society through its aggregation of social and economic institutions to reduce crime and recidivism. Our task in criminal justice is the performance of the duties to which we are assigned in the arrest, prosecution, adjudication, and disposition of criminals. We are accountable to the elected governors and legislatures who appoint and fund us. They in turn are accountable to the public. The responsibility of the governor, the legislature, and the press is to know what is going on and care enough to see to it that we have the will and the resources to do it right. The evidence is that not many governors, nor many legislators, see themselves as really accountable to the public for their part in maintaining and improving the criminal-justice system. The consequence of that failure in the chain of accountability is that many of our colleagues drift through their duties. We are not stonemasons building a cathedral; there is no such culmination for our efforts. But we had better become like the stonemason who knows his particular craft and sees to it that it is always done well. Not even the most naive layman will be satisfied with correctional sergeants who cannot see to it that locks are kept in repair, nor will he be impressed with our courage in setting goals that could never be achieved. Credibility is the reward of competence and cannot be achieved in any other way. But in our field of administration, incompetence leads directly to an inhuman and disgraceful blotch on the character of American civilization.

When Judge Frank Johnson announced his decision in the case of *James* v. *Wallace*, the governor of Alabama made a scathing response in which he said, among other complaints, that prison reformers were sentimental do-gooders. The contempt that some of our countrymen feel for those who wish to do good for others passes my understanding, as does the silence in which we suffer this strange opprobrium. My first commitment in criminal justice is that I will do no avoidable harm. My second obligation is that if I can, I will try to do some good. I must be hard-nosed about it; wishful thinking and airy promises will get us into just as bad trouble—though different trouble—as the callous indifference at Mount Meigs. We can and must manage by objectives, but our objectives are numerous— the fulfilment of the many duties we are obliged to perform with concern and efficiency.

Notes

1. *James* v. *Wallace*, 406 F. Supp. 318 (M.D. Ala. 1976).
2. Court Watching Project, Inc., *A Citizens' Study of the Franklin County Municipal Court* (Columbus, Ohio: The Court Watching Project, 1975).
3. Robert Martinson, "What Works?—Questions and Answers about Prison Reform" *The Public Interest*, no. 35 (Spring 1974):22-54.

5 What Do They Expect?

The annual Congress of Corrections gathers together the correctional establishment, as it is usually designated by unfriendly observers. There is something for everybody's taste. Sometimes the assembled Congress is in a mood for ruminations about the enduring problems confronting the field. At the Congress that took place in Philadelphia in 1979, there was good reason to worry, as I tried to show in this chapter that I presented.

What concerned me most, and still concerns me, is the uncertainty of leadership in our field. Public expectations of corrections are never specific. Most of my colleagues regularly deplore the indifference that they think they perceive, but not many of them are prepared to tell the public why they should take any interest at all in convicts and their keepers.

A couple of years ago, one of our numerous journals of criminal-justice studies published a paper of mine entitled "Doing Good with a Hard Nose."[1] The gist of the article was that doing good is a perfectly acceptable goal in life, "do-gooder" should not be an invidious epithet, but that the obstacles to doing any good at all in corrections are formidable and can be traced to human frailties that the realities of bureaucracy accentuate. I said some harsh things about the ideology of management by objectives, holding that if corrections has any objectives—and I am not sure that it does—they cannot possibly be achieved unless daily obligations are discharged humanely and efficiently.

I dwelt on some horrible examples of this self-evident truth, and in doing so I took a swipe at the kind of administrator who thinks that it is not his place to tell the public how the criminal-justice system should be improved. I mentioned a lecture once administered to me by an important official of that persuasion—now gone from a service for which he was ill-suited—who considered it to be inappropriate for correctional officials to advocate changes and new programs. I said that this reticence was not commendable humility but rather an abdication of professional responsibility and a recipe for creating correctional stagnation.

I thought at the time that that was a telling point, and I still do. But a month or so after the publication of that article I sat next to an old friend at

I have made some slight editorial changes in the chapter, which appeared in the *Proceedings of the 109th Congress of Corrections of the American Correctional Association* (1979). I am grateful to the editor of the *Proceedings* for permission to print it here.

a banquet. He was at that time the director of corrections in a large state, a competent administrator doing as well as he could in an extraordinarily difficult management situation. He chastised me for the argument I had made for the administrator's role as an advocate. In his opinion, my exhortation was far off the target. The task of a director, he said, was to carry out the policies of the governor and the laws enacted by the legislature. He was responsible for doing no more than he was told to do, but to do it as well as he possibly could. What he personally thought should be done might be inconsistent with what the governor had established as a policy. After all, the governor had a view of the larger picture that the director could not have. It was for him to fit into that picture, not to change it.

We were unconvinced by each other's arguments. I continue to hold that a governor's cabinet officer must recommend policy changes as needed to the governor, and when that policy is approved, he must take whatever course he can to put it into effect. For an elevated bureaucrat, this is a change in role that is inconsistent with all his training and experience. One of the most comfortable aspects of the bureaucratic career is the requirement of political neutrality. As President Truman used to say, a chief executive and his staff must work in a hot kitchen. A bureaucrat can keep cool, making decisions and carrying them out in accordance with policies handed down by his elected superiors. My friend had spent most of his life as just such a bureaucrat. His willingness to discharge his new responsibilities by the familiar bureaucratic model was entirely natural, though if literally carried out most likely to harm his agency.

No governor ever won an election on a platform of prison reform. Most governors rightly perceive a prison as a source of trouble. Riots, escapes, and scandals can undo them, but few votes will come their way for initiating enlightened changes. If correctional systems are to resolve the problems that confront them, their successes will seldom occur because of the foresight or the initiative coming from a governor's office. The director must consider, foresee, and project ahead. He must advise and prod, and he must tell whoever can help him what must be done. The life of the advocate is not an easy one. The evidence is that most directors in these times make few friends with the grim news they have to tell. Only a handful of the directors now in office have occupied their posts for more than five years. National leadership, if it is based on successful executive experience in corrections, is limited to a very few seasoned names.

Their task is not getting easier. Most of us can recall a simpler time when there were competing versions of correctional doctrine, but each was enunciated with authority and without ambiguity. Men like Austin McCormick, Sanford Bates, Richard McGee, Jim Bennett, and Myrl Alexander left no one in doubt as to what the public should expect of corrections if their versions were accepted.

At the other end of the continuum of opinion, more hard-fisted ideas prevailed, but their exponents were just as sure of themselves and of the tough policies of strict discipline and firm control that they propagated. Without disrespect to contemporary occupants of comparable positions, I think it must be said that no one is conveying the clear and unambiguous version of the correctional present and future that we used to hear twenty or thirty years ago.

Three Sources of Uncertainty

The reasons are not hard to find. First, too many of the innovations on which we embarked so confidently in the fifties and sixties have failed the test of effectiveness as measured on the scales of recidivism. Rightly or wrongly, a good many professional investments lost heavily, sometimes needlessly, on that count. We do not hear much about group counseling, intensive treatment, therapeutic communities, and a host of other promising ideas, nor do we seem to have many bright new ideas floated out for test. Relative to the total mass of correctional budgets, the costs of these programs were moderate, but measured by postrelease conduct, the benefits were indiscernible, as we should have predicted in the first place.

The second cause of uncertainty runs deeper. Like nearly all governmental institutions, corrections functions before a sceptical and distrustful public. Schools do not teach as well as they should, soldiers do not fight as well, regulating agencies do not regulate in the public interest—and corrections does not correct. Or so it seems. We ourselves share in the doubts that prevail. Many of us wonder uneasily whether we are doing the right thing at all and whether our programs are serving useful public purposes. To the extent that we feel this way—and I do not contend that all correctional administrators are so troubled—we cannot present a clear and confident message to a public not subjected to daily exposure to our realities.

The third source of uncertainty is the diversity of the problems that we face. Some of these problems are the consequences of profound social and economic changes that our whole society is experiencing. The correctional apparatus that we have inherited was designed to meet the needs of simpler times. It is poorly suited to adapt to the conditions brought about by social change of the magnitude that we have seen in our lifetimes. These are tides that we cannot reverse; we have to accommodate to them. But there are also artificial problems—laws, policies, and regulations that were meant to solve problems that no longer exist or that have changed in form. Laws that forbid work-release programs, laws that prevent furloughs, and laws that limit prison-industry production and sales are all removable obstacles needlessly hindering us in the accomplishment of our work. Too often we take these barriers to progress as though legislation could not be repealed and regulations could not be revoked. A thorough-going review of our governing legislation should identify these obstacles for removal. Corrections is hard enough work under the best circumstances; we do not need the dead hand of the past.

Our predecessors never had to face these three sources of perplexity and confusion. Now I want to go on to discuss in more depth each of these problem areas. I cannot sweep them aside for the perplexed administrator, but I can at least make some suggestions for clearing the air.

Effectiveness at What?

What made anyone suppose that a weekly-group-counseling program would have detectable effect on recidivism? It was less than twenty years ago when my California colleagues and I persevered in a fruitless effort to prove that point with meticulously controlled studies—controlled at least as to the data going into and out of the computer. We did not get anywhere at all. Later, three independent researchers at UCLA tried the same feat with much more elaborate research design than we in the California Department of Corrections were able to stage. They, too, got nowhere, but they did write a widely acclaimed book that may have sealed the fate of group counseling and similar interventions.[2]

Looking back, I see now that to expect a positive result from such an evaluation was like trying to square the circle; it should have been seen as an axiomatic impossibility. No matter how powerful an experience a year of weekly-group-counseling sessions might be—or a year of daily sessions, if that had been possible—the notion that this treatment would offset the harsh realities of postrelease existence of the parolee should have been seen as preposterous.

Our evaluations proceeded on that line because everyone, especially those who were controlling our budgets, thought that the justification of programs depended on their evaluation by the criterion of recidivism. We did not protest. Many agencies still engage in such evaluations. There are some who would carry this process one absurd step farther: they argue that a correctional program should not merely reduce recidivism, but it must prove its worth by reducing crime rates.

I do not argue that recidivism is a scale that we should never use. It is obviously appropriate for the study of the effectiveness of a parole system (though not as simple to carry out as some would suppose), and recidivsm is an indispensable parameter when planning the development of the system. Nevertheless, it was silly to think that a program with demonstrable value for the improvement of communications and the maintenance of understanding within the harsh and often violent prison climate should stand or fall on the recidivism of its participants. True, we do not have easy methods for studying the results of any program by its improvement of the institutional climate, but that does not mean that we will use a wholly inappropriate measure because we cannot find one that is convincingly suitable.

I have labored this example because it goes to the heart of the prevalent notion that nothing works. A correctional institution or agency is far too complex in the interaction of its components to be validly evaluated program by program. What we need and must insist upon is a second generation of evaluation researchers who are capable of studying the effectiveness of programs in achieving their immediate goals. Do students in adult-basic-education programs learn to read or do they not? Do prison medical programs provide competent surgical and medical treatment for cancer and heart disease or do they not? These are the questions that evaluation research must properly address. It is irrelevant that those who have learned to read or those who have had cancer surgery go out to succeed on parole. Not all prison treatment programs are as easy to assess as these two, but the same principles must apply in the evaluation of any of them when coming to a judgement about continued support, modification, or termination.

Can Corrections Succeed or Fail?

There is a steamy speech that is often heard from critics of corrections to the effect that if a private business had the record of failures reported for our correctional systems for the last fifty years, that business would have long since gone bankrupt. What nonsense! Such arguments can and should be put to rest. Their irrelevance seems too transparently obvious to debate. Nevertheless that speech survives, and it influences many people who should know better.

The power of a correctional agency to rehabilitate anyone is limited and unpredictable; commitment to the rehabilitative ideal can be no more than a good intention. The minimum requirement for correctional institutions and agencies is to hold in custody or under surveillance the people the court sends as punishment and to do what is possible to help them. Success and failure can only be measured within the scope of these obligations.

Social realism must enter into the process of measurement. Some of the men and women who come to prison have been so shocked by the crisis in their fortunes that they are only too eager to get whatever help they need to reconstruct their lives. In such cases the opportunities for success are obvious, and, when the program fails, the reasons must be sought.

But too many of the offender population have been severely damaged by their commitment to criminal careers and all the psychological and social commitments that a criminal career entails. Correctional agencies cannot be excused from trying to help them, but to charge the failure of the individual as a failure of the system is to defy common sense.

I propose that the measurement of correctional effectiveness should be carried out on the scales of efficiency and humanity. A lot of agencies and institutions fail on these scores, and they should be held to account for their deficiencies accordingly. To suppose that the success or failure of a correctional agency is to be traced on a graph of recidivism over the years is to attribute to corrections far more responsibility than it can handle for the social and economic failures of the whole society. America may teeter on the edge of social bankruptcy, whatever that is, but whether it is or it is not has nothing at all to do with the way the correctional officials do their jobs.

The notion that a correctional agency has a mission to rehabilitate its clientele is old and respectable. Many people have firmly believed it and still do. It is untrue. Correctional agencies should not allow themselves to be evaluated on the performance of a task that is impossible. Our responsibility is difficult enough to discharge with credit. We have to keep hope alive among men and women whose situation gives them little reason to hope for better things. Unless they can engage in programs that give them a realistic expectation of getting these better things, most of them will return to prison, worse off than ever.

No one needs to be reminded that people go to prison as punishment for crimes they have committed. They come out of prison, too. If all that has happened to them is the lawless brutality of the idle gang on the yard or the suspended animation of the custodial lockdown, we can be sure that that success or failure after release will have nothing to do with a program. We do have a responsibility for the recidivist criminal if we have given him no other choice when he was our prisoner. He can be expected to persevere in his predatory ways if we have not even tried to show him a believable alternative.

The Troubles We Have Seen and Will See

We can classify our main troubles under four headings: conceptual, control, fiscal, and program. The most important heading is conceptual. We must clarify for ourselves and for our public the nature of our responsibilities. We have onerous duties to discharge, and we should be held to strict account for the way in which we discharge them. We have to keep our prisoners safe from each other and our staff safe from them. Prisons must be clean and decent and safely administered. The twentieth or the twenty-first-century prison should exist for the containment of offenders for whom no lesser punishment or control will suffice. It should be a prison in which opportunities are visible for lawful employment after release and opportunities are available for prisoners to better themselves if they so choose. Every effort will be made to prepare the prisoner for citizenship and participation in the community outside. All these obligations, if they are imposed on corrections, will entail a radical overhaul of the conceptual basis of a prison system. We are not going to drift into changes of this kind, but unless objectives of this magnitude are adopted, the present drift will be toward worse trouble than we have faced in these years of tribulation.

The truth is that a prison system maintained for punishment only, without a concept that guides it into service to the community, will be a stagnating, drifting system, poorly led and staffed by the kinds of people who are content to do as little as possible in a service that does no more than hold people for specified periods of time. Under such conditions, prisoners will indeed be dehumanized, and the preoccupation of everyone will be to prepare for the worst. This noxious state of affairs can be avoided, but only by an effort to conceptualize an alternative and put it into being. The pessimism that is so frequently to be heard assures that nothing good will happen and makes it probable that the bad things that are always possible in prisons will be worse than they have to be when they do happen.

Control, the second heading of trouble, has always been the first aim of officials and rightly so. Maintenance of control is getting harder all the time, as no person active in corrections needs to be told. What can be done? Let us begin with the heavy burden of our terrible legacy of prison architecture.

What we have now in most states is a collection of prisons, old and new, that is derived from a model that was well suited to conditions in the nineteenth century. Then our correctional ancestors moved convicts in lockstep formations from cells to mess hall and thence to mills or shops and back again. The old Auburn prison was admirably suited to the efficient control of prisoners under this simple but rigorous routine. We are not operating that kind of prison any more and never will again. The prison in which convicts move freely calls for a different design, but we persist in building the Auburn cellblock with electronic modifications. Gangs and factions flourish in this environment, and the exploitation of prisoners by fellow prisoners is hard to thwart. There is much renovation and reconstruction to be done in the interest of safety, lawfulness, and order. Until this reconstruction is done, we shall continue to have troubles in our prisons that might be avoided with more appropriate design.

Architecture is not the only problem. The prison as we know it has moved far from an autarchic control that prevailed until well after World War II. In the properly managed prison of the old style, as—for one example—Stateville under the rule of Warden Joe Ragen, there was never any question as to where authority resided. It resided in the person of the warden, whose word was final and never slow in forthcoming. This is not the place to recite in detail all the erosion of the warden's authority that has taken place. The old-time warden, an autocrat with princely powers, has been transformed into a field manager for the department of corrections that employs him. The important decisions about penal policy are made in the state capital. It is for the warden to carry them out faithfully as a technician, not as an executive with unlimited authority. The evolution from autocrat to manager was inevitable and generally beneficial. But control has become ambiguous and more so with the flowering of civil-service rules and regulations that have compromised management's control thoughout all government services. To add to the dilution of authority, the phenomenal growth of public-service-employees unions has placed in negotiation many of the prerogatives that used to be considered exclusively managerial. Even if we could, we should not go back to autocracy in the front office, nor should civil service be abolished, nor should the unions be curbed. These reversals of historic trends are not going to happen, and they should not. But it is time that some new principles should be introduced to establish the boundaries between the correctional manager's responsibilities and those that the civil-service commissions must retain and those that are legitimate concerns of the public-employees unions.

How is this to be done? The aim should be legislation that clearly lays out these boundaries and provides the means to assure that they are respected. Eventually both the states and the federal government will arrive at this point for all the agencies affected. Eventually is a long time, long because there are powerful interests in conflict: the interest of the general public, the political interest of the governor and the legislative leadership, the interest of managers, and the interests of subordinate prison employees and of the convicts whom they keep. All these interests work with and against each other in different ways in different agencies. It is no wonder that no governor that I have heard of has taken steps to move into this dangerous swamp. Eventually some governor must. We cannot continue in a condition in which command cannot be exercised when it is needed, in which promotions cannot be made on merit, and where working rules interfere with control. Consider this anecdote told me by a warden who related that when he took over a certain prison not long ago, he decided to make a tour of his new domain. When he came to the administrative-segregation unit, he was informed by the sergeant in charge that the rules of the union forbade the warden's physical presence in the interest of employee safety. The warden was a large and forceful man who was not to be intimidated, and he was not. That such a restriction on the warden's movement could be seriously proposed indicates a trend that has gone too far already and threatens to reach heights of absurdity. It is time for correctional officals to think through the essentials of a concordat in which all boundaries of responsibility would be delineated so that we will have a consensus on what must be done, and we can begin to take steps to induce the political actors to help us do it. It will be an intricate task to perform, and it will not get easier by deferring it.

Concordats, gentlemen's agreements about spheres of authority, and even iron-clad legislation will not work if trained and talented people are not on hand to keep a firm hand on their application. The warden who has come up through the ranks to a managerial post has been accustomed to issuing orders that are followed and to following orders issued to him. Arriving at the top, he has to learn the arts of analysis and negotiation. There are places where these arts are taught and can be learned. They should be expanded and made available to those who must resolve conflicts rather than win them. Along with the new correctional manager the union business agent should be offered a curriculum that will enable him to represent the long-range as well as the short-range interests of correctional employees. It takes two to bargain; where both sides understand what is involved in a good negotiation, the outcome is more likely to stand up to the test of long-term compliance.

The fundamental changes in architecture and organizational structure are urged to increase our ability to respond effectively to the formidable problems of control that now face correctional management. Those problems can be expected to become even more serious in the foreseeable future. There can be no question but that in the large prison systems of the industrial states we are dealing with a more difficult, refractory, and aggressive body of convicts than we had as recently as ten or fifteen years ago. The sense of danger that is spoken of so often by people who work directly with them, the high incidence of violence, the ubiquitous problem of drugs all testify to the development of conditions for which new measures of control will be needed. As time goes on, technology will solve some of these problems, but reliance on electronic marvels will not save our skins. We have to put our own expertise to work. We are not using all we know about the classification of prisoners, about the exploitation of incentives and disincentives, and about the maintenance of clear channels of communication. I doubt that any prison in the country is making constructive use of its prisoner-grievance system to spot the points at which needless abrasion is occurring and where the operation of the facility is not in conformance with policies. Many prison officials still resist the idea of a grievance system, many others install a nominal program, thereby harming their own credibility with the prisoner population. They deprive themselves of information that cannot be obtained in any other way.

The management of a large body of prisoners calls for a system of realistic incentives and disincentives. That system should be the basis for classification. It will not work without information flowing freely in both vertical directions. In a prison so managed there will be at least a closer approximation to fairness than in the facility in which communications trickle through clogged channels and misinformation and rumor flash unchecked through the grapevine. Most of the unpleasant surprises that happen in prisons take place because the staff has not worked hard at keeping the channels of communication open. Reliance on snitches and stool-pigeons is a dangerous foundation for security these days, but there are still many custodial people who depend on the crude methods of their forebears. When wardens and captains delude themselves into the notion that all is well because no information to the contrary is coming in from their usually reliable sources, we know how far we have to go in bringing prison administration into a safe condition, free of preventable violence and corruption.

Turning now to a third set of problems, the lack of money, the state of corrections extends from austere to desperate. The costs of merely keeping a prisoner under lock and key and increasing, and the cost of buidling facilities for locking up more people is increasing even faster. At the same time, the taxpayers on whom we depend are less and less inclined to give us what we ask for or believe we need. Throughout the seventies, we supposed that the pressures on us might diminish as the population ages; with fewer young people to commit crimes we ought to have some relief in the number of admissions. It is too early to be sure, but the indications that we ought to be getting if this is the case do not seem to be in sight. Prison populations are increasing, and most systems in the nation are experiencing pressures that are close to unacceptable.

The only answer is a shift in sentencing policy. Legislators and judges must consider far more carefully the irreducible costs of prison time. A man-year in prison is far too costly a public expense to squander on anyone who does not need to have it. It is no news to us or to our most vocal critics that too many people are sent to prison to serve sentences that are unreasonably long. Our task is to assume leadership in making a national correctional policy that limits incarceration to a minimum number of offenders for minimum periods of time. It is not clear what the formula for such a policy would be. It is a reasearchable topic; we need studies that enable legislators and judges to make rational use of expensive prison time that we are now frittering away on men and women who do not need it. Some statistics suggest that about 15 percent of the felony convictions in most states will be the maximum number of felons who should be committed to prison. That indication may be too high or too low. Whatever the proportion should be, the disparity between Minnesota, with an incarceration rate 42 per 100,000 and North Carolina with a rate of 210 per 100,000 cannot be defended by appealing to the differences in the quality of human beings in these states—especially when we find that the crime rates are almost identical.

Reduction of prison populations and prison time is not to be expected without realistic alternatives to incarceration. Too many of these alternatives are either nominal—nothing at all happens—or they are so poorly thought out that there is no reason to suppose that they do any good. Judges will not use alternatives for serious offenders unless they are confident that a good result can be expected. There are good programs, and we should know more about them and how they function. But there are not nearly enough to take the load of serious offenders out of prison. We have more than enough people telling us that more use should be made of alternatives to incarceration. We do not have nearly enough telling us how to do it, or, better, volunteering to do it themselves.

Perhaps the lack of good community programs has to do with the culture of pessimism that was inspired by the "nothing-works" message. That episode in correctional history was a necessary purge of some of the absurdities that were passing as rehabilitative treatment, but it also did a great deal of damage. Both the general public and a good many of the correctional professionals learned to think that because research told us that nothing works, nothing could work. Innovation withered in this climate of gloom. A creative pessimist is a contradiction in terms. Never has there been a time when corrections stood in so much need of creativity and was getting less of it than the present.

There are faint signs on the horizon of better things to come. For most correctional officials it is an article of faith that for the adult offender, whether in prison or out, a full work-week is the essential program ingredient. With a very few notable exceptions, this article of faith is more of a frustration than a goal for realistic aspiration. We think that if an offender is out in the community he should have a full-time job, whatever else we want him to do or he himself wants to do. If the offender is in prison, he should not be loitering on the yard or in a dayroom or—worse still—dozing in a classroom or workshop. He should be putting in an eight-hour day at believable work and being paid wages worth getting.

But most correctional agencies function without the essential program ingredient. This state of affairs is unique to American prisons. In no other country that I have visited do we find so much make-work, so much outright idleness, and such a culture of redundancy. It is not too much to say that most state prisons prepare criminals for a return to the community confirmed in the belief that society has no other place for them but the career of a superfluous person.

If this situation could be easily remedied, it would have been corrected long ago. The legal, technical, and political difficulties are well known and generally seen as virtually insuperable. There are ways out of this impasse. With the exception of the Texas Department of Corrections, a special case, the only flourishing prison-industry progrm is operated by the federal

Bureau of Prisons. That is readily understandable; the Bureau of Prisons has exclusive access to the federal market. That market is big enough to accommodate more producers. The laws and regulations that keep state-prison-industry systems out of it should be changed. The barriers to state prisons are artificial and were erected decades ago to prevent abuses that can now be prevented by other means. This solution to an old problem has been proposed before, and I have yet to hear of a sensible argument against it. Of course there are many and obvious vested interests using any argument they can scratch up to support their intransigent opposition.

Those arguments are voiced in the state legislatures, too. I suspect that the state-use market in most states should be adequate to support a much larger prison-industry production that the license-plate factories on which prisons still rely so heavily. This revitalization of prison industry will not occur unless the quality of prison production is competitive. Satisfactory production cannot be expected from a factory in which too many prisoners are assigned to get them out of the yard and dayrooms and in which the pay is nominal. The movement toward a simulation of free-industry conditions is an essential element of the revitalization that is so urgently needed. It is heartening to observe that the Law Enforcement Assistance Administration has invested so vigorously in the Free-Venture program initiated by the American Foundation to achieve this simulation. It is even more heartening to go into a Free-Venture workshop and see prisoners actually at work. It has been a long time since the law and the courts sentenced prisoners to hard labor; that irony was intolerably crude. But the way toward hard work has been demonstrated. It must occupy the first place on the agenda of correctional administrators.

Out of the Doldrums and into the Community

The agenda for correctional leadership are much longer than I have outlined here. I have done no more than scrawl my graffiti in the dust of inaction. There is trouble ahead in American prisons. Much of it is beyond the power of prison officials to prevent. But much is preventable; the commissioners and directors who can translate their concerns into activism will achieve and deserve the modest immortality that prison reform has conferred on some of their predecessors. The situation differs from state to state; not every director will be safe in the venture into leadership that I urge. My friend who thought that change of the system should be left to the governor will be uncomfortable with the kind of advocacy I see as necessary. But I am certain that there are potential leaders and opportunities for them to show the way toward improvement of a system that cannot be allowed to drift in policy and bloat in numbers for much longer.

The picture I have painted is not equally gloomy in every state. But whatever the condition of corrections may be, there is absolutely no reason for complacency and every reason to work for the improvement of a system that will assuredly get worse if it does not get better. Those improvements cannot possibly be the spontaneous remissions of our manifold troubles.

What do they—that nebulous and seemingly indifferent public—expect of corrections? In a democracy any administrator who expects to succeed in office must see to it that the public gets as much of what it expects as he can deliver. Within reasonable limits, the administrator can tell the public what it ought to want, and the public will expect it. For years, the public believed what we said about the rehabilitative ideal; if it has been disabused of that notion, we were principally responsible. We still have a duty to our political supervisors and to the widest public we can reach to say clearly and honestly what should be expected of us. Having conveyed that message, our energies should be devoted to delivering in accordance with the expectations we have encouraged. Sometimes delivery will not match promises and expectations, and the explanation must be sought and published. But what the public must not expect nor receive is the aimless drift of the pessimistic administrator who seeks only to survive.

The Dangerous Juvenile Offender

Cruel Choices for a Baffled System

In 1977 my colleagues in the Dangerous Offender Project and I were engaged in the research that led to the publication of our book, The Violent Few, *by Donna Hamparian, Richard L. Schuster, Simon Dinitz, and John P. Conrad (Lexington Books, 1978). Each of us was asked to deliver our thoughts on the problems of the dangerous juvenile offender in various conferences and workshops. I presented this chapter at a conference on juvenile justice that took place in Ocean City, Maryland in 1977.*

The tragic account of Billy had a sequel that added horror to the tale. When I returned from the conference at which this chapter was delivered, I learned that Billy had hanged himself at the Franklin County Jail. The place he chose for his suicide was just outside the dayroom in which a number of prisoners were watching television. Nobody was watching Billy.

What Shall We Do with These Murderous Boys?

During a week in 1977 we were edified, if that is the word, by the televised prosecution in Florida of a 15-year-old boy, Ronnie Zamora, accused and convicted of the robbery and murder of an elderly woman. Only excerpts were available to me in Ohio, but they were enough to give me a general sense of the proceedings. As I listened and watched, I wondered what on earth would happen to Ronnie if the jury were to accept the meretricious defense that the murder could be explained as a transient episode of insanity, induced somehow by excessive exposure to the exploits of *Kojak* and similar depictions of urban violence. The jury rejected this contention, and Ronnie will spend a long time in Florida's prisons, attaining manhood and mature years in a community in which he must struggle for physical survival. Had the jury found him not guilty by reason of insanity, the state of Florida would have been confronted with a formidable problem, hardly to be solved by a program of permanent abstention from the watching of television. Yet the absence of appropriate dispositions for boys like Ronnie presents criminal-justice decision makers with a cruel and limited set of choices. Florida could hardly place Ronnie in a community correctional setting, his appalling crime and his wretched history being what they were. The selection of dispositions was limited to prison, some kind of youth facility, and, possibly, a mental hospital. Prison will use up most of his life, if he survives it. A youth facility would have kept him too briefly to satisfy a fearful public. A mental hospital might or might not provide the treatment he needs—if such treatment exists. At this distance, and with my limited knowledge of the case, of Florida law, and of the social resources available for his care, I can go no farther than to say that the most important aspect of the case was not the defense nor the telecasting of the trial but rather the poverty of our social imagination. We do not know what to do with a boy like Ronnie, so we pack him off to the human rubbish heap, where he will be out of our sight and out of our minds. The situation does not seem to have inspired anyone to search for a more responsible solution to the problem of reconstructing Ronnie's miserable life and prospects.

By coincidence, I was involved that same week in the problems of another youth accused of murder. The public defender of an Ohio county asked me to testify in a juvenile-court hearing to determine whether a 17-year-old boy whom I shall call Billy should be bound over to an adult-criminal court for trial. Billy had been accused of the robbery and murder of a 72-year-old man, a situation that, on the face of it, seems guaranteed to mobilize a maximum of antipathy for the defendant, but it transpired that there was more to the story than met the eye.

Billy is one of a fairly large Appalachian family living on the margins of our economy. His parents have been on welfare more often than not. Poor managers, they have been unable to provide their children with more than subsistence. Love and harmony seem to have been rarely manifest in a home chiefly remarkable for violence. Billy recalls having been beaten by electric extension cords, straps, belts, sticks, and boards from early childhood until one day, when he was fourteen, his mother came at him in a fury with a plank with which she was going to beat him. He knocked her unconscious, and from that time on he seems to have been mostly on his own.

School had been an arena of defeat. He had great difficulty in reading and was eventually discovered to be dyslexic, neurologically impaired so that letters do not arrive in his brain in intelligible order for words to be made out of them. He learned to think of himself as a "dummy," the word that other children applied to him. By the time he was 9, he had taken to sniffing glue, which certaintly did not improve his nervous system. When he was fourteen, he dropped out, perhaps because of his unrelieved scholastic failures, perhaps because of his assult on his mother.

He took to hanging around, sometimes in the company of an uncle who seems to have introduced him to homosexual practices. It was not long before he was making 20 dollars "a trick" as a homosexual prostitute. A large portion of his earnings went into the purchase of various narcotics, which did not include any "heavy stuff."

One of his customers was the old man who was the victim in the offense. The actual events that took place on the Fourth of July are necessarily hard to be sure about, as you will see. It appears that Billy, his uncle, and the old man took a motel room to pass the long weekend together. They drank heavily and smoked some pot. As they became more and more intoxicated, conviviality turned into acrimony. They ran out of beer and the old man told Billy to go out and get some more, calling him a dummy and a punk as he issued the order. The official account alleges that in a fury Billy attacked him and administered such a beating that the old man succumbed. The pathologist's report shows that the alcoholic content of the old man's blood was so high that his death was probably imminent anyway.

Juvenile-court jurisdiction in Ohio terminates at age 18, and Billy was 17 years and 3 months. The public defender was impressed with Billy's vulnerability. So was I, when I interviewed him. He is a slight youth with chestnut blonde hair, blue eyes, and a fair, beardless complexion. He speaks rather haltingly, unsure of himself with strangers. A nonverbal intelligence test elicited an IQ well above average. When asked what he would like to do, he says he would like to join the army, to serve his country, and after discharge he would like to go to Florida and work as a deep-sea fisherman, where, he understands, a person can earn as much as $30,000 a year. Last spring a friend took him to Florida and he liked the climate and the sea. He does not think of himself as a homosexual; he has had lots of girlfriends, but he can make so much money turning tricks that he doesn't see why he shouldn't.

His dreams and aspirations for a fisherman's life were predicated on the hope that he would not be bound over to the court of common pleas. If he had been committed to the Ohio Youth Commission, he could have been placed in a private facility for treatment, assuming that the Commission was willing to take the risk involved. The public defender had interested a remarkable man named Tom Peters in Billy's case. Peters is an entrepreneur of altruism, a man who has accepted the gospel of community-based corrections and has established a small halfway house, which he calls "Betterway," in a city in northern Ohio. He interviewed Billy twice, each time at considerable length, convinced himself that he could help him, and so testified in the juvenile-court hearing.

Thus there were three options for the court to consider. If Billy were to be bound over to the court of common pleas he would be committed to prison for life or for a considerable term. If jurisdiction were to be retained by the juvenile court, he would be committed to the Youth Commission, which could assign him to one of its secure institutions and sooner or later might place him at Betterway, an action that, I think, the Commission would seriously consider if the court were to recommend it.

Ohio prisons are overcrowded and underprogrammed. Naturally an effort would be made to protect Billy, but such measures would seriously restrict his participation in the educational and remedial programs that he badly needs. In the dense throngs of men and boys in American megaprisons, people get lost, sometimes until it is too late. A careful prison warden would try to see to it that a pretty youth like Billy would be kept out of harm's way, if only to prevent rivals for his favors from doing battle. Billy would not be a welcome prisoner, nor is it conceivable that he would eventually become better for the experience.

The Youth Commission facilities are smaller, and programs relevant to Billy's serious educational and psychological problems are at least in principle available. Again, his vulnerability would require a responsible superintendent to take measures for his protection. We could hardly expect that Billy could have the full benefit of the programs provided; I think the willingness of Betterway to take him on would be likely to strike a responsive chord.

Whether Mr. Peters could do as well as he hoped we shall probably never know; the court decided to bind Billy over for trial as an adult. I am certain that this decision was made with regret and concern. The cruel choice between a child's best interests and the protection of society had to be resolved. Billy stands accused of the most serious of crimes, and his background and personal situation inspire no confidence at all in his ability to change. To argue that he is not dangerous is to dismiss the horrible affair on July 4th, a record of violent family relation in his home, and a life without adult control for at least three years. Commitment to the Youth Commission would have to end when he reached age 21, whether he were doing well or badly. If he were to escape from custody, especially if he were to leave Betterway, the court's vulnerability to charges of undue leniency and disregard of its responsibility for the protection of society would be difficult to answer. We can hardly blame the troubled judge, but we can wish that our powers of social invention could have provided him with a better way of disposing of this pathetic youth. I am not sure that Mr. Peters' Betterway was indeed the better way that we needed. Whether it was or not, the decision must have been agonizing. To commit anyone, even a confirmed recidivist, to a long term in prison is a hard decision for a judge, especially if he has some knowledge of what a long term in a contemporary prison must be like. To commit a naive and beardless boy to such a maelstrom must be a painful action, no matter how justifiable it may be.

The similarity of the problems posed by Ronnie Zamora and Billy needs no underlining. The juvenile-justice system has been troubled by boys like this throughout its history. Their crimes are so grave that it is incongruous to use the standard juvenile-court rationale and assign a priority to the protection of the child's best interest. So we bind them over to an adult-criminal court, thereby assuring the maintenance of control for whatever number of years is deemed appropriate in the state criminal code. In doing so, we force the boy into premature manhood and abandon serious effort to reconstruct his life; in most cases we assure that he will be even worse when he leaves the hands of the state than he was when he came.

If we are to believe what we read—and I believe some of it—Ronnie and Billy would not be much better off if they were kept in the jurisdiction of the juvenile court. Newspaper reports insistently convey the message that the situation is out of control in the largest cities. We are told that the courts are so burdened that due consideration of cases is impossible and that vicious young thugs are able to "get away with murder," because nobody really knows what is going on. Although I do not doubt the veracity of at least some of these reports, data are insufficient to give us a clear picture of the discrepancies between serious delinquency and its disposition. If the conditions in the family and juvenile courts of our largest cities are as bad as they are said to be, it is unlikely that any amount of data could be assembled to make this sort of assessment.

But even if the workload is not as unmanageable as it is represented, even if we could be sure that in every city most serious juvenile offenders are picked up by the police and promptly placed under the court's control, the fundamental problem would remain. It is not an organizational problem, to be solved by the improved training of the police or the selection of more and better juvenile-court personnel. It is a conceptual problem of deciding on a constructive and effective response to the serious juvenile offender. In this respect, I contend that we are virtually bankrupt. Our ideas are threadbare and our problems are worse; all too often they continue the production of the "state-raised youth," so well described by John Irwin in his memorable book, *The Felon*.[1]

Irwin identifies four themes in the world of the state-raised youth. First, violence is the proper mode of settling an argument, and a man must be ready to inflict it and face it. Second, membership in cliques commands loyalties and defines values. Third, homosexuality defines an exploitative and often violent caste system, whereby sexual conduct is based on the ability to exercise force and the complementary deprivation of masculinity that results from subjugation. Fourth, there is a fantasy of the "streets" as a temporary sojourn for orgiastic pleasure, a place for holidays from the real world of the institution.

No one wants to raise youths like this. Indeed, legislators, judges, and correctional officials will be unanimous that this is precisely the kind of result that they do not want to get. But this is a kind of young man that reform schools have been raising for many decades. Such young men are still being raised, mainly because the state does not know what else to do with them once it gets them.

The Circular Misery of Wrongs

The absences of ideas and the inappropriateness of programs for the management of the serious juvenile offender as a separate class is a familiar state of affairs. The inadequacies of youth correctional facilities are staple items for reformist rhetoric. The traditional reform school has been denounced roundly for many decades. Modifications of architecture, program activities, and staff orientation have indeed taken place. But the more it changes, the more it is the same. The hideous old battlements that our nineteenth-century forebears built with the apparent intention of scaring kids into better behavior have been demolished or at least remodeled. The occasional survival of these legacies of oppression is unanimously deplored, and their use is justified on account of the absence of funds for replacement. Discipline by "cadet officers," which was once the mainstay of order in the reformatory, has gone for good and so has the humiliating lockstep. The vestiges of military programming that remain are the harmless remnants of a noxious tradition. Generally it is accepted that youth-corrections facilities should be quite small and that staff should be qualified to administer a resocializing program.

The new dilemmas confronting state agencies in planning residential treatment for youth have only recently become matters of general recognition. We have not been accustomed to differentiating the dangerous juvenile offender or any other class in the workload of juvenile delinquency. For years enlightened judges and probation officers have operated on the principle that it is desirable to limit the penetration of the juvenile-corrections system so far as possible in considering the disposition of any delinquent boy or girl. Therefore some kids went on probation, and only those who seemed to be unmanageable in the community went to training schools. The nature of the offense obviously had something to do with the disposition, but the ideology prevailed, and still does, that the nature of the child's personal situation rather than the nature of his offense should determine his treatment. The population mixture in the institutions includes delinquents of an extremely serious order and others whose infractions of the law have been close to insignificant. But once arrived at the institution, treatment tends to be undifferentiated except as to its duration. Its content depends on present behavior rather than on the events that brought the youth into the custody of the state. Considering our uncertainty about measures that can be expected to prepare people in custody for a return to the community, this lack of differentiation is entirely understandable. So far, our experiments in differential treatment have been inconclusive for the formulation of new policy.

The need for change is in the air. Perhaps we may attribute its recognition to research that has shown that treatment is much less effective than we had hoped and that recidivists from youth facilities are prolific and frequent criminals. Perhaps it was the alarm of a number of juvenile-court judges who have been critical of youth corrections but have not had any alternative disposition available. Perhaps it has been the fascination of the media with the youthful mugger and rapist that has put the entire juvenile-justice system on the defensive. Whatever the sources, we now have a consensus that there is a dangerous juvenile offender and that the state's response to him is inadequate for the protection of the public.

This order of classification is new and inconsistent with the traditional suppositions of the juvenile court in the years before the Supreme Court's decision in the *Gault* case.[2] During that long period in which our ideas about youth crime and its treatment took form, became standardized for practice, and eventually came under such fundamental challenge that they could not survive as constituting a paradigm controlling further development, the presumptions about delinquency were simple. The juvenile delinquent was by definition a child in trouble. It then became the task of the court and the correctional system to remedy the trouble. The nature of the offense was not the determinant of the decision. Rather, the child was to be seen as a whole person, and the magnitude of his offense was not necessarily the measure of the intervention needed. No practice is as simple as an elegant theory that prescribes it. Of course steps were taken to assure that such an exceptional person as the teenage murderer would be kept under control for a longer period of time than a peer whose offense was less grave, even if the lesser offender's social or psychological problems might be more severe. The post-*Gault* court has discarded some of these assumptions. The parental role will undoubtedly be further dismantled. The primary difference between the juvenile court and the criminal court will be found in the limits on sentencing procedures. The way is clear for a new and more rigorous disposition of the serious juvenile offender.

It is at this point that we encounter the root issue, the most serious problem, among so many other serious problems, now confronting American jurisprudence. Legislators and judges must bring about changes in the administration of juvenile justice if severely damaged children are not to be further damaged by the actions of the state. The circular misery in which the chronic delinquent is entangled is both personal and social. The ruin of his lifetime begins early and menaces everyone around him.

It should be a primary consideration in the administration of justice that the court shall do no harm. The prospect ahead is that harm may well be routine. We must concern ourselves with the modification of that prospect; we wish to minimize the damage done to children under the protracted control of the state. As for the larger world of creative jurisprudence, I ask, in what other domain of the law must judges and lawyers confront the probability that decisions they make and actions they take will not redress wrongs done but rather will initiate new and even more grievous wrongs?

A Way Out of the Conceptual Vacuum

Our anxieties about the dangerous juvenile offender have not propelled us far into the realm of innovation. Public discourse seems to be limited to four major themes for the modification of the official response to the problem of violent crime when committed by children. I will discuss these options specifically because each of them illustrates the obstacles to constructive change.

First, there is the response of the juvenile court to the exceptionally serious offense, ordinarily committed by a minor whose maturity in criminal behavior is all too apparent to everyone in contact with him. Such a case as Billy's can be and often is declared inappropriate for adjudication in the juvenile court and "bound over" for regular criminal proceedings in an adult court. It would be interesting to know how many cases are handled this way, of what types, and with what consequences. Unfortunately, the statistical picture is murky. Relying on the *Uniform Crime Reports* we can only say that in the universe of juvenile dispositions the referral to an adult court occupies an inconspicuous space, about sixty-nine thousand or 4.4 percent of all juveniles arrested.[3]

There are no firm data as to whether there is a trend to use this option more frequently. We know nothing of the types of cases bound over, the actions taken by the adult-criminal court, or the consequences of those actions for the individual, for the correctional system to which he is committed, or to the community at large for the supposed protection of which the juvenile is converted into an adult. We shall have to wait patiently for data that can facilitate an informed discussion of these issues.

Although we cannot measure, we can inspect the logic of the waiver of juvenile-court jurisdiction and consider where it will lead us. In the days of the pre-*Gault* court the rationale was logical. The custodial facilities that the juvenile court can command are juvenile institutions. Jurisdiction over any ward is limited to the duration of his minority—with some adjustments in the law of some states. If the court has to consider the case of a 17 year old charged with a heinous crime, it is understandable that it would wish to assure control beyond the maximum of four years to which its jurisdiction is limited.

The commitment of an experienced young violent offender with previous commitments to juvenile institutions to yet another such facility is difficult to defend as in either the boy's interest or in society's. The institution for older delinquents is balanced on an opposition between a staff culture and a criminal culture—a balance that is easily tipped. The contribution of the boy to the criminal culture is likely to outweigh the positive benefits he may gain from the commitment. The court has every reason to ask, why on earth continue the pretense that this young thug is a child in trouble? Why should he not be counted as a young adult in the prison system rather than an old child in the youth-corrections system?

The answer to these questions if anything but obvious. For the boy himself, the advantage of yet another youth commitment is less time to serve, although in states that are experimenting with mandatory sentences for juveniles, the advantage will be narrower than it used to be. For the state the value of more time served by an adult commitment is increased incapacitation of a young man of whom the community is afraid. There is also the popular belief that an adult commitment will be more effective in achieving the goals of general deterrence and intimidation. This belief has yet to be convincingly verified, but sceptical critics of the system have not yet shaken it with data. Whatever the truth may be about these issues the chances that the offender himself will be better for the experience of incarceration in either system are negligible. The bindover will accomplish a longer incapacitation and a more vigorous expression of community outrage. These are negative accomplishments, and their value is impossible to verify.

The bindover is an option available to the juvenile court, and it is exercised in different ways by different judges. Indeed, we hear that in some communities minors ask to be bound over, evidently believing that the chances for leniency are greater in adult than in the juvenile courts. But the uncertainty about the propriety of the bindover hides a conceptual vacuum. We do not know what to do with this apparently dangerous youth, so we put him away for as long as we can. The most we can hope for is that the experience will be so unpleasant that he will do whatever he can to avoid its repetition.

I do not know of any evidence on the effectiveness of incarceration in the intimidation of any offenders from the commission of further crime. The data on recidivism available to me appear to show that a majority of the people released from prison—perhaps as many as 60 percent—do not recidivate.[4] I doubt that they have been rehabilitated, so I will tentatively conclude that intimidation has motivated them to keep out of trouble. But we are talking about a dangerous juvenile offender. He is usually a chronic recidivist for whom incarceration holds few unacceptable terrors. Even if intimidation is effective for many prisoners, it is least effective for him.

Is this all we can do? Is it reasonable to concede so much to the prevailing pessimism? The worst aspect of the consensus that "nothing works" is the corollary to which it leads: nothing can work. As logical as the bindover seems to the judge and the public, the consignment of the young aggressive recidivist to prison is an admission of defeat. The record of youth-training facilities with such young men is discouraging, but the structural and programmatic faults in most of them glare at us so obviously that it is clear that improvements must be possible if we have the will to undertake them. To excuse the juvenile-justice system from the effort on the ground that "nothing works" is to admit that society is indifferent about results.

Against the occasional bindover of the truly exceptional delinquent as an individual case I will not complain. But to define a class of offenders who may be bound over is to create a policy that closes out the prospect of change. There must be continuing pressure on administrators, clinicians, and researchers to generate a better solution for this troublesome fraction of the delinquent population than the deep-six to which the tough-minded, so-called realists are willing to consign them.

The reverse of the bindover strategy is the mandatory sentence for the dangerous juvenile offender. Instead of sending him off to an adult prison, he is to be kept in the juvenile-justice system until he is old enough for prison, a model that has been adopted by the state of New York. I do not hear from advocates of this policy any suggested activities to fill up those years. That would not matter if the professionals who are responsible for the design of programs appeared to have any treatment innovations in mind. They do not. We are asked to make the same act of faith in the usefulness of a mixture of incapacitation and intimidation that is implied by advocates of more bindovers.

The emerging solution, as the category of the dangerous juvenile offender takes form as a class for which there are criteria for selection, is the secure facility, usually rather small, usually well provided with staff positions, and usually quite expensive to operate. If dollars were the only measure of our concern, it would be clear that despite my jeremiads our society has not given up on these young people. But again, we have a conceptual vacuum.

Two examples will illustrate the point. The publication last year of *Juvenile Victimization* by Bartollas, Miller, and Dinitz provides us with an account of how things go in a well-designed, fairly new (1961), and generously staffed (145 staff for 192 residents), facility designated for aggressive older boys in Ohio.[5] Although most of the problems in maintaining control are recognized by the staff, the culture is exploitative and criminal. Some of the staff are so fearful of their charges that they hide in the security of their offices. A constant testing of the courage and resourcefulness of the others seems to go on. When residents are out of the sight, there is considerable violence and sexual imposition, following, as if by prescription, the theoretical analysis that I have quoted from Irwin. In the air is a climate of intimidation with all the roles that result from that kind of interaction.

The program itself consists of the usual mixture of counseling, remedial education, and vocational training. It is supported in the institutional-mission statements by such language as: "[Our goals are] to promote positive attitudinal and behavioral change within an atmosphere of mutual respect and personal dignity; to provide a resident with opportunities to gain an increased understanding of himself, others, and his environment;

and to learn to meet his needs in socially acceptable ways."[6] The institution described is not atypical, except that the discrepancies between intentions and performance have been documented with painful thoroughness. This is a situation in which the staff still has the last word, but the dominant boys among the residents enjoy most of the control. Those familiar with the literature of youth-training schools or who have had access to oral accounts of how things have been for the last half-century, will recognize this facility as the legitimate heir of an old and disgusting tradition. One can account for the persistence of the tradition; staff idealism erodes in the incessant backwash of unrealized expectations; training is insufficient to prepare recruits for the interactions ahead; leadership by seniors is perfunctory and rhetorical—the list can go on. To my mind, the primary failing to which this dismal list of failings is attributable is the compromise with residents over lawful conduct. Once that compromise has been made, and unlawfulness has been overlooked, the hope for creating a civic culture is gone. As the authors of this powerful book put it: "instead of modeling themselves after other professional staff, the professional staff is subverted and adopts the style and values of the residents. . . . [A]s long as personnel are in the institution, they must react and respond in resident terms. The turf belongs to the inmates.[7]

These failings of the conventional youth-corrections facility are well known, and an understanding of them certainly is not my special preserve. Because the youth correctional facilities of Massachusetts shared most of these unpromising characteristics, along with some special handicaps peculiar to a bureaucracy too long entrenched, Commissioner Jerome Miller initiated his celebrated experiment with deinstitutionalization. It has been described so frequently that one hardly knows which account to cite, but I will call attention to the most recent one, that of Ohlin, Miller, and Coates.[8] Massachusetts has never been able to deinstitutionalize its youth-corrections program in the strictest sense of the word. There are still "Secure-Care Units" for the management of extremely aggressive youth in units of a dozen, with a staff almost as large. Although data are hard to come by—these are not the programs on which Miller and his disciples wish to rest their case—the usual length of stay seems to be less than a year, and the administrative pressure on the staff is to get kids out rather than keep them in.

My own observation of this element of the Massachusetts program was brief and quite possibly unrepresentative, but it was provocative. The facility was at some distance from downtown Boston, an enclave of delinquents on the grounds of a mental hospital. It was in the charge of a pleasant young man whose commitment to the cause shone through his realistic estimate of the prospects for success as it is usually understood in activities of this kind. He noted that most of his twelve youths had no family interested in them;

most had been committed for extremely serious crimes of violence; and most had educational and social handicaps of massive dimensions wholly apart from the handicap of a record of frequent and grievous delinquency. In his words, "most of these guys have been moving so fast through life that they decide what they should do after they have done it. All we can do is to slow them down." He gave as an example of the process of deceleration an incident that had occurred that morning, before my arrival. Pointing to a small stereo speaker on the floor opposite his desk, he said; "One of the boys threw that at me this morning because I had turned him down on a home visit—he wasn't ready for the privilege. I asked him why he did it, and he said it was because he was so mad at me. Then after thinking it over for a minute, he went on to say, 'I guess I wasn't as mad as I would have been a month ago. I wouldn't have missed you then'."

The program consists of remedial education, some athletics, and some group counseling. Except for the lack of a vocational-training program, the very small size of the population, an its undiluted composition—everybody's tough—the program has a family likeness to the program in the much larger Ohio institution. I would suppose the Massachusetts people would subscribe to the official Ohio objectives as I transcribed them earlier. But slowing violent delinquents down, the realistic stated goal of the Massachusetts program manager, does not seem to me to be a sufficient objective. It is a step ahead from the treatment that such boys receive in most states. It may be that its success will be more apparent than its staff expect. After all, the history of corrections is strewn with blasted expectations, and the wise manager will mute his hopes with modesty. But when experience with this kind of offender is considered as a frame of reference for assessment of the Massachusetts adventure and its underlying concepts, I do not see much reason to expect a greatly improved performance. The Harvard report to which I have referred found that recidivism from secure-care units was in the order of 60 percent, much higher than any of the other residential or nonresidential placements. An interesting additional finding is made: there seems to be less recidivism among those who began in secure care and ended there when compared with those who were transferred from a less secure program to secure care. In a system like this, the impact of program failure has its own special significance.[9] A possible interpretation of such a finding is that where the system is as eager for success as is the case in Massachusetts, the client's failure within the system adds a confirmation to his expectation of failure in the conventional world.

Massachusetts is not the only state with experimental work under way to discover a more effective way to hold and help the dangerous juvenile offender in spite of himself. The very small living unit that is characteristic of the Massachusetts program may well be an essential feature of the system of the future; at least it offers the most likely laboratory for the development of whatever successful approach may be feasible. It is too early to say what we can expect, but at least it is probable that many of the repulsive effects described by Bartollas and his colleagues can be entirely avoided. I suspect that the Massachusetts planners believe that there is a way to be found for improved control and treatment that will not require the maintenance of even the tiny secure-care units that now seem necessary.

As mentioned earlier, there seem to be four approaches to the problem of the Dangerous Juvenile Offender. Binding over the older ones converts them into adults. To require a mandatory sentence of two or three years is tantamount to changing part of the juvenile-justice system into an essentially adult system in which incapacitation is the primary goal. To modify the existing system by developing specialized secure units constitutes an act of continuing faith in the state as a vehicle for treatment. Each approach calls for the state to continue raising youth.

These three propositions contain within them the foundations of doubt. As to the first two, we back down on our national commitment to a fair start for children. Perhaps we can give up on the adult offenders, or some of them, as too scarred, too damaged to be accessible to help. I do not think we are yet willing to give up on the sixteen or seventeen-year-old kid who has foundered in delinquency because of the mismanagement of his early years by the adults in his life. As to the third proposition, the placement of these minors in small state institutions, we have only too much reason to believe that state agencies for the extension of help to people needing help will become bureaucratized, impersonal, and preoccupied with procedures. There are many things that only the state can do well, but the management of human relationships is not one of them.

So the fourth policy option is the regeneration of the private sector. In a sense, this choice has always been available. Children of the upper classes who get out of control have for many years been sent away to military academies or similar residential schools for attention and discipline that they could not get at home. Some of these facilities may be well managed; some are certainly frauds against distracted parents. We do not really know much that is objective about these places, but there are suspicions that in keeping the bad rich boy out of a reform school his parents may not be getting a much better bargain from the boarding school that is willing to take him in.

The state as *parens patriae* has money to spend, too. Nobody really knows anything definite about the traffic in difficult children, often across state lines, which gets them out of institutions in which they are unmanageable and into group homes, camps, or private institutional situations that are willing to manage for a price and able to make a profit from that price. Obviously there should be much more known about this situation, and it may well be that it is one of those many entrepreneurial activities of modern times that needs a federal regulatory agency to assure the maintenance of standards.

All that is by way of recognition that the private sector is not necessarily a reliable resource for converting the dangerous juvenile offender into an inoffensive but productive citizen. Nevertheless, I think there are a number of reasons for supposing that most of the future progress to be made in improving the state's response to this figure of our concern may lie in this direction. I shall conclude this chapter by outlining my reasons for believing that enlightened policy should go as far as it can in the encouragement of the private sector to care for these youths and to create programs for their socialization.

First, as I have already indicated, the state is not well adapted to the helping role. I think that is as it should be. The state should prevent avoidable misery, but it has no business making individuals happy or morally better. Its tools are those of management and order; its procedures are bureaucratic; its agents cannot express the state's love or concern because the state is not an entity capable of love and concern. Impersonality, fairness, and rationality are what we expect from the state. It is not to take risks, and although it may and does experiment, the experiments it conducts are directed at the improvement of state services, which sets a special boundary to the possibilities for improvement.

Second, the kinds of services that dangerous juvenile offenders need do not lend themselves to the kinds of careers for which civil servants are recruited and around which they build their lives. The pattern of thirty or so years in the same service, with promotion by seniority, civil service and union rules about hours, duties, privileges, rights, and training is workable for a fire department or for highway construction and maintenance. It is much less appropriate when the work to be done is in the influencing of others by example, counseling, and control. It is even less appropriate for the special tasks that those assigned to the dangerous juvenile offender must carry out.

All of us must know in our bones what the problem is. The best of intentions and the highest of motivations will erode with emotional fatigue. It is a rare man or woman who can confront hostility professionally and constructively for the duration of a normal civil-service career. Some day some salty young resident will sling a stereo speaker at the civil-servant counselor and the response will be inappropriate, not because the counselor is new and untrained but rather because he is too experienced and burnt out. I suggest that ways have to be found to enlist energetic and well-disposed young people to work for a few years only in facilities of this kind. I do not think that such a way can be found in the civil service.

The third problem is one of leadership. It has been my observation that the best programs revolve around the personality of a manager or director who possesses charisma. Examples come readily to my mind, and probably to the mind of anyone else who has watched schools, counseling services, group therapy, and even prisons. We should make it easier for people of this kind to build programs that fit their potential contributions. I do not think that conventional state procedures lend themselves to the kind of voluntarism that the charismatic leader requires for scope, happy accidents to the contrary notwithstanding.

Fourth, a private employee is much more easily hired or fired than the civil servant. Although it is untrue that civil servants cannot be fired, (I have seen it done), the difficulties will daunt all but the most determined manager and will certainly detain him from more profitable uses of his energies.

Finally, it is a lot easier to get rid of an unsatisfactory program that is on a service contract to the state than it is to phase out a budgeted state program. In either case the commissioner of corrections—or whoever he may be—does not have an easy task. Other arrangements have to be made for service, pressures to continue the program in spite of poor performance will usually be heavy, and the Commissioner is in the politically unenviable position of making a considerable number of enemies and few, if any, friends. But it is easier to refuse a new contract than to close down a bad state program, and failure is a contingency for which provision must be made.

I cannot prove that the private sector is the best hope in this unpromising challenge to the state's competence. Obviously if we are to choose this route, we cannot expect an overnight transformation. Legions of young men and women are not out there eagerly waiting for their chance to show what they can do with these troubled and sometimes frightening young offenders. Nor is there an obvious category of people serving organizations who can channel their energies into constructive service.

And even more obviously, once we have state funds transferred to private organizations for the provision of services, there will be abuses and shortcomings and failures that could have been prevented had adequate precautions been taken. The state will still have standards to set and practices to regulate. It will, however, be out of the business of regulating itself, but it will still be the teacher.

Many years ago, Mr. Justice Brandeis wrote: "[O]ur government is the potent, the omnipresent teacher. For good or ill, it teaches the whole people by example. Crime is contagious. If the government becomes a law breaker, it breeds contempt for the law; it invites every man to become a law unto himself; it invites anarchy."[10] He was not writing about the operation of facilities for the management of the dangerous juvenile offender, but his point extends to our problem. What the state finds itself doing in even fairly well run juvenile facilities is condoning unlawful conduct by allowing a criminal culture to control the turf. This is exactly the example that cannot be permitted in residential facilities. It may be possible to avoid it in a state facility, but I suggest that we will all be a lot safer if we turn the task over to the concerned entrepreneur who is willing to comply with the state's guidelines, to do as the state requires but not as the state itself has so commonly done in the past.

What do we want the state to teach? I think that whatever else is taught—from welding to the primal scream—the lessons have to take place in a lawful community, one in which either violations of the criminal law do not occur or, if they do, they result in immediate adverse consequences. Obviously life outside is not like that. The dangerous juvenile offender usually comes from a nearly lawless society and will return to it. That cannot excuse the state from its duty to assure that while he is in custody he is safe and prevented from unlawful conduct. We do not know what good observance of this principle will do, but we know all too well what harm will be done by not observing it.

This chapter began with a discussion of the problems posed by two dissimilar boys, Ronnie and Billy, charged with identical crimes. It is superfluous to add that any conceivable regeneration of the juvenile-justice system will be an inadquate solution for the problems they pose. It is too late: too late for the victims, too late for boys who seem to have been programmed for violence. Obviously the country needs services that can channel such young people into life patterns that are not patently dangerous to themselves and to others. Such tasks are beyond the capability of the state. The immense task ahead is for the philanthropic community working in partnership with the state. Ronnie and Billy are symbols of the urgency of what has to be done.

Notes

1. John Irwin, *The Felon* (Englewood Cliffs, N.J.: Prentice-Hall, 1970), pp. 26-29. For another and confirming account, see Malcolm Braly, *False Starts* (Boston: Little, Brown, 1976), pp. 36-60.

2. *In the Matter of the Application of Paul L. Gault and Marjorie Gault, Father and Mother of Gerald Francis Gault, a Minor, Applicants.* United States Supreme Court, October Term 1966. 1 Criminal Law Reporter 3031-3054.

3. Federal Bureau of Investigation, *Uniform Crime Reports* (1976) table 57, p. 220. (Washington, D.C.: Government Printing Office, 1977).

4. See *Uniform Parole Reports*, December 1976, published by the National Council on Crime and Delinquency, for the most optimistic estimate of prison recidivism.

5. Clemens Bartollas, Stuart J. Miller, and Simon Dinitz, *Juvenile Victimization: The Institutional Paradox.* (New York: Halsted Press, 1976).

6. Ibid., p. 31.

7. Ibid., p. 273.

8. Lloyd E. Ohlin, Alden D. Miller, and Robert B. Coates, *Juvenile Correctional Reform in Massachusetts* (Washington, D.C.: U.S. Government Printing Office, 1977).

9. Ibid., pp. 77-78.

10. *Olmstead* v. *U.S.* 277 U.S. 438, at 485 (1928). I regret to add that Mr. Justice Brandeis wrote in dissent in a case involving wire-tapping. He was joined by Mr. Justice Holmes.

7

Who's in Charge?

The Control of Gang Violence in California Prisons

I left the California Depatment of Corrections in 1967 to join the staff of the U.S. Bureau of Prisons. After twenty years with the same department, I kept in touch with developments that became more and more alarming as the years went by. Although the level of violence had been increasing before I left, the events of the next ten years were taking place in a prison scene vastly different from the one I had left, which almost seemed placid in contrast. Neither the political violence of the Soledad Brothers nor the almost unfathomable violence of the Mexican Mafia and La Nuestra Familia matched any of my experience in the seemingly old-fashioned prisons I used to know.

At the same time a brief exposure to the realities at Stateville, Joilet, and Pontiac in Illinois had given me much to think about with respect to the problems of gang violence once it was out of control in the conventional American megaprison. When I was invited to discuss the implications of gang violence at a symposium on correctional-facility planning, to be attended by many of my old California colleagues, I accepted with considerable interest. It was a time for thinking through the implications of a new problem. I have to concede that, although the principles I proposed were obvious enough, their application is difficult, once the troubles have gone beyond the customary methods of control to resolve.

Power and the Prisoners

Ten years have passed since I left the California Department of Corrections for different pastures a continent away from Sacramento. Various welcome professional assignments and sheer nostalgia have brought me back frequently enough to keep superficially abreast of developments in the bureaucracy in which my career took form. But the world changes, and nowhere in my personal experience have the changes been so striking and so disconcerting as in California prisons.

My perspective is particular. Only the veterans of the Department will recall that for six years, from 1954 to 1960, I was intermittently the Supervisor of Inmate Classification—or to mention an alternative title against which I struggled in vain, the Head Rover Boy. Then as now, the responsibility of this office included the distribution of prisoners among the Department's facilities in accordance with an estimate of their individual requirements for custodial control and program opportunities. There were other responsibilities as well, but there was no question of the primacy of my responsibility for a decision-making apparatus that would assure that prisoners would be under sufficient control to prevent their infliction of violence on staff or other prisoners or their victimization in the case of men who were peculiarly vulnerable in the general prison population. It was a job with a number of morbid fascinations. Typical concerns were the potential for escape in the case of young men considered for camp or minimum-custody assignments; whether a Folsom prisoner under consideration for movement to San Quentin had surviving enemies at that destination; the possibility that a youth who had to be held in the Adjustment Center at the Deuel Vocational Institution could hack it in the dayrooms at Soledad. These and many other kinds of decisions were based on record review, consultations with the staff, and, not often enough, interviews with the prisoners concerned. My staff and I were constantly traveling from prison to prison; hence the not entirely respectful sobriquet.

I will not contend that those were the good old days when all was well in the best of all possible departments of corrections. Escapes did occur, and sometimes they were serious. There were not many murders or assaults, but those that did take place brought into bold relief the precarious nature of our control. Too often for our comfort, the classification staff found itself making conservative decisions about custody because we feared the consequences of the alternatives.

All that has not entirely changed. In my recent conversations with members of the present classification staff, I learn that there are still the same concerns about escape, the same interest in finding men for minimum-custody assignments, and the same interest in assuring that people needing major psychiatric care should be transferred to Vacaville. But two elements have come into the work that transform the classification process out of easy recognition. Those elements are murder and the ascendancy of ethnic gangs which acquire and maintain power through the exercise of violence.

The statistical particulars will be much better known to observers closer to the scene than I am as I write in Ohio. What I do know is shocking enough. I am told that there have been sixteen murders of prisoners in California facilities since the beginning of this calendar year. This figure compares to the number of killings in 1976, which was twenty. Murder is not yet an every-day event, but the fear of it must be uppermost in the minds of most California prisoners. It is a fear that serves the special interests of those who impose it, the leaders of the gangs which have staked out their turf in several prisons. To an extent that I still find hard to believe, these gangs control jobs, housing, and protective custody. The most credible kind of intimidation compels prisoners to request job changes so that a gang member can take over a desirable assignment. Men who belong to gangs not recognized by the dominant prisoner leadership must be immediately transferred out if they are to survive their terms. A gang leader can order another convict into protective custody, an order that neither the warden or the convict himself can safely defy. The Mexican Mafia have exclusive rights to the turf at San Quentin and Soledad but cannot be moved to Tracy, which "belongs" to La Nuestra Familia. A classification staff representative is assigned to special responsibility for maintaining a formal and informal information bank about gang membership, activities, and alliances.

There may be exaggerations in what I have been told, but unless I have been systematically misinformed, the situation in broad outline is that at several California prisons—Folsom, San Quentin, Tracy, and Soledad—a substantial share of power has been seized and kept by ethnic gangs. Prisoners at these facilities quite literally have little to fear from the staff but everything to fear from each other.

Sociologists once believed that the prison community could be best understood in terms of the solidary opposition model, in which an uneasy balance of power was maintained between staff and prisoners by concessions made by the staff to obtain cooperation, and concessions made by prisoners to maintain tranquillity and "to ease the pains of imprisonment." We have to revise that theoretical model in the light of what seems to be going on in California prisons now. I doubt that in the maximum-security prisons there is much fear of the uniformed staff among the ordinary prisoners; the terror comes from one's fellows, and the guards are the best protection against them.

The Diminished Powers of the Warden

What has happened and what can be done to correct this sickening tilt into bloodshed? I am at an obvious handicap in attempting a diagnosis and prescription at such a distance. But since I have been asked, I shall offer what can be generated from a remote perspective and some familiarity with thought about prison management, antisocial gangs, and the social changes that our country has been experiencing during the last two tumultuous decades.

First, let us consider the evolution of ideas and practice in prison control. If we turn to the historians of nineteenth-century penology, we discover a universal pattern of consistent and unregulated autarchy. The warden was sovereign—so long as he was in favor in the governor's office—and could do as he pleased within extremely broad limits.[1] In a sense that sheds light on both institutions, the slave plantation and the prison were enclaves of absolutism in a democratic polity. They were indigestible and unassimilable to the larger society. Slavery had to go and did, but we have never persuaded ourselves that we can do without the prison. It has survived. For generations wardens managed as all successful autocrats have done, mixing terror, incentives, and favoritism as best they could to keep their subjects fearful but not desperate, hopeful but always uncertain. The absolute power of the warden extended to the guards, who were kept dependent on his favor for security on their jobs and hopes for some advancement.[2] A wise warden kept some of his powers latent and in reserve, never depending on fear alone. If a conqueror of nations relied on a policy of "divide and rule," a successful warden would go farther; he would atomize the community under his control by assuring that his intelligence system seemed so pervasive that no one, guard or prisoner, could trust anyone else. Bloody uprisings could and did occur, but the warden—or his successor—would regain control with measures that would be swift, terrible, and none too scrupulous as to due process in finding and punishing the ringleaders. Those of us who started work in California prisons in the early days of the McGee regime can remember the tales of old-timers about grotesque abuses of power and privileges by wardens and captains and con-bosses. Some documentation can be found in the memoirs of Clinton Duffy, Kenyon Scudder, James A. Johnston, and Leo Stanley.[3] The life of an autocrat was hard, and success required peculiar talents that not many who chose this calling possessed in sufficient measure.

But one of the constant principles which the old warden faithfully observed was the prevention of groups among prisoners. The fish at San Quentin was exhorted to do his own time. The seasoned old con at Folsom observed this maxim and knew that it had to be taken literally. When the Captain intimated that whenever three men were gathered on the yard he was represented, it was not an exaggeration. The Captain had to know what was going on so as to maintain control, and one of the by-products of his intelligence system was an atmosphere of distrust that prevented the formation of groups.

That was the legacy of the prison autocrat. Absolutism was supplanted by bureaucracy and the limits of control established by central-office management. It would go too far afield to enter into an analysis of all the changes brought about by the removal of absolute authority from the warden and his conversion into a managing officer enjoying specific, limited, and delegated powers. For the purposes of this theoretical discussion, it is important to recognize that accountability became a reality. The warden was accountable to the director for the maintenance of law and order and for the operation of industrial and educational programs. He could not be an autocrat, and the limits on his powers were imposed not only by Sacramento but also by the specialized and professional nature of the duties to be carried out by his staff. Instead of a czar who could rule as he pleased, he had become a field officer to whom his subordinates were accountable for results, but he was subject to a multiplicity of constraints. His own performance was reviewable in the central office. Civil-service rules settled for him his decisions about hiring and firing and on what terms. Professional associations held him responsible for meeting their requirements as a price for getting services from their members. Unions and employees' associations imposed on him rules of their own about working conditions and promotions for their members. Civil libertarians and the courts subjected him to scrutiny of his compliance with the constitutional requirements for due process of law in administering discipline and redressing grievances. The transformation of a sovereign into a bureaucraat was rapid, and many improvements in the conditions of incarceration were thereby made possible.

But all these new constraints that reduced the prison czar into a mere manager were imposed by forces that were and are by no means compatible with each other. The prison autarchy had been a single locus of power, subject to no organized challenge. It now existed in an arena in which factions competed for fragments of authority. The famous dichotomy of power between custody on the yard and care and treatment in the front office was never entirely papered over. To add to the fissures, external movements further challenged the legitimacy of control.

It was maintained on the momentum of custodial practice. The traditions of the indeterminate sentence, whereby release depended on reasonable conformance of the prisoner to the requirements of discipline, assured the survival of the old routines for a considerable period of time. The climate of mistrust was maintained in the prison community by custodial insistence on prisoners doing their own time but keeping the captain's office well informed about those who did not. Spontaneous groups did not coalesce. The conspiracies necessary for escape and the marketing of contraband were organized often enough and from time to time succeeded briefly. Such combinations were necessarily small, usually infiltrated by agents of custody and usually broken up with ease and in time. Their objectives were limited and specific. An escape could necessarily involve only a few prisoners, and the manufacture of hooch seldom could be managed on a large enough scale to benefit more than a handful. Even the introduction of contraband from outside seems in retrospect to have been usually a very small-scale operation. The atomization of the prison community continued to be impressively effective. The routines of managerial control survived for a long time, in spite of all the fissures in the no longer monolithic staff because convicts could not find ways to combine in lasting organizations.

As we all know, that has changed. As I look back, I think the crumbling began with the success of the Black Muslims. Although the custodial establishment throughout the country made a determined campaign to pulverize it, this movement endured and prospered. Its leaders were systematically separated from their followers, usually by administrative segregation. Muslim groups were denied the right to meet, but met anyway. Outside imams and ministers were kept outside; the right of chaplaincy was rigidly closed off. Nevertheless, the commitment to doctrine, the observance of a discipline calling for complete loyalty to brothers in the movement, and the impermeability of the group to subversive infiltration combined to establish the Muslims as a prisoner organization that had to be legitimized. By 1977, of course, public opinion and appellate-court decisions have long since allowed the Muslims equal status with other religious faiths. Fifteen years ago, their emergence was an alarming problem for custodial control, made more alarming by their resistance to ordinary procedures for dissolution. That they are now a relatively benign presence in the prison testifies to growing good sense on both sides of what was once a bitter and dangerous contest of power.

The Muslims proved that prisoners could organize. Their example was not lost on prisoner groups with far less exalted objectives. The combination of ethnic solidarity, intimidating discipline, and common cultural backgrounds made possible the open functioning of gangs aiming at temporal power rather than spiritual benefits. There is some evidence that there was gang activity in California prisons as far back as the late fifties or early sixties, but it was subterranean and small scale compared to the formidable supergangs that now confront the prison administrator.

I have already outlined the administrative changes that have reduced the powers of the warden and made impossible the vigorous response to subversion that would have been mounted in the era of absolutism. It is futile to speculate as to whether the ruthlessness of the prison autocrat would have prevailed against the contemporary prison gang, but I think it is highly probable that the uncertainties of the prison manager and his superiors have contributed to an unhealthy situation in which authority shares power with the prison supergang.

At first, intelligence procedures failed. The significance of gang killings at San Quentin in the early sixties went unrecognized until many years later. Attempts at cooptation followed the recognition that the gangs could not be extirpated, but the leadership could not readily be coopted. Now I hear of a policy of violence control whereby gangs are kept separate from each other through classification procedures restricting transfer of gang members to particular institutions. Some murderous hostilities are thereby prevented, but this quasi-legitimation of gang authority has resulted in their achievement of unprecedented power to control work and housing assignments. It certainly has not eliminated violence; the number of prison homicides indicates how far this problem is from a satisfactory resolution.

Although the Mexican Mafia, La Nuestra Familia, the Black Guerilla Family, and the Aryan Brotherhood appear to have had their formal origins in prison, I do not think they can be understood as prison artifacts. The juvenile gang has been a feature of slum life in American cities for generations. Thrasher's classic, *The Gang*, describes vividly the characteristics of the juvenile gang in the Chicago of the twenties.[4] His account has an uncanny validity for our times. Unemployed boys and young men, disenchanted with school, without prospects for stable careers, living in neighborhoods in which the common denominator is the irregular life of the American underclass, find comfort and manhood in the gang. Petty crime and narcotics keep them provided for. Status is gained by defiance of the law and is verified by arrests and jail terms. Experience in such gangs on the streets is imported to youth correctional facilities and eventually to prisons. The contemporary prisoner arrives on the yard with considerable knowledge of the necessary principles of organization. He knows that an intimidating discipline is essential and accepts it as proof of his virility. Ethnic and territorial solidarity reinforce the discipline. A man proves his worth to the gang and his worth as a man by carrying out dangerous and sometimes homicidal assignments for his superiors. The ethos of the gang is obviously compatible with the characteristics of the "state-raised youth," so well described by Irwin.[5] By Irwin's account, the state-raised youth lives in the real world of the prison. His values are conditioned by the necessity to inflict violence and to face it from others as a proof of manhood and as the only proper way of resolving conflict. Homosexual imposition further defines manhood; a man subjugates his sexual partner, and those who are subjugated are deprived of manhood. The real world is behind the bars; the streets are the locale for fantasies of orgiastic pleasures and occasional respites from the real world. Youths with this perspective on the daily routines of incarceration are obviously candidates for dedicated gang membership. On the streets or on the yard, such young men can be relied on to lead or to follow with absolute fidelity to the values of the gang. The extent to which they will go is reflected in the terrifying violence they carry out. It is eloquently expressed by a quotation from an interview with a prisoner reported in Jacobs' remarkable report of gang violence at Stateville, where there are problems strikingly similar to those confronting similar California prisons. In this interview, a black prisoner says: "The gang leaders have absolute control. T_____could just have told his men to tear it down and they would—a lot of these guys would die for their gang—dying doesn't mean anything to them. They'd rather die than let it be said that they wouldn't go all the way."[6] Clearly cooptation and negotiation are processes with limited prospects for success when confronted by groups characterized by this state of mind.

Action and Avoidance—Nine Prescriptions

The gangs have had their small successes in California prisons. It will be natural for them to reach for larger achievements, and their chances for such victories are obvious. No easy solution to the problem is conceivable, and that makes urgent business of the formulation of policies and programs leading to the restoration of legitimate control. The underlying concepts of such policies are not hard to state, but carrying them out will present formidable, almost insurmountable, difficulties. I will offer here six principles for action and three principles for avoidance. I cannot pretend to exhaust the possibilities, but I am certain that not much headway will be made on the road back to control unless these principles are observed. If California is really about to engage in a prison-building program, it is essential that architecture and staffing be designed to further the execution of these directives, for which I make no claims for originality.

To begin with the principles for action:

1. Increase work and activity: The slum gang thrives on unemployment. The gang relieves boredom and inactivity. One participant observer in a slum gang in Glasgow reported a universal experience: "Life with the gang was not all violence, sex, and petty delinquency. Far from it. One of the foremost sensations that remains with me is the feeling of unending boredom, of crushing tedium, of listening hour after hour to desultory conversation and indiscriminate grumbling. Standing with one's back against a wall, with one's hands in one's pockets, . . . was *the* gang activity."[7] There is never enough work to do in California prisons. Probably there is no topic in the agenda of prison reform that recurs so frequently as the need for the full-employment prison. The prison gangster standing with his back against the wall, his hands in his pockets, and sharing malevolences with his comrades is reinforcing his commitment to his gang. He is bored, but the gang promises to relieve the boredom. Narcotics may be on the way, or there may be a new punk to rape, or a score to settle with a rival gang, or perhaps a defector from one's own true faith. The prison provides him with the basic necessities for survival, but the gang offers him life. Part of this life is the tedious business of waiting. Authorities should not mistake it for tranquility.

The full-employment prison will not solve this problem, but without full and genuine work and activity it is inconceivable that the gangs will attenuate in influence, numbers and violence. It is beyond my scope to suggest measures for increasing the prison-industry program to its proper dimensions; that has been urged repeatedly ever since I was first employed in corrections, and long before. The choice is more stark than ever. Either expand prison industries or face the grim and intolerable consequences of expanded gang influence.

2. Reduce unit size: Rhetoric deploring the megaprison—the archetypes of which are to be found in San Quentin and Folsom—is insufficiently specific. Indeed, some people who should know better insist that there has been nothing to show that a large prison cannot be as satisfactory as a small one if it is properly managed. Others, who should also know better, point out that so far as they can see the recidivism rates of convicts released from large prisons are no worse than those of convicts released from small prisons. These contentions are beside any important point. The large prison is limited to reactive control; it is a place where preparations must be made for the worst because the worst is certain to happen. Neither guards nor prisoners can know each other or initiate activities to relieve hostilities. The small prison—or a medium-sized prison divisible into small units—can be a terrible place, too. Indeed, some of the worst prisons I have ever seen are relatively small. But a unit size of no more than thirty, preferably less, is an essential tool for control aiming at prevention of violence rather than its mere limitation.

3. Increase staff: We have to reconsider the kinds of staff that are needed in maximum-security facilities. The prevailing style at San Quentin and Folsom, I understand, is to pair off the guards so that one can protect the other. I must suppose that this expedient is necessary, given the hazardous conditions of these prisons. But staff working in pairs will be in little contact with prisoners. They will see and be seen, but they will be in impersonal communication. Two officers patrolling together will cover far less of a cellblock or some other building than two men patrolling separately. Violence is still a furtive activity that takes place where it cannot be easily seen. Guards cannot be everywhere, but the more frequently they get around, the more out-of-the-way places will be covered.

4. Intelligence: It is unlikely that stool-pigeons can be found to infiltrate the gangs, and I would not recommend an attempt to recruit them. That does not mean that we can or should give up the attempt to know what is going on. The patrolling guard is there not only to see and be seen, but to hear and be heard. An officer who is trained to interact casually, informally, but significantly with prisoners will eventually be entrusted with information useful for the purposes of control. That will not happen if he is always one of a pair, but it can happen if he regularly is in contact with a small unit for which he is responsible. A mass of hundreds of men in a cellblock is an impenetrable murk, an inscrutable beast whose actions cannot be predicted. A decent man who is seen every day and understood by a small group with which he is working may become a confidant of some and will be at least respected by the others in his domain.

5. The lawful community: A prison should be lawful, and all persons working in a prison should enforce the law. The difficulties in achieving this objective are obvious and well known, but they require emphasis at a time

when the considerations of due process tend to obscure the necessities of crime control. I must tread carefully here; along with most persons committed to the objectives of prison reform, I have welcomed the tardy recognition that due process of law is necessary, desirable, and possible in our prisons. I would not wish the courts to resume the hands-off policy that used to prevail. Having said this, I must add that prisons still have to be lawful, and that violations of the law should and must be investigated and prosecuted. The unwillingness of district attorneys to add to their workload and the reluctance of criminal investigators to engage in the unrewarding process of crime detection on the prison yard must give way to a rigorous policy of law enforcement. Prisons cannot be as lawful as convents, but they certainly will become less dangerous if the consequences of law violation are regularly seen. Wrongdoing must have adverse consequences wherever it occurs, especially when it occurs in prison. Whatever resources are required to increase the effectiveness of investigations and prosecutions should be applied to this end. Statutes articulating the penalties for felonies committed in prison should be severe. Incentives to prisoners supplying information leading to convictions must be carefully administered to assure their protection, but it should be remembered that gangs cannot function unless members can count on the absolute loyalty of all other members.

6. Increase participation in prison programs by minority-group leaders: The gang leadership still makes use of the rhetoric of the civil-rights movement and the vocabulary of the political prisoner. I mention this point because it suggests that gang members are still accessible to the example and concern of minority-group leaders. Organizations such as the National Association for the Advancement of Colored People, the Urban League, and the United Farm Workers should be actively encouraged to present alternatives to gangsterism. It would be naive to suppose that the "hard core" would succumb to such blandishments, but I think it is not unreasonable to expect that legitimate leadership would make the recruitment of new members considerably more difficult.

The question will arise as to whether the National Prisoners' Union might help in offsetting the power of the gangs. I think that the introduction of the union in a prison in which gangs are entrenched would complicate the problem. The uncertainty about the role of the union, the inexperience of its leaders, and the numerous intrastaff conflicts that already exist would make positive contributions by the union most improbable.

I suggested that there were three principles of avoidance, by which I mean concessions that must not be made by the prison management:

1. Gang leadership must not be overtly or tacitly recognized. Under no circumstances should negotiations or concessions give gang leaders a basis

for estimating their power or the extent to which they can go in intimidating staff or prisoners. It is an illusion to suppose that they can be coopted, and attempts to establish a laissez-faire policy are doomed to failure. Gang leaders must not be arrested or held on mere suspicion, but when they violate laws or rules they must not be allowed to do so with impunity.

In this connection, insignia of memberships should be confiscated when it is certain what they are. Meetings can never be allowed, and communications must be carefully controlled. I am opposed to routine censorship of all mail, but I think there is an overriding necessity to have competent censorship of all mail to and from active members of known gangs.

Necessarily the prison management will have to be in contact with gang leaders. Sometimes these contacts will be unwitting; I am told that custodial intelligence is not always reliable as to the identities of these leaders. I do not mean the proscription of negotiations with gangs to be interpreted as a requirement that gangsters be ostracized from the community. On the contrary, where a council of prisoners is assembled for management's purposes, it is to be expected and even to be hoped that gang leaders will be present. Such a council will not be a forum in which negotiations can take place on gangster terms. It wil be most effective when it is an occasion for the firm articulation of community relations acceptable to management.

2. Power must not be shared: I do not know to what extent an exaggerated impression has been spread about concerning the sharing of power over job assignments and housing with gang leaders. If the accounts I have heard are accurate, steps must be taken to withdraw these concessions. Known gang members must not be assigned to privileged jobs. A report of intimidation should be the object of intensive investigation, and the person responsible for making threats must be placed under severe and prolonged control. There must be no advantage accruing to membership in a gang, and it should be clear that the unaffiliated prisoner is in a more favorable position.

3. Prevent the introduction of contraband: The importation of narcotics and other contraband is obviously undesirable, even without considering the influence that contraband assures the leadership of these gangs. The life of the gang depends in part on contraband rewards. It can be assumed that efforts are made to prevent forbidden articles from coming into the prison. These efforts should be reviewed to determine whether additional procedures or new resources would increase their effectiveness. A prison in which a narcotics traffic is flourishing is a prison in tenuous official control. In this situation, the gangs have the management about where they want it to be—in a condition of relative impotence. Prosecution of anyone, free or prisoner, who is engaged in contraband traffic should be swift, and conviction should automatically result in a term in prison.

The Restoration of Control

I hope I have been sufficiently drastic. Murder, homosexual rape, and ag-
gravated assaults are drastic events in themselves. An organized gang
responsible for such crimes cannot be left to its own devices. When the state
tolerates such a gang it becomes an accomplice to its deeds, an outcome that
is incompatible with the state's obligation to set the example of lawfulness.

A situation that is not improving is certainly getting worse. The campaign I have outlined is obvious to the point of platitude. No experience in
prison administration is needed to appreciate its difficulty. Victories will be
partial, and their consequences will be real only if the staff is resolute in its
determination to regain control.

Our deliberations are in the interest of formulating a plan for correctional facilities in California. It is appropriate here to cite the architectural
maxim: form follows function. The design of a structure should correspond
with the purposes that structure is intended to serve, whether it is a church,
an office building, or a prison. Prisons have been changing in purpose, but
they have been constrained by the design principles of the nineteenth century. As I have already tried to show, the early-American style in prison architecture was admirably suited to the principles of control then prevailing.
The silent system of Auburn and the repressive measures that made it possible closely corresponded to the form of the megaprison. If management's
operations call for the atomization of the prison community and the prevention of a prison culture, then the vast prison in which faceless men march
from place to place in lockstep anonymity is the proper form.

Even if we wanted to, we could not go back to the old Auburn system.
Instead of trying to accommodate ourselves to the stringencies of Auburn
architecture, it is essential that we should design a form that follows the new
functions and exigencies of the prison. What we are doing now, as we see in
the confident power of the prison supergang, is the adaptation of the an-
tique and obsolete structure of a century ago to the purposes of violent and
antisocial power. It cannot be stressed too often that the structure of most
of our prisons suits the gangster far better than it suits the warden.

Our forebears in the prison business used to control their convicts by
preventing the development of a prison community. Changes in the
ideology of criminal justice have developed a prison community that in
many respects cannot be controlled. The immense cellblocks at San Quentin
and Folsom facilitate the objectives of the gang leaders. So do the smaller
but still excessively large wings at Soledad and at the Deuel Vocational Institution. The design principles of the last century frustrate control instead
of facilitating it. The task before us is to create a form in which the function
of maintaining a lawful prison community is furthered. I am no architect,
and I cannot prescribe all the details of such a form. But I am confident that

it will be found necessary to reduce unit size to no more than thirty and probably in some situations to less than twenty. Units will be grouped to constitute a facility of from 250 to 400 people, and it may eventually be found desirable to make these new prisons "cocorrectional," including both sexes. The core of the new prison will be industrial, and it will be expected that everyone, except unusually determined recalcitrants, will work an eight-hour day.

Both money and innovative talent will be needed in abundance if the new prisons are to conform to these principles, and the old prisons are somehow to be adapted. It will be an ironic failure of nerve if, at a time when we know what needs to be done, we content ourselves with half-measures and myopic economies that will plague our successors for generations to come.

The Department of Corrections is in charge of the gates and the walls of the prisons of California. I do not think it can be said that it is truly in charge of the yards and cellblocks and housing wings at most of the closed prisons. The plan for California correctional facilities should aim at eliminating all doubt. The Department of Corrections must be in complete and unquestioned charge of all the facilities for which it is responsible. Whatever else is done, control is not to be shared; violations of this axiom lead only to brutish anarchy.

Notes

1. The best recent example of the sovereignty of a prison warden is to be found in James B. Jacobs, *Stateville: The Penitentiary in Mass Society* (Chicago and London: University of Chicago Press, 1977). A concise account of the regime of Warden Joseph Ragen is to be found in pp. 28-51. See also, W. David Lewis, *From Newgate to Dannemora: The Rise of the Penitentiary in New York, 1796-1848* (Ithaca, N.Y.: Cornell University Press, 1965) for nineteenth-century antecedents, especially the account of Warden Elam Lynds, of Auburn (pp. 84-89).

2. Jacobs, *Stateville*, pp. 40-41. Conditions at San Quentin and Folsom were as stringent as at Stateville according to my conversations with veterans of the early years of this century. During a long probationary period, San Quentin guards were allowed to leave the reservation for no more than one day and had to get the captain's permission for this indulgence.

3. See Clinton T. Duffy and Dean Jennings, *The San Quentin Story* (New York: Doubleday, 1950); Kenyon Scudder, *Prisoners Are People* (New York: Doubleday, 1952); James A. Johnston, *Prison Life Is Different* (Boston: Houghton Mifflin, 1937); Leo L. Stanley, Men at Their Worst (New York: Appleton-Century, 1941).

4. Frederic M. Thrasher, *The Gang: A Study of 1313 Gangs in Chicago* (Chicago and London: University of Chicago Press, 1927).

5. John Irwin, *The Felon* (Englewood Cliffs, N.J.: Prentice-Hall, 1970), pp. 26-29.

6. Jacobs, *Stateville*, p. 138.

7. James Patrick (pseudonym), *A Glasgow Gang Observed* (London: Eyre-Methuen, 1973), p. 80.

8

Function Follows Form

A Note on Prison Architecture

One of the absurdities that some of the more ardent prison abolitionists repeat as though it were an axiom is the notion that it is the height of futility to attempt to improve prison design. One such zealot explained to me that "a pig-pen is a pig-pen, even if its colors are pastel." A neat epigram perhaps, but I remain unconvinced. I have seen prisons of all kinds, from the dreadful—but fairly new—prisons of Alabama before Eighth-Amendment litigation stripped away the horrors, to the humanely designed prisons of Sweden. I conclude that architects can make a difference in the character of the punishment meted out by the state. Social scientists, working with architects, could make the prison easier to endure for those who must serve time in them—and also for those who must work in them. Even the experience of incarceration is relative. If we must build prisons—and I am certain that we must—let us put our minds to doing it right. American penology abounds with bad examples with which the nation will have to live for centuries. The shame is that so many are of such recent construction.

Once, when I was a parole officer for the California Youth Authority, I had occasion to return a parolee to the Preston School of Industry. He was a nice kid of about 15 or 16 who stole cars, and, having stolen several while on parole, he had been recommitted to the Youth Authority. We had to drive from San Francisco to Ione, about three hours away in the Sierra foothills, and it was a comparatively pleasant trip, as such trips go. My young companion chattered amiably about the things that interested teenagers then and now—sports, girls, school, and his special interest in stealing cars. All went well until we rounded the fateful bend where the Preston School of Industry (PSI) came into sight. The approach is a long one; you could see the looming tower about 10 miles away, and the sight never failed to make a sombre impression on kids being returned to PSI. It was tall and dark and ugly; it was a menacing symbol of what lay in store for a boy as he traveled the last few miles of the free world. Silence fell on both of us. Then, looking out at a pasture, my parole violator said: "I wish I was a cow out in that field for the next 11 months."

This chapter was a contribution to a discussion at the annual meeting of the American Society of Criminology in 1978. It is a scratch on the surface; this topic needs much more frequent and thorough discussion.

He had a fair idea of how much time he would have to do, and an accurate idea of how miserable those months would be. Preston was an atrocious reform school in those days in which a lazy superintendent allowed an oppressive tradition of lockstep management to prevail while spouting the vernacular of rehabilitation.

The tower is gone, the superintendent has long since been forgotten, and Preston has been transformed into a smaller school with a program that has eliminated the cadet corps, the special cottages for the kids who caused the various kinds of trouble that bothered the staff, and some pretty sophisticated programs have been instituted. What I want to comment on here is the cunning way in which architects have captured the intentions of penal administrators and made their work easier for them. When PSI was built, nearly a century ago, our forebears knew that kids should not be in penitentiaries; they should be reformed separately from convicts. The prevailing wisdom was that a juvenile delinquent needed to be intimidated; he needed to learn what was in store for him if he did not mend his ways. The buildings were large and oppressive in design. Bad kids lived in cells, better kids lived in dorms, strong kids were "dukes" in charge of cadet companies, weak kids were punks who never achieved the manly traits that they were supposed to acquire while locked up. Probably some boys came out of this hideous experience better, or at least no worse, but the recidivism rate was very high. I think it is significant that the leadership of the California Youth Authority decided that these fearful old buildings had to be demolished, and demolished they were. Preston now looks more like a boarding school than a reformatory. I do not know what the recidivism rates are; even if they are no better than they used to be, Californians no longer have on their conscience those ghastly buildings and the senseless regime we imposed on those boys in those days.

Things change more slowly in prisons. Some years ago I was a member of a task force appointed to think through the design requirements for a new maximum-security prison to be built in California. Putting our heads together, we produced a campus of small units, each related to small workshops and schoolrooms. The particulars are unimportant; I am glad to say that the prison was never built, despite all our efforts. What is important is that we did not apply the principles of the inside cellblock—the great contribution of the Auburn prison to penal architecture. Looking over our tentative plans, one of the senior wardens of the department, a man who would probably have been appointed to run the new facility, commented in disgust: "Why do you people want to make my job harder?" So far as he was concerned, a maximum-security prison had to have a long inside cellblock to facilitate counts and control. Any other design merely added difficulty and needless expense to the management of a prison.

The inside cell-block admirably carries out the functions that its designers had in mind. The warden who ruled over it for many years, the famous Elam Lynds, was frank about his objectives. He held that the ultimate aim of a prison was to "reduce the inmate to a silent and insulated working machine."[1] To do this it was necessary to "break his spirit" along the way. Anyone who has seen the classic inside cellblock knows the efficiency it adds to the function of locking up a lot of men at the appointed time, unlocking at another appointed time, and moving them from cell to messhall to workplace and back to the cell again. It is far easier to be a working machine than to be a man in such an architectural setting. Rusche and Kirchheimer in their history of punishment hold that society has always chosen methods of punishment that were consistent with the economic requirements at the time.[2] Those were the days when America needed a lot of working machines.

We no longer build the classic Auburn prison, but we still have dozens of them in use, and we still adapt the inside cellblock, with its dreary, closed-off atmosphere, to a more modern design, usually something like a telephone pole with living and work units sprouting from a long central corridor. Prisoners in this familiar model of penal architecture may be inside cellblocks, but they are easier to control because the living uits are smaller and troublemakers are easier to set apart from their fellows. The convenience of this design for control of a large mass of prisoners has been tested and apparently not found wanting. It does not matter much that a determined effort must be made by the prisoner to get a breath of fresh air; he could go for weeks without seeing the sun or the sky. The telephone pole is a considerable advance over the Auburn style, but it still gives primacy to control, and it will produce a working machine if there is any work to do. Unfortunately, many of these prisons have to be designed for an alternative—loitering—and there are dayrooms for loitering, schoolrooms for loitering, and gymnasiums for loitering. Even the industrial wings usually contain more loiterers than workers.

What kind of prison do we want? I suggest that no criminologist has thought through what directives the architect should receive from the scholars who know criminals best. What we have is a prison designed for work, if there is work to be done, and intended for firm control at all times. What we think we should have is a prison is which prisoners can experience citizenship in a community. Communities in normal living are composed of small groups of people living in neighborhoods. Although neighbors are not what they used to be in the good old days that none of us really remember very clearly, a strong community must surely consist of such groups rather than anonymous individuals clumped into large mobs. Nothing but mistrust and fear can thrive in the mob; everyone is justified in preparing for the worst, and sooner or later the worst happens. Someone is stabbed or shot or taken hostage. The wonder is that we can still find men and women who are willing to work as guards in such places, but there is no wonder about the convicts—they have no choice.

There are signs that architects, at least, are beginning to think about what the modern prison should be like. The new Minnesota High Security Facility, now under construction, is intended to house a true community. The intent of the Department of Corrections of that state has been imaginatively carried out by an architectural group which understands that there are more considerations than security to be borne in mind in designing for the penology of the future. There are a few other examples in this country of prison designs that have been created with a view to community building rather than oppression.

What we do not know is whether they will work, and, if they do, what it takes in addition to humane intentions to make them work. What seems clear to me is that it is futile to continue to rely on decent people to create decent prisons in the ancient cages designed for the obsolete function of oppression. It should not be beyond the capacity of social science to answer some of the questions that prison administrators inevitably ask us when they back us into a corner to get our help. What can we say about the size of a prison? How many prisoners? What can we say about the characteristics of a unit that can maximize the opportunity for choice? What can we say about the proper size of a prison cell? I tend to stammer my guesses when asked these questions, and there are plenty of prison administrators out there who want to know the answers.

Some years ago, I visited the Maple Lane School for Girls, a correctional facility operated by Washington State for delinquent juveniles. As the superintendent drove me down the lane of maples that leads to the campus and gives the school its name, he commented: "Notice what they've done for me here. This lane leads down to the receiving cottage. When a sheriff drives a girl down here, we hope that she gets the message: 'Maybe they've all given up on you where you live. The state of Washington hasn't given up and this campus tells you what we intend to do for you.'" That is the communication of one institution to its residents. It will not work unless the program matches the architecture. But no program will be effective in a setting where no program was intended. I think the expansive notions about abolishing incarceration and putting a moratorium on any prison building collide at this point with the universal obsolescence of the physical plant of American penology. We have a lot more to do in bringing prison architecture out of the nineteenth century; our contributions must consist of more than pieties about the evils of prison life as we find them in our studies. Those evils will persist unless we have something more to say about the physical enviroment that can be expected to eliminate them.

The maxim of modern architecture is that form follows function. Having seen how boring modern architecture can be when it takes the maxim too literally, many leaders of that profession have begun to play it down. But in prisons, function tends to follow form, because the forms are so perdurable. Inevitably more prisons are going to be built during the coming decade. It is urgent that our research and our thought should influence the design of forms for the new community-building function.

Notes

1. W. David Lewis, *From Newgate to Dannemora* (Ithaca, N.Y.: Cornell University Press, 1965).
2. G. Rusche and O. Kirchheimer, *Punishment and Social Structure* (New York: Russell and Russell, 1968).

9

Who Needs a Doorbell Pusher?

The Case for the Abolition of Parole

My career in corrections began in 1946 when I spent a year as a parole officer for the California Youth Authority. Although I thoroughly enjoyed the work and the association with colleagues of my age and background who were as new as I was to the field, even then I had twinges of doubt about the usefulness of what I was doing. Those twinges were magnified into outright; scepticism as I continued to work in the system. Asked by the American Society of Criminology to make the case for abolition of parole, I made it in the chapter that follows.

Nearly thirty years ago, I was a parole officer, Grade I, employed by the California Youth Authority. I was the bottom of a ladder which I intended to climb as rapidly as possible in the interest of my other roles as a husband, father, and mortgagor. My caseload consisted of all the Youth Authority parolees in the city and county of San Francisco and also all the parolees in the North Coast counties up to the Oregon border. There was a representation of young thugs from San Quentin, younger thugs from the Preston School of Industry, and children headed for thuggery and thievery, released on parole from the Nelles School for Boys, and the Fricot School up in the Sierra foothills. They all fascinated me. I liked talking to them, I liked even the chase they led me when I went looking for them, and I liked the endless bull sessions about our experiences with them which took place during coffee breaks, luncheons, and after hours with my three colleagues. Each of us has gone on to what may or may not be better things, but we all look back fondly to that year as the time of our lives.

We had a crusty supervisor of the old school of parole whose message was uncompromising and explicit in his official directives in each case record: *See the Boy in the Home.* It was clear that we should see as many boys in the home as possible and that the way up the ladder was at least partly numerical; it was essential to do what I rather enjoyed doing anyway, seeing my young hoodlums out in the field.

I almost excelled. Each month, the monthly report listed my name as the second-most-diligent parole officer in all the Youth Authority in the

This chapter was originally printed in *The Prison Journal* 59 (Autumn-Winter 1979):17-26. I am grateful to the editors of the *Journal* for allowing me to reprint it here.

matter of field calls. The first-most-diligent colleague was a veteran officer of many years of service who covered a vast area out of the Sacramento office. Frustrated at my inability to catch him in this monthly competition, I finally cornered him at a staff meeting and asked for the secret of his success. He smiled enigmatically and indulgently attributed his nearly complete coverage of his widely distributed caseload to the many more years of experience that he had to his credit. He implied that I was doing well for a youngster and no doubt in the fullness of years would match his presently matchless achievement. A few months later he was fired for falsifying his records, and I went on to other employment, not involving the pushing of doorbells.

Years later, my seniority in the system led me to sit on a civil-service-examination oral board in which my role was to determine the eligibility for promotion of about a hundred Grade I parole officers in the California Division of Parole. Remembering the competitions of the old days, I found myself enquiring of these candidates how many field calls they had made in the previous month. Most of them were able to quote an acceptable, even an impressive figure, but I still remember with bemusement a young man who staunchly replied that he had seen two parolees in the field. He was not going to play a numbers game with me, he said, and anyway he preferred to see his clients in the office. Unfortunately, his ideas about the supervision of parole officers were equally unconventional, so our Board flunked him, but I wished that I had had the time and opportunity to find out what really had happened on his caseload. Had his indolence made a difference?

One more vignette, and then I will get on to a consideration of the meaning, if any, to be found in all this effort. One of the intermediate rungs on the ladder I was climbing was a position known as classification and parole representative at the California State Prison at Soledad, later to be redesignated as the California Correctional Facility. In my day, Soledad was a prison and little known to anyone outside the California correctional circuit. One of my most momentous tasks was to act as the institutional representative at the monthly hearings conducted by the Adult Authority, as the California parole board was rather grandly designated. Usually this task occupied most of a week, and good lord! How hard we all worked! The gentlemen of the Board, eager to get back to their homes in San Francisco, would hear cases all day, dine in the only acceptable local restaurant, and return to the prison for night hearings until we could hardly keep our eyes open. The basic routine was unvarying. Inmate enters, gets a courteous greeting from the interviewing member while the other two colleagues read records on the cases to come. Interviewing member compliments inmate on his improving work and school record, then asks how he now accounts for the course of conduct which led him into the commission of the offense for which he is serving time. Inmate's account seldom satisfies the interviewer, who probes for details and indicates that he cannot be conned. Questions are asked concerning the reasons that make the inmate think he can stay out of future trouble. Usually there is an answer to that, an invocation of the influence of a family, a job, and good habits learned from thinking it all over. Anything else he would like to say? Well, the Board will let him know.

There were variations for notorious or exceptionally interesting cases, for inmates who could not speak English, and for especially talented fellows who could capture the Board's interest with a sad tale, an amusing slice of underworld life, or an insight into the causes and prevention of crime. Some Board members administered homilies on law and morality, on self-pity and a sense of responsibility; some laboriously pointed out the error of the inmate's ways; some stressed the incredible difficulties ahead in the world outside. After the inmate had left, there would ensue a discussion of his "readiness" for parole, ordinarily beginning with a consideration of whether enough time had been done. Intuitions and precedent governed the routine decisions—or nearly all of them—but exceptional cases would get extended reflection, even calls for further reports on the man's mental state, the present attitude of the chief of police in his home town toward his release, or other topics on which the Board would want reassurance.

These sketches represent the essential elements of parole practice in California as I knew it when I was a part of that renowned system. The structure has changed to accommodate an ever-increasing caseload and to provide for experimental innovations in service. I think it is fair to say that the fundamentals are still about the same and that there are no really exceptional variations in the practice of parole in any state where it is taken seriously. I have used broad strokes, but the picture is not intended to be a caricature, nor do I think that those familiar with actual parole service will consider that I have exaggerated grossly.

So what is going on? I think a fair consideration of parole operations as they have been conducted in this country for most of this century clearly support the case that the concept of parole is redundant. This is not a new contention. The positions taken by Fogel,[1] McGee,[2] and several other writers have included most of the points I will advance here. But it is a hard thing to abolish a familiar and long-established public service. Indeed, it is difficult to think of a comparable example, and the consequences of such a drastic move are not entirely predictable. So in what follows, I shall briefly make the case against parole, arguing that it should be abolished, but with care. I shall also suggest that, although the institution of parole should go, there is a continuing problem, the relocation of the prisoner into the community, that will continue to require attention. I shall suggest some alternatives that will meet identifiable needs and urge that criminologists give some consideration to their design and acceptability as effective means of solving the relocation problem.

The Case against Parole

In his article on the indeterminate sentence, McGee recites the evidence of
the injustice and inefficiency inherent in the administration of a system
based on the individualization of sentencing.[3] If there is no reason to
believe that the rehabilitative programs of the prison have any consistent
and detectable influence on prisoners, there is no apparent basis for differentiating sentences in accordance with change in the social and
psychological status of the offender. There being no way to judge change
for the better or worse, there is no reason to wait for it to happen. We are
therefore reduced to basing the decision about sentencing on the considerations of punishment, incapacitation, and deterrence. So far, we have
been unable to provide the criminal-justice system with empirical guidance
on the principles by which sentences can be best fixed to meet these goals.
Until criminologists can make such a contribution, arbitrary limits should
be set by the legislature. In doing so, I think that we should call attention
to the general opinion of the informed that no discernible purpose is served
by long terms. The data we have suggest that recidivism does not
significantly or reliably vary with perturbation of the sentencing
parameter. We have no idea how many burglaries are spared the community by locking a hundred burglars up for a year or any other given
period of time, nor do we know how many potential burglars are deterred
from breaking into premises that do not belong to them by consideration
of the miseries of burglars in confinement. Until some evidence sheds light
on these murky issues, we would do best to flatten out terms, keep them
short, and try to design a sentencing structure that will not overcrowd our
prisons or necessitate building large units of additional capacity. The
charge to social science is clear, and we should take such satisfaction as we
can in the opportunity to explore such relatively unploughed fields as the
differential effects of various forms of punishment, the whole topic of
general deterrence (in which we now contemplate the spectacle of
economists glowering at sociologists with conclusions drawn from data
that both sides agree to be seriously defective), and incapacitation, on
which no work at all has been done.[4]

But we do not need to wait for research to advocate the end of indeter-
minancy in sentencing. Our explorations of the topics I have mentioned
will scarcely lead to any principles that will require differentiation of
penalties to make them fit the criminal. The flat term structure proposed
by Fogel will do well enough, subject to careful advance assessment of the
increase or decline of prison populations as a result of the actual terms fixed
by law.[5]

The parole board exists to administer the indeterminate sentence. It has no evident function if flat-term sentencing is to be imposed by the courts with remission for good time to be administered by the prison warden on strict conditions laid out in the law and audited by functionaries independent of the correctional system. Who these functionaries might be is an issue that need not detain us long. They might be members of a council appointed by the chief justice of the state supreme court. They might be inspectors-general designated by the governor; they might be independent civil servants with ombudsman prerogatives. There should be some right of remedy against an unjust deprivation of good-time remission, but the apparatus should be simple and decisions should be expeditious and final. There should be no reference to irrelevant questions such as progress in treatment, educational success, postrelease plans, or insight into the reasons for criminality.

We should not disregard the obvious reasons for allowing for good time in remission of parts of a sentence. A prison is a difficult and dangerous place for all concerned, and its administration must be directed at the personal safety of staff and inmates. Those who suppose that procedures that assure the compliance of all personnel and all prisoners are somehow invalid impositions are indifferent to the tenuous controls available to those in authority. Messinger has clearly shown how the indeterminate sentence has been seen by the designers of the California correctional system as an essential element of administrative control.[6] Although good behavior in prison is no guarantee of early release, bad behavior is an insuperable obstacle. If we are to eliminate parole, the provision of credits for good time—archaic though the terminology seems to the contemporary penologist—is an essential strategy for control. It must be explicit, systematic, and equitably administered, but it is all that is required for the maintenance of discipline.

Let us turn to the parole officer and his daily rounds. In her acutely observed study of the California parole system, Studt divides the functions of the officer between the headings of surveillance and service.[7] She concludes with some conviction that the parole officer seldom accomplishes any significant contributions in either direction.

The fleeting contacts that the diligent officer makes with the individuals in his caseload hardly constitute surveillance in the sense that any assurance is gained concerning the lawfulness of the parolee's behavior. The various studies of caseload size have never shown differentials in favor of the smaller caseload. From this situation it is certainly impossible to infer any effectiveness from intensified surveillance. We are really unable to construct a model of parole supervision that provides for effectiveness in surveillance. Such a model would have to allow for the development of a costly network of information about the activities of each parolee such that the parole officer would have continuous knowledge of what his charges are doing and about to do. But even if such a model were feasible, what would we do with it? Increasingly we find it repugnant to due process to "violate" the parolee on account of his tendentious behavior. We prefer to await a violation of the law, an event that obviates the need for surveillance—except, of course, that the parole officer might know better than the police where to find the parolee if he is wanted for arrest. We can hardly justify parole services on the basis of the surveillance model. What the parole officer can do, if it should be done at all, can be better done by the police. The pushing of doorbells, the recording of "contacts," and the requirement of monthly reports all add up to expensive pseudo-services. At best they constitute a costly but useless frenzy of activity. But more often than not, I suspect, they harass and humiliate the parolee without gaining even the illusion of control.

It is a little different story on the service dimension. There are many kinds of assistance that a parole officer can afford his charges, and they should not be written off as useless. There is something of a knack involved in locating employment for a young man without credentials but nevertheless imbued with imperious expectations. It can be done, and many parole officers are remarkably good at it. Some parole officers excel at the advocacy role, helping the parolee out of tight situations that may or may not be of his own making. The negotiations with the police or prosecutor when a parolee is suspected of further law violation may well be crucial to his future survival in the community. Finally, we should admiringly acknowledge the kind of man who exemplifies the supportive role of the good correctional caseworker. I think here of officers whom I have known to hold an almost continuous open house for their parolees, mostly listening to tales of their personal misfortunes. Sometimes the help is tangible, mostly it is in the nature of the needed sympathetic ear. I do not think we can do without them, but, of course, we do. Very few parole officers are endowed with the qualities of endurance and empathy that this role calls for. I do not think that any system can create them, but that is not to say that we can do without the altruism and intelligence that they represent. Most parole officers function on a much more businesslike level, making their calls as I used to do, hustling jobs for men who are as likely as not to disappoint them, and trying to talk a skeptical cop or prosecutor out of pushing charges. It is a tough job, calling for endurance, patience, and a tolerance for failure. I do not denigrate those who pursue this thankless career when I say that their talents and energies could be put to better use.

Let me recapitulate the argument so far by reviewing the history of the concept of parole. It began as an essay in leniency, an attempt to relieve some of the miseries of confinement through hopes of early release. Decisions were made by various functionaries, usually lay boards, concerning the eligibility of prisoners for an "act of grace" by the state. These acts of grace were determined by predictions of future conduct based on whatever rationales and policies that the boards could improvise. Awareness of the unreliability of such predictions led to the establishment of the system of supervision with which we have become so familiar. I think it is fair to say that parole systems began with an exclusive emphasis on surveillance and only gradually metamorphosed into their present hybrid condition in which the officers of parole attempt to combine surveillance and service. The apparent need of the parolee for service was obvious. Certainly no one could be blind to the precarious state of the released prisoner, a man under deep suspicion, often friendless, usually without skills, usually all too aware of society's rejection. It is understandable that parole agencies have wanted to incorporate the function of social work. Experienced parole officers know that their usefulness in the mission of surveillance is almost negligible. But somehow the needs of the parolee for reintegration—that usefully vague objective in current fashion—must be met. Who else can meet them but the parole officer?

The answer is that if the parole officer makes the attempt, no one else will compete with him. The social agencies whose mission it is to help people in trouble will concede to the parole system the task of helping offenders. If the parole officer, a specialist in administering such help, cannot reintegrate the offender, what reason is there to suppose that a service without such expertise could do better?

The answers to this question are becoming clear. First, parole research has now been conducted in circumstances that have refined the experimental model to an almost impractical optimum. Studt's study of the California parole system clearly is based on the work of well-trained and sensitive personnel, motivated to do their best to help, well aware that their efforts at surveillance are obsolete superfluities.[8] The recent study of the California Community Treatment Project by Lerman is based on the analysis of data from services differentiated by a theory of treatment addressed to the problems of defective personality development.[9] Despite the sophistication of the concept, the successes of the treatments administered in small caseloads have attested to the supportive decision making of the Youth Authority rather than the effectiveness of the parole officer's intervention. The earlier San Francisco Project, reported by Wahl and Carter, was unable to show any differential success for optimized services. Farther back in time, the old SIPU (Special Intensive Parole Unit) studies of the California Department of Corrections, followed by the work unit project of the same department, have failed to demonstrate consistent experimental success. It is true that most of the work I have mentioned has been carried on in the California correctional departments, but the research has been well controlled by agencies that have hoped that results would demonstrate the success of the experiments. To my knowledge, no parole research conducted elsewhere has produced findings that suggest a better outcome under other auspices.

In the second place, theory of an admittedly crude sort stares us in the face. Anyone familiar with correctional practice is soon uncomfortably aware of the conflict between coercion and assistance. Like everyone else in the treatment sector of corrections, the parole officer carries the handcuffs of authority in the same briefcase with his casebook. The symbolism is blunt but suggestive. Its signigicance is even weightier when the parole officer packs a pistol as well. The attempt is made to combine the authority of the state with the human concern and the professional skills of the helping occupations. Years ago I used to hope that we could construct a theory of parole that would be based on improving the relationship of the offender to authority through some kind of reconciliation with this ambiguity. Although there have been some experiments to prove this point, none of them have really come off in the data analysis, and I have never seen a situation in which this putative process has actually taken place. We do not hear about it any more; we are increasingly reconciled to the idea that the conflict between coercion and assistance is unbridgeable.

And in the third place, we should be considering the nature of the assistance that one human being or one agency can offer to any individual in a society organized like ours. Of what real value is it in the helping process to be expert in the operations of the criminal-justice system? Is it not of considerably greater value to have a full knowledge of the resources of the community, to be able to offer services according to determined needs rather than according to present and past status? For a man who needs a job, a decent place to stay, or simply good and disinterested advice, the terms of reference should not be his legal disabilities or the stigma of retribution and control. He should be helped as a person in need by an agency with experience in meeting these needs. What reason is there to suppose that a counselor of a vocational-rehabilitation service cannot do as well as or better than a parole officer in getting an exoffender placed in employment? But neither the vocational-rehabilitation services nor any other social services will tread far into the parole officer's turf so long as the parole officer attempts to carry out a job-finding service.

This interpretation of the parole function has been as inexorable as I could make it. Nevertheless, no one who knows the work of the men and women who administer and perform parole services can fail to concede that many work hard, many are skillful, and that goodwill and hopefulness persist in the face of the inevitable disappointments and failures. These attributes of the parole system are social assets of which better use can be made. They should not be smothered in a system that is rooted in obsolete and exploded notions about human conduct and its control.

The Application of Lessons Learned

A whole new generation of radical social criticism has become intoxicated with the appeal of abolitionism. If a social institution such as the prison, the juvenile-training school, or parole can be demonstrated as oppressive, redundant, or just undesirable, let it be abolished in the interest of freedom and enlightenment. Let me conclude this disquisition with a disavowal of any such intent. I think abolitionism, as applied to social institutions, is an impractical and thoroughly undesirable program. I do not want to abolish those parole services that are needed; I want to reconstruct a system that cannot be counted on to administer them, as it is now organized.

I have already made plain my advocacy of the flat-term concept as a replacement of the indeterminate sentence. There is a little to add to what I have said. Flat terms must be administered with conscious safeguards of due process and administrative control. With all its conceptual defects, the parole board does provide for statewide equalization of the sentencing process. Some may argue that it is only an equalization of caprice, and in a sense we may never be able to eliminate that element. But it is certain that if we are to turn the sentencing process back to the judiciary, even with the rigorous constraints of the flat term, there should be provision for an appellate process, open to both prosecution and defense, that will assure that judicial error in the sentencing process as well as in the trial of the case can be rectified. Similarly, the administration of the good-time provisions of the law must be scrupulously monitored by an independent functionary with powers to assure that where good time has been lost as a result of circumstances in dispute the situation can be responsibly reviewed.

The flat-term concept eliminates the notion of parole for surveillance. Sometimes a released prisoner will need surveillance, in which case let us be serious about the need and let the police do it, as they would and should in the case of any persons suspected of committing a crime. But this is a needless and unproductive process where no crime is suspected. Institutionalized distrust is a futile indignity outside of the prison. When it is operationalized in the community it leads to alienation rather than reintegration. It is an impossible foundation for public protection.

But the released prisoner does need help and often. If there is to be no parole service, he will have to be guided to the help he needs. I suggest that this bridge might consist of two elements. First, a referral service should be readily available to prisoners needing and wanting help in preparation for release and in dealing with whatever problems are beyond their capacities after release takes place. This service might be publicly administered, but, if so, it should be clearly independent of the prison administration and without any mandate to participate in the control of the prisoner before or after release. The agency might also be in private hands, which would assure independence but in circumstances of unstable fiscal support.

The second element of the new model of after-care should be a revival of voluntarism in prisoner assistance. One of the more significant disadvantages of the parole system that we have allowed to monopolize the assistance of prisoners has been the attenuation of the old voluntary services, the Societies for the Alleviation of the Miseries of Prisoners, which used to flourish in some states. If reintegration is our objective, we need these societies as never before, although with less ponderous titles. They should mobilize prison visitors, assure that they are provided the necessary supporting services, and might also operate the referral services that are essential to successful reintegration. Here is where the altruism and goodwill to be found in parole services can be put to most successful use.

In the years when I worked as a parole officer criticisms of our work usually evoked a standard response: "What does he know about it—he's never pushed a doorbell!" I doubt that this dismissal counted for much outside our ranks, but it somehow made us feel good; nobody could understand what we were up against who had not pushed doorbells in search of cons and excons. But time has gone by. The answer to my question is that the doorbell pusher is now redundant, and public services should be not maintained around his function. What can never be redundant is the quality of altruism, that aspect of citizenship in a democracy assuming the preservation and strengthening of the social bonds that can once again bring the crime problem under control.

Notes

1. David Fogel, ". . . *We Are the Living Proof . . .*" (Cincinnati: W.W. Anderson, 1975).

2. Richard A. McGee, "A New Look at Sentencing," *Federal Probation* 38, no. 2 (June 1974):3-8, and 38, no. 3 (September 1974):3-11.

3. Ibid.

4. As of the time of that writing. But see Alfred Blumstein, Jacqueline Cohen, and Daniel Nagin, eds., *Deterrence and Incapacitation* (Washington, D.C.: National Research Council, 1977). See also, Stephan Van Dine, John P. Conrad, and Simon Dinitz, *Restraining the Wicked* (Lexington, Mass.: Lexington Books, D.C. Heath, 1979).

5. Fogel, *Living Proof.*

6. Sheldon Messinger, "Strategies of Control" (Doctoral diss., University of California, 1969), see chap. 3.

7. Elliot Studt, *Surveillance and Service* (Los Angeles: University of California at Los Angeles, Institute of Government and Public Affairs, 1972).

8. Ibid.

9. Paul Lerman, *Community Treatment and Social Control: A Critical Analysis of Juvenile Correctional Policy* (Chicago and London: University of Chicago Press, 1975).

10

Fifty Years in a Squirrel Cage

The Past, Present, and Future of Evaluation in Corrections

The history of my uncomfortable involvement in evaluation research is partially recounted in this chapter, which was prepared for a conference on this topic conducted by the University of South Florida. As will be apparent, I was plunged into this marginally useful line of inquiry with very little preparation. A new approach to parole was to be initiated, and it had to be evaluated to discover whether the increased benefits would offset the increased cost. Wiser heads than I assured the department that the experimental-research design would be the appropriate model for the assessment. Even at that time, I thought the value of that design was open to question. As the years have gone by since the launching of the special intensive parole unit my questions have become better informed and more insistent. The appearance in the early seventies of the "nothing-works" message on the effectiveness of rehabilitation programs convinced me that much damage had been done by the kind of evaluation that we had done. The structure of interpretation that has been erected on a far-too-simple research pattern goes far to account for the conceptual doldrums in which correctional thought has been becalmed.

This chapter was my manifesto on the futility of the experimental design in correctional evaluation. The line of thought presented here has inexorably led me away from the goal orientation that has been articulated, although not pursued for the last century. Common sense should have told us long ago that the evaluation of a special intensive parole unit consisting of parole officers with nothing more in common than the size of their caseloads would be a meaningless exercise, and so it proved to be. Social scientists have always mistrusted common sense—and sometimes with good reason. But fifty years of counting recidivists? A squirrel cage can come to seem the most natural place for a statistician, especially if one can always think of yet another refinement that might lead to statistical significance the next time around.

The Power of Empiricism

Most of the great paradigms of science can be proudly traced to an ancestor. Aristotle was the so-called father of logic, Newton the father of physics, and Osler the father of modern medicine. The parentage of most of the social sciences is still in dispute, but there is no question about the paradigm of correctional evaluation. That intellectual tradition had parents, and they were married to each other.

So when I was asked to weave a historical perspective on correctional evaluation, I turned respectfully to the works of Sheldon and Eleanor Glueck. I am old enough to remember well the publication of *500 Criminal Careers*, the first fruit of their long and assiduous collaboration.[1] It created quite a stir in 1930, when it first appeared. That was long before a whimsical fate propelled me into the prison business, but a high-school student in touch with the serious book reviews could not fail to notice the controversy and wonder about its implications. I got hold of the book, read it with awe at the industry of its authors and perplexity about its implications. I am still perplexed, forty-six years later, after a far more thorough immersion in the subject matter than I ever expected to have when the book first came into my hands.

Evidently it is not much read now. The copy that I borrowed from our university library was last checked out in 1970, and that was the first time since 1963. But let me call to your attention the remarks of Dr. Richard Cabot, who wrote the foreword:

> The important fact established in this book is that out of 510 men who left the Massachusetts Reformatory during the years 1911-22 *eighty per cent* [author's italics] were not reformed five to fifteen years later, but went right on committing crimes after their discharges. This is a damning piece of evidence—not against that Reformatory in particular . . . but against the reformatory system in general. Here it does not work. No one knows that it works any better elsewhere.[2]

Now this was a shocking discovery. Until then, the prevailing belief had been that reformatory training was remarkably successful. The Gluecks' review of the literature elicited numerous expert opinions that, of the young men released from the nation's reformatories, about 80 percent "refrained from crime and became helpful members of society." I am bemused to note that one of the authorities cited was James A. Leonard, superintendent of the Ohio State Reformatory at Mansfield, architecturally one of the most depressing bastilles I have ever seen, whose experience and observation led him to believe that three out of four young men discharged from reformatory institutions lived good and useful lives after their release. Apparently alone among the authors reviewed, E.H. Sutherland was sceptical of the rosy estimates of the professional-reformatory operators. It is clear from the Gluecks' review that the ingenuous American public was not accustomed to challenging its correctional experts, who themselves seemed to have enjoyed an enviable confidence in the rightness of what they were doing.

In the face of this innocence, the discovery that the facts were the exact opposite of the claims of the professionals must have been a thunderous disillusion, even in the age of H.L. Mencken and a whole culture of debunkers. For consider the methods of the Gluecks. They rejected the comfortable review of prison records, the interviews with wardens and parole-board members, and the annual reports of reformatory superintendents, all of which had theretofore combined to give the world a reassuring view of the success of contemporary penology. Instead, they set out to trace the whereabouts of each man released from the Concord Reformatory over an eleven-year period, to find him, interview him, and report on his further involvement, if any, in crime. Their success in accomplishing this task can still plunge the social scientist of the seventies into a state of envious awe. Not only were they able to report on the parole histories of 477 of their cohort of 510, but they were also able to locate 422 of these worthies five years after the expiration of their paroles.

The findings for the parolees were grim: over half of them were violators, and at least 70 percent of the violations were for new crimes. The average length of employment on a job was about three months. Parole supervision in most cases was nominal; parole agents in over half the cases did not see parolees even once on their own initiative. As to the postparole followup it was found that almost four-fifths of the group of 422 traced to their abodes had committed criminal acts. The authors' conclusion is worth repeating in full:

> In comparing the criminality of the men during the three stages of our inquiry, it was found: (a) that there were measurably fewer total failures and more successes during the supervised parole period than during either the post-parole or the pre-Reformatory period; (b) that the Reformatory and parole supervision, together with the passage of time had exerted some influence in curbing the criminal tendencies of our group. The large majority of the men, however, have not abandoned their careers of crime.[3]

The study is replete with findings about the programs of the Reformatory, the processes of parole, and the employment histories of the cohort group. It then goes on to some explanations of the discouraging findings cited. Their elaborately cautious exploration of the reasons for the institution's failure was compressed by the impatient Dr. Cabot, their senior, as follows:

> Why should men thoroughly accustomed and habituated to crime . . . change all (their) bad habits and acquire good ones merely because they are confined for a little over a year in an institution in which they are forced to do work in which they have little or no interest, . . . and pursued not principally for its educational value, but for its economic results, for which the prisoners care nothing? . . . Why should this regime reform anyone? In my

experience, there are few tougher and more unyielding structures than a bad habit. It does not change as the result of a few months of forced, un-paid, and unpalatable labor. I doubt if anyone knows what will change such habits within a short time and under the conditions of institutional life. So far as I have seen such reforms . . . there has been at least one necessary condition: That someone should come to know and to under-stand the man in so intimate and friendly a way that he comes to a better understanding of himself and to a truer comprehension of the world he lives in. Out of this prime reorientation there may grow supplementary and reinforcing factors such as:

a.   A new interest in an honest job.
b.   A new affection for someone for whose sake it now seems worthwhile to behave decently.
c.   A perception that crime does not pay.[4]

Much later in the book, the Gluecks report on the sacrifice of program and human interaction in the interest of maintaining a well-oiled ad-ministrative machine. But optimism prevailed. Although the "deadweight of inertia and routinization" was recognized for what it was, it was clear to them that a program consisting of classification, psychiatry and social work, education and vocational training, and the "personal touch" might yet "render . . . rehabilitation possible."

It would be simple to comment here that we have come full circle, like my squirrel in his cage. But history is not all that simple, nor do I know what went on in the Concord Reformatory superintendent's office when he and his staff digested all the bad news that these pioneer researchers had to tell about their institution. This was a book that smashed illusions and stripped off pretenses. That was the end of the Elmira Reformatory as a model for American penology. Until then, it had been the centerpiece of progress, a goal for correctional aspiration. The Gluecks and their mentor, Dr. Cabot, had shown it up for the meretricious scheme it was; instead of 80 percent success, it achieved 80 percent failure. It did not work, and the Gluecks came close to showing why it did not work. Obsession with adminis-trative mechanics had drained out all humanity, all hope, all reason for being.

The Gluecks then went on, as I have mentioned, to urge on the state a program of uplift. Instead of a pointless industrial program, they said, create an individualized-treatment program, complete with a truly indeter-minate sentence. And it was done, more or less, over a geat many years, sometimes with soaring hopes, sometimes with contemptible hypocrisy. It would be wrong to assign the credit, what there was of it to assign, to the Gluecks. I am enough of a determinist to believe it probably would have happened anyway. But certainly *500 Criminal Careers* gave a powerful im-petus to the movement. Young psychiatrists, social workers, parole agents, and teachers drifted into corrections, moved by the authority of the Gluecks to believe that there was a job to do. It took time for the model to crystallize, but it always does. Sixteen years after the publication of that book, I found myself trying to find ways of applying that "personal touch" that the Gluecks extolled to my caseload of parolees in San Francisco. The work of this industrious pair may not be read so much now, but their influence lingers on. That was the power of empiricism, coupled with an unshakeable belief that somehow these young poeple could, for the most part, be helped to a better kind of life. Before moving on, I cannot resist one last archaic quotation from Dr. Cabot's memorable foreword: "Knowing as I do the men and women who did this work and the amount of ingenuity and persistence which they expended, I predict that it will be a long time before such a thorough and accurate piece of follow-up work is done again. It took the larger part of three years and cost eleven thousand dollars, the money being supplied through grants from the Milton Fund of Harvard University."[5] A long time indeed! Aside from the Glueck's own subsequent efforts, we can hardly say that even an attempt has been made to match it. But how much computer time would those eleven thousand dollars buy today?

The Practice and Pitfalls of Empiricism

Let us leave the Gluecks and pass on to more recent history. The scene shifts from Boston to Sacramento, and it is now 1953. Little of consequence happened in correctional evaluation in the twenty-three-year interval that elapsed after the publication of *500 Criminal Careers*, but in California we have taken the Gluecks' prescription to heart, and their recommendations could not have been more conscientiously followed. Our leader was Richard McGee, an impatient director of Corrections who was never able to let well enough alone. At his side was Norman Fenton, the deputy director for Classification and Treatment. Fenton was a persistent and believing meliorist, exactly the right man to charge with the creation of a departmentwide treatment program that would do something for each of the department's twenty thousand inmates, from the hardened old cons at Folsom to the beardless young hooligans at the Deuel Vocational Institution. I was one of Fenton's acolytes, having risen from practice to administrative duties, then as now, a necessary metamorphosis for the upwardly mobile.

Every year the department went to the legislature with an innovation that would cost money but improve the effectiveness of the correctional program, or so we thought and claimed. In 1953, the great push was for a halfway house, which one of our staff had conceived and planned in convincing detail. In spite of our enthusiasm, the legislative analyst, our mordant critic, would have none of it, pointing out that he would not like a halfway house in his neighborhood and doubted that anyone else would, either. But he astonished us by going on to recommend that if a reduction in prison building was what we wanted, we should consider an "intensification of parole." Why not allot a sum of money to establish some experimental-parole caseloads? He even suggested a no-cost, self-financing way of doing it; let the Adult Authority advance by three months the release of each person assigned to an experimental caseload. The money thus saved would pay for the experiment. And this was how the memorable Special Intensive Parole Unit (SIPU) came into being.

I was involved in the planning and eventually inherited the job of managing the unit. Suddenly research was the fashionable role in corrections, and several of us who had previously been committed to the administrative grindstone were now preoccupied with unfamiliar problems of research design. In spite of our naiveté, in spite of our venture into a domain of research that had lain fallow for so many years, we enjoyed two advantages. The first was an advisory committee composed of eminent and sympathetic social scientists who seemed to be fascinated at the spectacle of prison officials trying to use the experimental method to improve their work. We also had the incomparable Ronald Beattie, the statistician who had almost singlehandedly designed and organized the California Bureau of Criminal Statistics, still far and away the most comprehensive and best-integrated collection of crime and delinquency data in existence. With guidance on the scientific method from our committee and with access to a working statistical data bank, we were sure that we could soon prove that intensive parole supervision was cost effective. None of us had any patience for the null hypothesis.

At first, it looked as though we were going to match the success of Dr. Jonas Salk, who was at that time proving his methods of immunizing children against poliomyelitis by the use of a similar research design calling for randomly selected control and experimental groups. His successful example was frequently invoked for the inspiration of our parole officers.

Experimental caseloads were limited to fifteen parolees, and there were fourteen of them scattered through the state. Control caseloads were kept at the ninety-man level prevailing before the experiment, and care was taken to assure that the control caseloads were each drawn from the same geographical areas as the experimental caseloads. The research design called for five cells. Four cells were established by caseload size and the variable of parole advancement. Parolees with advanced- and nonadvanced-release dates were randomly distributed to the two kinds of caseloads, with the thought that we might as well know whether early release of parolees made any difference to their adjustment. We were careful to conceal from the parolees their status in this respect, but of course they had to know that if assigned to an experimental caseload they would be seeing a lot more of their parole agent than they had expected. The fifth cell in the design was reserved for high-risk parolees with a view to seeing whether the Adult Authority could release with impunity a sprinkling of really dangerous offenders by assigning them to the small experimental caseloads. This was the uncontrolled part of the experiment, and, although some of the risks were obviously authentic, nothing very untoward happened.

The early returns were good; the intensive caseloads seemed to "pay off" with fewer parole violations. But the drift was away from statistical significance, and at the end of my year of stewardship the margin in favor of the experimental unit was tenuous. It disappeared during the following year. In the years that followed many variants of the experiment were tried with only one success, and that a dubious one, in which minimum supervision for high base-expectancy parolees succeeded as well as regular supervision for a control group. The conceptual validity of this difference is open to obvious question, but there seems to have been a money saving.

So concerned were we with the perplexing task of finding how various adjustments of parole supervision might increase effectiveness that we missed the two lessons of the experience that now seem to be of real significance. First, our data invariably showed that advancement of release dates made no difference in the recidivism rates. Whatever readiness for parole might mean, the Adult Authority could not determine it within a three- to six-months margin. The meaning of this discovery should have been obvious and should then have been reflected in vastly altered Adult Authority policy, but twenty years had to pass before the Adult Authority abandoned the notion that some combination of wisdom, experience, and intuition would enable it to perceive any given inmate's readiness for return to the community.

The second lesson has yet to be applied, because no one knows what to do about it. Quite early I noticed that different parole officers had different results as to the recidivism in their caseloads. These results could not be entirely accounted for by social conditions in the districts in which they worked. In Oakland, for example, the SIPU agent was an irrepressible enthusiast who kept his office open until late hours at night to dispense advice to, and to conduct bull-sessions with, any parolee who cared to happen in, as most of his caseload seemed to enjoy doing. His violation rate was extraordinarily low, but I never saw any reason to believe that there was a special ambience in Oakland that favored parole success. Across the Bay in San Francisco the SIPU agent was an enthusiast of a different stripe. He liked to rise in the small hours of the morning so that he could descend on unemployed parolees and remind them that early birds get the available worms and slug-a-beds do not. How he managed to conduct these sunrise raids on his charges without dismemberment of his person I have never understood, but his parole violation rate was high, even after he was convinced that his strenuous counseling technique was unwise. It may well have seemed to his parolees that his brand of supervision was too high a price to pay, even for the privilege of living in San Francisco.

The conclusions to be drawn from SIPU, an experiment with exceptional longevity—it lasted for over twelve years in all its mutations—will differ from observer to observer. What it accomplished was quite rigorously controlled evaluation of the processes of parole. Because the conclusions were not statistically significant, the meaning of their inconclusiveness still has not sunk into the consciousness of correctional administrators, planners, and policy makers. A decade after the conclusion of SIPU, most parole boards still believe that they can determine parole readiness and try to individualize sentences accordingly. We still maintain elaborate parole agencies for the purpose of supervision, despite our inability to show that it makes any difference at all in the prevention of recidivism. Finally, the occasional cues about the value and nature of help that we get from gifted human beings like my friend in Oakland are disregarded as accidents of personality because we cannot find a way of putting a numerical value on them.

SIPU was followed by the Pilot Intensive Counseling Organization (PICO), the Intensive Treatment program (IT), and the Increased Correctional Effectiveness program (ICE). There was also the evaluation of group counseling at the California Men's Colony memorialized by Kassebaum, Ward, and Wilner in their elegant report, *Prison Treatment and Parole Survival*.[6] In each study a serious effort was made to maintain research control. All were addressed to the value of different forms of treatment by counseling. The criterion of success in each was postrelease recidivism. We knew how to conduct this kind of research, and as time went on, we became rather good at it. We never established a difference in favor of the experimental group in any of these evaluations, even though our bias in favor of the experiment often showed all too plainly.

One other California venture into evaluative research must be mentioned here to complete the picture. I refer, of course, to the Community Treatment Project of the California Youth Authority, a complex project that was based on the differential treatment of youthful offenders in accordance with programs of treatment related to their "interpersonal maturity," as assessed on a scale derived from the conceptualizations of Piaget and Erikson on psychological development. The work of Warren in designing the project,[7] of Palmer[8] in collecting the data with which to evaluate it, and of Lerman in challenging the claims made for its success are all available elsewhere and far too voluminous for me to recapitulate here.[9] For some years, there was a general belief that a successful method had been found for treating certain categories of delinquent youth, although the originators have always been careful to be highly selective in their claims. Nevertheless, the coming of a theoretical basis for differential treatment of delinquents in custody was intellectually satisfying to professionals in corrections, and the principles of this model of treatment have been widely copied. For a time, indeed, both the model and the methods used for evaluating it were held up to the criminal-justice public as evidence that progress could be made in this discouraging field, despite all the evidence to the contrary. The use of a coherent theory as a basis for distributing both experimental and control groups was the secret to a meaningful evaluation, or so it was held, because in an undifferentiated program failures will cancel out successes and nothing will be learned from experience.[10] Lerman's strictures about the Community Treatment Project raise doubts that have not been satisfied about the project's apparently favorable outcomes. They do not shake the significance of the differentiations within the treated group. Unfortunately, differentiations of this kind are extraordinarily difficult to sustain.

And so ends my account of evaluative research in California. Our methods were copied elsewhere, but replications have not significantly altered the bleak conclusion that treatment programs in prison, differential parole-board decision making about release, and parole supervision after release make little difference discernable through the application of the scientific method.

Empiricism and the Refinement of Concepts

The stage is now set for the entry of Dr. Robert Martinson and his retinue. From about 1969, I had been aware, along with a number of others in the correctional-research community, of the studies of Martinson and his colleagues on the effectiveness of correctional treatment. Because of a tiresomely intricate administrative and legal situation, these studies languished unseen and unread for over five years, but they were frequently summarized, and their significance for the future of correctional policy was endlessly debated. We would be hard put to find such a *succes d'estime* of an unpublished and unavailable document anywhere in scientific literature.

Finally Martinson published a summary containing the fateful pronouncement: "With few and isolated exceptions, the rehabilitative efforts that have been reported so far have had no appreciable effect on recidivism."[11] This conclusion was based on a laborious review of the results of 231 studies of the effectiveness of correctional-treatment programs. Not all of these studies used the criterion of recidivism, but enough of them—137, to be exact—were measurable on that dimension to justify Martinson's now-famous conclusion.

We should note here that the widely circulated interpretation of Martinson's cautious language proclaims that no rehabilitative method "works."

He wisely avoided the claim that he had proved a negative, and indeed he specifically rejected the imputation that his studies show that correctional rehabilitation does not work. He also pointed out that the research reports analyzed in his study took place between the years 1945 and 1967, accepting the possibility that recent work may have been more effective in execution or more sensitive in research design.

But here I shall cast caution to the winds and proceed on the bold assumption that Martinson's interpreters were right the first time. I will argue here not only that rehabilitative efforts have failed to produce appreciable effects on recidivism but also that it is most unlikely that any systematic application of any rehabilitative program will seriously reduce the recidivism of the offender population to which it may be applied. I will be exhilarated if Martinson and I are proved to be wrong, but I think the reasons for pessimism are convincingly persuasive.

First, the processes of rehabilitation in the psychological and social domains outside of the criminal-justice system have been notoriously unpredictable. Psychiatrists and clinical psychologists have wrestled with the proof of the effectiveness of their treatment methods for many more years than correctional workers have been engaged with the problem. They have not enjoyed the advantage of so convenient a criterion of failure as recidivism, it is true, but objective evidence that their methods are predictably effective is virtually nonexistent. We must take note here that psychiatric therapy is addressed to troubled people who genuinely desire help with personal difficulties that they, themselves, recognize to be pathological. But in corrections we are trying to help people who, for the most part, do not feel that anything is wrong with them other than the stigma of conviction and the deprivation of liberty, two conditions for which treatment is of no relevance. Not many offenders feel the need of better psychological insight, more education, or even more vocational skills. Once in prison, they will attend school, participate in group counseling, and engage in vocational training, but it is exceedingly doubtful that their involvement arises from genuinely felt needs. I will come back to this point later. In the mean time, I hold to my speculation that the unpredictable processes of rehabilitation are unlikely to be effective with a population of subjects who generally feel no special need for relief from their personal deficiencies.

Second, the incentives for change are meager. It is true, of course, that offenders who are motivated to lead law-abiding lives will not have their liberty in jeopardy again. Unfortunately, the connections between the offerings of a rehabilitative program and satisfied conformity are tenuous. Not the insights gained from psychotherapy, not the possession of a high school diploma, not even the acquisition of an advanced vocational skill—a rare development—convincingly point to a life more attractive than the career that led to trouble in the first place. Indeed, it might be cynically argued that for most inmates all this effort at self-betterment leads nowhere at all. In prison, time can be filled in with these activities, but they have little relation to a believable future in which prisoner and society are fully reconciled. The essential ingredient of any incentive is a promise on which delivery can be made. Our society cannot credibly promise anything to a prisoner.

Third, for those who try to benefit from prison treatment, even for those who have achieved clear benefits, there remain the inescapable handicaps of severely impaired status and a hostile environment. Consider how you and I would cope with the formidable problems confronting us if we were released prisoners. There are the barriers to employment, the ostracism imposed by former friends and associates, the scepticism of even the most sincere well-wishers, the sense of degradation, and one's own self-doubt. To add to these psychic burdens, there is poverty of the most humiliating kind. Honest money is to be had for only the most precarious hand-to-mouth existence. These are massive obstacles to the realization of personal change. Few of us can be sure that we could surmount them if they blocked our way to a better future. The released prisoner has less experience of success, much less reason to believe that he can cope with adversity. The help that any correctional institution could offer him is frail support against the buffeting of the real world. What can a parole officer, even a SIPU parole officer with a fifteen-man caseload, offer to arm the excon for success in a world that does not want him?

Fourth, there is implicit in rehabilitation the expectation that the person receiving it will be enabled to lead a normal life. For many prisoners this expectation is not unreasonable. After all, the idea of rehabilitation in the medical context is that a patient who, having once led a normal life and now suffering a handicap as a result of illness or accident, will be assisted to compensate for his handicap so that he can again engage in normal pursuits. But what is normal about the life of the unemployed black, Chicano, or Indian, subjected to the daily humiliations of redundancy? Life at the bottom of the social barrel is abnormal. There is no way of preparing a man to adjust to it. A prisoner released to a community in which no one is working, or even worse, where most adults have never been regularly employed, is not likely to remember for long whatever it was that he learned in prison.

Fifth, coercion constricts volition, and volition is the essence of favorable personal change. Unless a man can choose freely, he can never learn to choose well. In prison a man can hardly choose at all—except to cheat or deceive those who control him. The pretense of change is the game that prisoners play with parole boards and prison staffs. It is a game that prisoners inevitably win, if only because nearly every prisoner must some day be released to make room for the continuing tide of replacements.

This has been a dismal recital of the reasons for the unhappy ending of a magnanimous dream. I could go on. Personnel are lacking to carry out programs. Prisoners are assigned to inappropriate treatment for reasons of incompetence, indifference, or simply to keep them occupied. Staff training is usually superficial and unconvincing. Pervading all efforts to overcome it is the culture of failure. Achievement and success are foreign to the prison and its inhabitants, both staff and prisoners. The wonder is that we ever thought that the rehabilitation of the prisoner could work. Hope springs eternal, and our hopes do much credit to our generosity and compassion. Nevertheless, the Martinson finding is all too credible. Rehabilitative programs have not had, and almost certainly cannot have, an appreciable effect on the rates of recidivism.

The importance of this proposition, the truth of which many had long suspected, can hardly be overstated. It has influenced the whole spectrum of opinion, despite lingering doubts in some quarters about its validity. On the correctional left, it is argued that the collapse of the claims of rehabilitation should lead to the abolition of the prison. If we cannot rehabilitate offenders in confinement, why lock them up at all? Punishment can be carried out by means less destructive to the individual's social survival; incapacitation merely defers crime, and no one has conclusively proved that prisons are essential to the general deterrence of violations of the law. This extreme view is too much for most people, no matter how much humane men and women must be repelled by the hideous and unnatural miseries we inflict on others through an agency of the state.

Closer to the center, the argument is made that prisons are necessary for a while longer, until we can think of what else to do with dangerous offenders. Realism compels us to recognize that our society regularly generates a few violent men who must be kept in restraint. Most of the advocates of this position maintain that there are few enough of them so that we should manage well enough with the prisons we have without building more.

In the center is the reasonable proposition that if rehabilitation does not work, then let us have done with the pretense that it does and with all the apparatus that is built on that pretense, namely, the indeterminate sentence and the administration of parole. From this position there flows the contention that it is unjust to practice the "medical model" further and that we should instead concentrate our efforts on making the criminal-justice system just. This is the well-known "justice model" proposed by David Fogel, who identifies as a needless instrument of oppression the model of rehabilitation as a prerequisite to release from prison. If Fogel has his way, prisoners will know their terms immediately after conviction, but they will earn remission by good behavior during the course of their incarceration. The derivation of Fogel's "justice model" from Martinson's conclusion is clear. If prisons could predictably rehabilitate, the indeterminate sentence would be logical and necessary. But as they cannot, the flat term is as fair as we can have. We should accept the incapacitating and deterrent effects it brings in the wake of justice.[12]

Moving to the correctional right, the argument is made that if we cannot improve prisoners through rehabilitative programs, we can at least assure that they are incapacitated and that the potential criminal is deterred by the consequences incurred by those who violate the law. Hence the argument for the mandatory sentence, which ranges from relatively mild deprivations of liberty to the most draconian severity. Both social scientists and political figures lean more and more to a punishment model. James Q. Wilson, who may be our most influential social-science commentator on criminal justice, has put this position starkly: "Society at a minimum must be able to protect itself from dangerous offenders and to impose some costs on criminal acts; . . . society really does not know how to do much else."[13]

Two full generations elapsed between the founding of the Elmira Reformatory in 1876 and the coup de grace administered by the Gluecks. The implementation of their program took another twenty years. The publication of *The Effectiveness of Correctional Treatment*, by Lipton, Martinson, and Wilks, is another such landmark event, although we must doubt that these authors will ever be so widely read as the Gluecks.[14] Nevertheless, it has provided empirical support for an unprecedented discussion of the fundamental issues in criminal justice. The present elevation of the crime rates demand change in law and policy, and it seems inevitable that the swing is toward a hard and severe line toward criminals.

The evaluation of the Gluecks' model of correctional rehabilitation has been brought to an end by the researchers whose work Martinson has surveyed. He has said that the present is a rare historic moment when choices must be made about the future. He denounces the misinterpretation of his position to carry the meaning that rehabilitation does not work and asserts that such a position is a "thought-killer." I must respectfully disagree. That version of his conclusion has provoked me to a lot of thought concerning the future of correctional evaluation, and to the refinement of its underlying concepts. It is to these reflections that I will now turn.

From Objectives to Duties

I began this disquisition with a reference to the Gluecks as the progenitors of the paradigm of correctional evaluation. Perhaps this estimate of their significance distorts the actual role they have played in the furtherance of empiricism in correctional evaluation. The longitudinal studies that we associate with their names certainly gave us a perspective on the effectiveness of correctional intervention and posed questions never before asked. But longitudinal studies are expensive, and they have obvious limitations for the purposes of evaluation. The Gluecks have had few emulators; the questions their methods could address have been asnwered.

The controlled experiment model that characterized the California evaluation program of the fifties and sixties had different conceptual origins. Borrowed from natural science, the method has great power in measuring the impact of an independent variable if it is administered to an experimental population and withheld from a control population. The independent variable must be carefully defined in terms of both its actual nature and the expectations of its effects. The administration of the treatment must be verifiable and verified. Finally there should be some theoretical link to the dependent variable, some reason grounded in a falsifiable theory to believe that the introduction of the independent variable will cause some measurable effect on the dependent variable.

Now I have gone through this painfully obvious although necessarily compressed account of the principles of controlled experimentation because I think we have to consider carefully the limitations of this kind of evaluative research. In the first place, we will not be allowed to test all propositions of correctional interest by this kind of study. Imagine, for example, a study of the effects of benign-milieu therapy under minimum-custody conditions for a random sample of maximum-custody dangerous offenders. Allowing our imagination more rein, we can think of a lot of studies that would be useful but legally or ethically impermissible. We agree to their impossibility and deal with the indicated propositions by other conceptual methods.

But much more important for our purposes is the virtual impossibility of maintaining the integrity of the independent variable—as for example my two SIPU parole officers in Oakland and San Francisco—and making some acceptable theoretical connection with recidivism as the customary dependent variable. If you have stayed with me so far, you know that I have a good deal of trouble with the assumptions on which this connection must rest. I believe that the chain of events between intervention and outcome must be very short if we are to attribute variations in the latter to the former. From the reading of literally thousands of case histories, I have emerged a sceptic about the chain between prison treatment and parole survival, or for that matter, between parole supervision and parole survival. There are a myriad of variables at work in different proportions on different people, and it seems incredible to me to conclude that rehabilitative efforts can have a measurable impact on recidivism.

Nevertheless, we have learned a good deal from this paradigm of evaluation. We certainly know that where correctional populations are not differentiated treatment variables do not show up in the measurement of the dependent variable. We know this proposition is true for a great number of treatment variables, so many that it seems unlikely that we will find a significant exception. Some of us have become dubious about the value of the entire parole system, and these doubts have extended to the indeterminate sentence itself. The question of time served in prison and its effect on recidivism is still open, but we know that if differences in the length of sentence do make a difference on that scale, they must be very large differences indeed.

These are important findings, and I take them seriously. But I think we have gone about as far as we can with this model of research. Not everyone will accept the notion that rehabilitation must be a subsidiary, incidental feature of corrections rather than a major objective, but if we can prove its feasibility as a goal we will have to find other ways of doing it.

In other words, we face the exhaustion of a paradigm, to use the language of Thomas Kuhn.[15] We have solved all the major puzzles that the recidivism paradigm can handle. Further studies based on this research model can only trivialize the effort to expand knowledge. This is not to say, of course, that for the purpose of justifying a budget or checking the efficiency of a variant program it may not be useful to carry out such a study occasionally. But as a means of understanding the interactions between individuals and the system, the control-group study, using recidivism as the dependent variable, has little more to offer us.

There is a more powerful reason for this conclusion than the inefficiency of this kind of research design. We have indeed shown that rehabilitative efforts have little or no impact on recidivism. If this is so, the justification for a correctional service cannot be teleological. In other words, we no longer have to think of a goal that must be achieved. We can forget the medical model and the hospital into which we were trying to convert the prison. The painful attempt to adapt the management-by-objectives strategy in administering corrections and justifying its budget can be consigned to the same boneyard of useless analogies as the medical model. Let us face corrections as a necessary process for the disposition of offenders and agree that the justification must be deontological. In other words, our task is to find out what is right and do it. Our values are not related to goal achievement but to the achievement of a moral and ethical system of control.

The questions for evaluation now become a vastly different sort, the kind that Judge Frank Johnson asked in Alabama when he closed down Governor Wallace's prisons because they offended basic decency. We are not concerned with the tedious question as to the relationship between a weekly group-counseling session and the future recidivism of those who participate in it. We will be concerned with the use of group counseling as a means of easing tensions within the institution in which it is practiced. We will stop fretting over whether inmates exposed to enough high school to pass a GED examination have a lower rate if recidivism than some other group, and we will try instead to find out how many inmates really want high-school courses while in prison and discover the most efficient way of packing knowledge into their heads. And we will stop experiments aimed at discovering whether thieves who receive income supplementation after their release from prison steal less than those who do not—instead we will try to find out what a man needs to survive at all after he gets out of prison.

What I have said so far is not to be construed to mean that we should desist from our efforts to rehabilitate inmates or prisons and those who are paroled from them. I am saying that we should create a prison in which a man can make an honest dollar if he chooses or subsist on a lean ration if he prefers not to work. He should be able to choose education, vocational training, or an appropriate psychotherapy if he wants to, but he should also have the privilege of being left to his own devices, so long as those devices do not impinge on someone else's freedom, safety, or convenience. A man is entitled to hope; to deprive him of that is nearly the ultimate cruelty. The opportunity to better oneself is a basic right in this country, and if prisons are ever to turn out citizens instead of excons, we will have to keep that opportunity realistic for all those who want it.

Deontology will require us to reexamine practically all our assumptions about the correctional enterprise. The duties that we must examine include duties to the public as well as to those we confine. We need empirical guidance on the appropriate scales of punishment for the purposes of retribution, incapacitation, and deterrence. What effect does punishment have in deterring the people on whom it is inflicted from the commission of new offenses? This is an obvious question so that I can answer it. How many burglaries are prevented by locking up a thousand burglars for a year? James Q. Wilson believes that ways have been found to answer this question, but neither he nor I know the answer.[16] And if we double the punishment for armed robbery, how many robberies are deterred? Is there a way of answering that question, and, if so, how do we balance the answer with the other process questions asked?

So let us have done with life in the squirrel cage, chasing after the bait we call recidivism, going around in endless circles, and ending with a correctional system that is about as bad as and possibly worse than the one we started with fifty years ago. We need evaluative research, not to tell us the truth about recidivism, which we can do precious little to affect, but to find out more how to perform our duty to mete out justice in a decent manner, consistent with the standards we hold to be American.

Notes

1. Sheldon Glueck and Eleanor T. Glueck, *500 Criminal Careers* (New York: Alfred A. Knopf, 1930).

2. Ibid., p. vii.

3. Ibid., p. 192.

4. Ibid., pp. ix-x.

5. Ibid., p. vii.

6. Gene Kassebaum, David Ward, and Daniel Wilner, *Prison Treatment and Parole Survial* (New York: John Wiley, 1971).

7. Marguerite Q. Warren, *"The Case for Differential Treatment of Delinquents,"* Annals of the American Academy of Political and Social Science 381 (January 1969): 47-59.

8. Numerous unpublished reports on the Community Treatment Project have been prepared under the general direction of Dr. Ted Palmer. They can be obtained from the California Youth Authority, Division of Research.

9. Paul Lerman, *Community Treatment and Social Control: A Critical Analysis of Juvenile Correctional Policy* (Chicago: University of Chicago Press, 1975).

10. National Advisory Commission on Criminal Justice Standards and Goals *Report of the Task Force on Corrections* (Washington, D.C.: U.S. Government Printing Office, 1973) pp. 516-517; Ted Palmer, *"Martinson Revisited,"* Journal of Research in Crime and Delinquency (July 1975): 133-152.

11. Robert Martinson *"What Works?—Questions and Answers about Prison Reform,"* The Public Interest, no. 35 (Spring 1964): 22-54.

12. David Fogel, *". . . We Are the Living Proof . . ." The Justice Model for Corrections* (Cincinnati: W. Anderson Company, 1975) pp. 245-260.

13. James Q. Wilson, *Thinking about Crime* (New York: Basic Books, 1975), pp. 172-173.

14. Douglas Lipton, Robert Martinson, and Judith Wilks, *The Effectiveness of Correctional Treatment* (New York: Praeger, 1975).

15. Thomas S. Kuhn, *Structure of Scientific Revolutions* (Chicago and London: University of Chicago Press, 1962).

16. Wilson, *Thinking about Crime,* pp. 200-201.

11 Beat the Dead Horse, but He Rises Again

Except for the publications of the American Correctional Association, there is little said and less written to constitute an apologia for the American prison. Denunciations are customary, and the kindest words are to the effect that these necessary evils must become less evil. Not many programs for the achievement of such an improvement are advanced, although the evils are always described in painful detail.

I am in full agreement with this position; I know that something must be done if the nation is not to be shamed again by such tragedies as the horrifying events at Santa Fe, New Mexico, in early 1980. We cannot continue to administer prisons as though they are about to disappear and therefore need no improvement. Yet the literature of prison abolition and reduction allows no credit for the people who hope to make prisons less unbearable. Indeed, advocates of moratorium on prison construction often respond as though the improvement of conditions is a futile endeavor, which, if it succeeded, would only make the task of dismantling the system more difficult.

"No enemies to the left!" So goes the old slogan of French socialists. I know and admire the advocates of extreme reductivism, but my involvement in prison-reform litigation during recent years has convinced me that it is urgent both to rebuild the physical plants of our generally repellent old fortress-prisons and also to rebuild the staffs of these places from top to bottom. The abolitionist movement does not make such a campaign easy to undertake.

In 1977 the editors of the Journal of Criminal Law and Criminology *offered me the opportunity to write a review essay of recent books by two prominent advocates of abolition or extreme reduction. I took that as a chance to urge that the emergency in corrections will not be settled by a moratorium; the need is measures to make prisons safe and lawful. I do not think that, alone, the "correctional establishment" can accomplish this task.*

Ever since the publication of that uncompromising polemic, *Struggle for Justice,* by the American Friends Service Committee, the American prison

I am grateful to the editors of the *Journal of Criminal Law and Criminology* for permission to reprint this chapter. The original will be found in vol. 68, no. 1, pp. 160-164. I have made some minor editorial changes.

has been an easy and frequent target for attack from many and widely divergent quarters.[1] Events have kept them in public view. Attica, the tragedies at San Quentin and Soledad, and spectacular disturbances at other prisons throughout the country have reminded all concerned parties that something must be done about the hideous conditions in which we keep our convicted offenders. The federal courts have set some limits to those conditions through a succession of decisions, with supporting opinions, that have established rights for men and women who had previously been treated as civilly dead. The powers of wardens and guards, formerly limited only by their estimate of public tolerance, are now curtailed by the application of due process. The jaded aphorists are wrong when they assert that the more prisons change, the more they are the same. No one should assume that there has been substantial improvement in the ugly routines of cellblock management, or that contentment reigns in the nation's prison yards. Nevertheless some abuses have been abruptly stopped by firm and courageous judges, and the conditions have been created by which changes for the better can be made by administrators minded to make the possible real.

The five years that have elapsed since the Quakers' frontal assault on the practice of incarceration have seen the flowering of a whole literature of penological commentary and criticism. To bring order to this proliferation, Gordon Hawkins proposed in his recent disquisition, *The Prison*, a typology of prison critics.[2] Abolitionists wish to do away with prisons altogether. Rigorists want to make them tougher. Reformers advocate continued pursuit of the rehabilitative ideal. Reductivists reject the ideology of rehabilitation and argue that although prisons are necessary, they should be used as little as possible. In this chapter I shall make some use of the taxonomy, even though it is too neat for the clash of ideas it is intended to classify.

The two books under consideration here fall into separate bins. Murton's *The Dilemma of Prison Reform*, is a reductivist tract, aimed at the penological liberal.[3] Sommer's *The End of Imprisonment* argues the abolitionist case.[4] Murton is a practical man with little stomach for the practice of incarceration as he has known it but unable to foresee an early end to it. Hawkins points out that the true abolitionist is a rare bird indeed, best exemplified by that eloquent nineteenth-century anarchist, Prince Peter Kropotkin. Until the publication of Sommer's book, Kropotkin's nearest modern counterpart was Jessica Mitford.[5] Like Mitford and Kropotkin, Sommer advocates the abolition of the prison as a phase in the fundamental overhaul of all our social institutions.

Both abolitionists and reductivists take naturally to the recital of correctional horrors, and both Murton and Sommer lay about them with admirable vigor in ticking off the wishful euphemisms and brutal actualities of correctional control. Both writers try with might and main to beat the horse dead. Neither succeeds. The horse plods on. His route leads nowhere, but he seems more likely to gain in strength than to collapse from the belaboring he receives from these authors.

The adventures of Thomas Murton in Arkansas and elsewhere are well known to the criminal-justice public and beyond. It is not difficult to dismiss the strategy of confrontation that he exemplified as quixotic and self-defeating. He was sent packing by a state government unwilling to face up to horrors that it had ignored, or to change its ways as fast as Murton's unwelcome discoveries required. Nevertheless, ever since that confrontation the Arkansas prisons have been emerging from a slough of brutality and incomparable misery. Some of the credit for change must be Murton's, some of it must go to the federal judiciary, which pronounced the Arkansas prisons unconstitutional. None of it can go to the late Governor Winthrop Rockefeller or to the political villains in the legislature whom Murton denounces. A forthright stand against iniquity is inconsistent with the style of the times. We prefer to administer our way out of nastiness, but it should not require a blue-ribbon task force or even a staff committee to smell out a wrong that has been done and to prescribe the steps for putting an end to it.

Murton tells his story as a chapter in the long and miserable history of punishment. Much of what he has to tell has been better told by others; he is not a trained historian. Many pages are given over to heavy-handed irony, angry rhetoric, and the denunciation of evil. He would have done better to allocate that space to a careful account of what actually happened in Arkansas as a case study in the politics of prison reform. The mighty thwacks that Murton administers to all the correctional rogues who have come to his attention would have been more effective if they had been better documented.

It would not have required an investigation in depth of the callousness of Murton's villains to identify in them the same banality of evil that Hannah Arendt discovered in Adolf Eichmann. I am well enough acquainted with some of these penal ruffians to venture a perspective on their infamy. Most of them are godly bureaucrats by their own lights, kind to their families and considerate of their subordinates. Caught in a system in which the resources provided them are grossly insufficient for the decent performance of the tasks to be done, they lapse from helplessness into inertia. Their rationalizations for the conditions over which they preside are laced with cynicism. The public may hear from them a resounding "commitment" to the rehabilitation of offenders and the reform of the system, but the annual rejection of their budget-augmentation requests does not prompt them to resign their posts in favor of a campaign to remedy conditions. As seniority overtakes them, they are called on to testify concerning the conditions in the facilities ruled by brother wardens. They are always supportive. In their own domains, paperwork fills their days; inspection of their facilities is left to subordinates. They do what they think they must, and they explain their inability to do more by pointing to the law, the budget, and the indifference of the general public. They find ways to justify, or at least to excuse the promiscuous use of force, they tolerate the filth and the disorder in their institutions, and they indignantly resist the attempts by outsiders to improve the system. It remains for the federal judiciary, prompted by a few boat-rockers like Murton and a few persistent convict writ-writers to correct the most egregious abuses. Judges may interfere, but it is not within their province to manage the system or to remedy the fundamental causes of mismanagement.

There is indeed a *Dunciad* to be written about penal bureaucrats, but Murton is no Alexander Pope, in spite of the passion of his invective. Nor does he have the scope for a theoretical formulation that would furnish the reader with hope for better things to come. He concedes that this country will need prisons for as long as our troubled society generates the level of violence from which we now suffer. To remedy the awfulness of the American prison, he urges a model of participatory management in which prisoners would be allowed a maximum share in the administration of the communities in which they live. Citing the examples of Alexander Maconochie, Thomas Mott Osborne, Howard Gill, and his own brief efflorescence in Arkansas, he proposes a sort of village life for correctional staff and residents. Around a "downtown" of central services, residential "suburbs" would be clustered in which life would resemble as nearly as possible the polity of a democratic small town. Murton does not tell us how he would maintain an approximation of normal community life within coercively enforced boundaries. Although he takes note of the abrupt termination of the four experiments on which he draws for his model, he does not explain how his plan for participatory management could avoid the same melancholy fate.

Sommer's anger at what he has seen, read, and heard suffuses his book. A psychologist of distinction and unusual originality, he has made important contributions to an understanding of the interaction between man and manmade environments. Invited by the Law Enforcement Assistance Administration (LEAA) to participate in studies of the impact of the manmade prison on prisoners and staff, he expected at first to help modify the oppressive models in which correctional restraint has taken place for nearly two centuries. This undertaking was part of a major effort by LEAA to assure that its investment in correctional construction would be held to standards of rationality and humanity that had not hitherto characterized American prison architecture.

From this initiative LEAA received more than it bargained for. Moyer and Flynn produced their immense *Guidelines for Correctional Design* and organized the National Clearinghouse for Criminal Justice Program and Architecture, by which the processes of design review were institutionalized for the time that LEAA provided substantial funding for prison and jail construction.[6] Nagel undertook and completed a survey of recent prison construction, documenting the inadequacies and suggesting new approaches to the design of such prisons as society continues to need.[7] Johnston wrote a companion study, a history of prison architecture, which defined the monstrous errors of the nineteenth century and the assumptions about human nature on which they rested.[8] Sommer described his initial approach to the assignment of making connections between environmental psychology and prison architecture:

> I believed that the problems of the prison could be solved by building small, modern institutions close to the inmate's home, with ample amenities, privacy, provision for family contact, counseling, academic and vocational training, and access to community facilities. This was a liberal dream which might have worked except that it didn't take into account the obvious facts that prison is used for only a small number of offenders in a highly discriminatory manner and that most of these offenders are losers who are marked indelibly by the experience.[9]

Examining the liberal dream insofar as it was realized in the California correctional system, in which brains and money have been applied in the attempt to make prisons both humane and useful, Sommer concludes that the task is hopeless. The only honest course is to bring the prison as an institution to an end as quickly as possible. Relentlessly he asserts the prison's failures, insisting that it survives only by reason of a childish strain of thought about human beings which he calls "paleologic," following Arieti's coinage of the term as a tool for understanding the thought patterns of schizophrenics. Rationality in approaching crime and correction would discard the idea and practice of incarceration as an ineffective waste of resources when such less destructive alternatives are available as fines, reprimands, public ridicule, banishment, and restitution.

For the present, Sommer thinks, the first step is to empty the prison of the 85 to 90 percent of its inmates who are not "violent, predatory offenders." This figure recurs frequently in the rhetoric of abolitionism. It is usually attributed to an unidentified prison warden who proffers the estimate based on data as he does not specify. Although it is obvious in any review of prison records that there are many prisoners whose crimes hardly merit incarceration, no one has undertaken a survey to determine the proportion they make up of the total prison population.

Sommer does not make clear what he thinks should happen to the residue of violent predators. At one point he suggests that with "ample back-up staff and money" they might be released into the community (p. 181). Elsewhere, he endorses a proposal to sentence all offenders to a short term of detention, no more than six months. Those who are to be confined for longer would be presented for jury consideration, to determine whether they presented a sufficient danger to society to justify their continued imprisonment. In such proceedings, the burden of proof would be on the state to establish the dangerousness of the offender. "Since this task is extremely difficult, and most expert opinion in this area is suspect, the state is probably not going to attempt to hold many people beyond the initial six-months period." In a footnote, Sommer adds that "the development of suitable procedures to protect the rights both of convicted offenders and of society will require a considerable amount of both legal and legislative work" (p. 175).

If it is uncertain how the detention of the offender is going to work out in the friendly new world that Sommer foresees, the justification for the uncertainty is explicit. He cites with approval the position laid out by the Norwegian criminologist Thomas Mathiesen in his carefully reasoned *The Politics of Abolition*.[10] Mathiesen's disquisition distinguishes between positive reforms that aim at abolishing the present system and negative reforms that perpetuate it. Thus, if Sommer has correctly understood Mathiesen, either of the approaches he suggests can be justified if they are planned within the conceptual framework of abolitionism. Maybe all prisoners can be turned loose, or maybe it would serve the ends of abolition better if all offenders were subjected to brief incarceration. These matters can be decided later, once society has agreed to abolish the whole system of corrections.

But Mathiesen does not conclude his advocacy of abolition on any such note. Essential to his position is the principle that social change is never finished. To him, the abolition of the prison is only a step in the endlessly unfinished business of abolition. In his suggestive explication, "the maintenance of an abolition implies that there is constantly more to abolish, that one looks ahead and toward a new and still more long-term objective of abolition, that one constantly moves in a wider circle to new fields of abolition."[11]

This is the politics of continuous revolution, not far from the principles once propounded by the late Mao Tse-tung. The returns on the strategy of Chinese communism are still awaiting final assessment, but it is obvious that Mao's successors intend to bank the fires of perpetual revolution. However that may be, a cultural revolution is an improbable eventuality in the United States. Our business is certainly unfinished, but the sense in which this is true is the gradualism that the revolutionary finds distasteful. Until and unless we abolish the prison as a part of an encompassing abolitionist strategy, it seems inevitable that we will have to use the prison as a social control of last resort. If the signs of the times mean what they seem to mean, we shall almost certainly build a good many new prisons in the near future. The question that now confronts us is the question that Sommer refused to address: What can be done to make the future prison more bearable than the present?

We return to the liberal dream, the failure of which caused Sommer to embark on his abolitionist course. The prospects for improving our prisons are conjectural at best. Throughout the nation prisons are seriously over-crowded, and the condition is getting worse. Some far-sighted ad-ministrators are trying to muster support for plans to build what Sommer scorns as "modern, pastel-hued prisons," of the kind that he considers without merit. Elsewhere the choice lies between building new megaprisons and toleration of severe overcrowding. Some reductivists hold that over-crowding is to be welcomed because it will force the state to release all of-fenders who are not demonstrably dangerous. This is the position taken by the American Friends Service Committee in the *Struggle for Justice*.[12] Other reductivists, myself included, believe that new construction cannot be avoided if our prisons are not to become more shameful than they already are. Public impatience with the present level of crime will not be eased by alternatives to incarceration, nor will it be put off by the prospective reconstruction of the social order that the abolitionsts urge as the only hope for urban peace. The increased use of alternatives to incarceration is surely feasible if the public could be persuaded to accept such apparent leniency as appropriate for the punishment of serious criminals. It is beyond any doubt in my mind that the connections between urban crime and grave social and economic injustice are close and getting more and more noxious. Until the country accepts these propositions and acts on them, men and women will continue to be jammed into old prisons that should have been demolished decades ago.

The source of our confusion is in the muddy reasoning that allowed the idea of success and failure to be applied to the operations of criminal justice in general and of prisons in particular. Here is a peculiarly American habit of thought, indispensable in economic endeavors but fatally inappropriate for the evaluation of the processes of justice. A business succeeds if it makes a profit and fails if it does not. A football team succeeds if it wins all or most of its games, and fails if it does not. For a good many years after World War II, which was a great success, Americans were persuaded that the criminal-justice system could be properly assessed by its effect on the crime rates, as measured by the Federal Bureau of Investigation. By the same reasoning, a correctional system's success could be measured by its rate of recidivism. Few police chiefs or judges were replaced because the crime rate rose in their jurisdictions; few correctional administrators, whether competent or not, have been inconvenienced by a rise in the recidivism of offenders released from their facilities. Yet we hear from both Murton and Sommer, and many of their colleagues leaning to abolitionism, that prisons have failed and therefore should be abolished.

The truth is that the criminal-justice system can never eliminate nor even significantly reduce the incidence of crime. Whatever the prison is able to do, it certainly has never shown any power to influence the crime rates. We should never have expected that such a goal was achievable. We declared war on crime, anyway, and pumped billions of dollars into the support of our "crime fighters" just as resources were unstintingly poured into the military during the war against the Axis powers. An authentic war against the military forces of an enemy can be won or lost. A war against crime is a metaphor and not a very useful metaphor at that. Out of the campaign we have learned a little: the police can prevent very little crime, the courts can do little to deter it, and the prisons do not seem to be able to do more than intimidate some of the offenders who are committed for a first time.

Criminal justice must be seen as a process without goals or long-range objectives. Its success or failure cannot be measured by statistical dents in the slopes of the crime rates. Instead we must learn to think of the system as consisting of interacting agencies of the state, each with immediate and well-defined tasks to perform. These tasks can be and must be performed well. What is intolerable is the cynical acceptance of nonfeasance and misfeasance. The police should apprehend more criminals, prepare the cases against them better, and deal fairly and efficiently with the victims of crime. The courts should dispense justice without delay and with even hands. The prisons should hold offenders securely, safely, and humanely, providing such assistance as is possible to promote resocialization. Success is to be judged in the performance of these tasks. Unfortunately, there is little evidence that anyone, even the performers, is prepared to assess the achievement of the system in these terms. For too many years we have all been mesmerized by a teleological perspective on criminal justice. In that baleful light, no success is conceivable. If crime is out of control, it must be because there are not enough policemen—so this reasoning goes—or because judges are soft-headed, or because prisons are failing to reform prisoners. The first step toward realism in crime control is to abandon teleology and long-range goals. We must expect less of the criminal-justice system; we must expect no more than the decent and efficient performance of its immediate duties. The second step is to expect much more of our other social institutions.

Here we will find the sorest point of all. Our human-service institutions are generally losing public confidence but in no sector of society so much as among the poor. The poor have always received poor services, where they have had any at all. Their schools are usually the oldest and most dilapidated in any city, poorly staffed and overcrowded. Their hospitals are smelly theaters of death and despair. Welfare offices are neither sensitive to clients' needs nor efficient in meeting them. The worst services of all are generally to be found in our prisons, which until recently have mostly been inhabited by poor people. The crimes they commit can best be understood as adaptations to the conditions of poverty. There are other adaptations: casual labor, dependency on welfare, drugs, and alcohol—and for a lucky few, upward mobility out of poverty. It is a sore point that both the criminal and the noncriminal poor, standing in the most need of human services, get the poorest quality. But even the American prison spruces up its management and its services when it has to cater to middle-class offenders, as though to demonstrate that the typical prison—the Big House—is really intended for the poor, who somehow do not require the amenities and consideration afforded to malefactors of more affluence.

There are exceptions to the rule that the poor are poorly served. Religious orders and societies do what has to be done in accordance with what they perceive as a divine mandate. Altruists form societies to relieve distress. Even in the civil services many are to be found who are motivated to help and who possess the training to help efficiently. In these kinds of exceptions to the dreary rules that govern the lives of America's poor are to be found hopes for change for the better. Our prisons can be better and it is worthwhile to try. The contrast between the wickedness to be found in the mismanagement of some and the altruism to be found in the management of others establishes the possibility of hope within the least promising of our public institutions.

So far as he goes, Mathiesen is right. Society is always unfinished. The way out of stagnation and oppression is to recognize this endlessly unfinished state of affairs. But Mathiesen is wrong in his stand that abolition is a route to a better world. We have to identify the sources of the wrongdoing performed in our behalf by the state, as Murton and Sommer have done, but we have to build on what we have. We must consider the meaning of our occasional successes and our frequent mistakes in doing what has to be done. We have no other choice.

Notes

1. American Friends Service Committee, *Struggle for Justice* (New York: Hill and Wang, 1971).

2. Gordon Hawkins, *The Prison: Policy and Practice* (Chicago and London: University of Chicago Press, 1976), pp. 5-29.

3. Thomas O. Murton, *The Dilemma of Prison Reform* (New York: Holt, Rinehart and Winston, 1976).

4. Robert Sommer, *The End of Imprisonment* (New York: Oxford University Press, 1976).

5. Jessica Mitford, *Kind and Usual Punishment: The Prison Business* (New York: Knopf, 1973).

6. Fred D. Moyer, Edith E. Flynn, Fred A. Powers, and Michael J. Plautz, *Guidelines for the Planning and Design of Regional and Community Correctional Centers for Adults* (Urbana, Ill.: Department of Architecture, University of Illinois, 1972).

7. William G. Nagel, *The New Red Barn: A Critical Look at the Modern American Prison* (New York: Walker, 1973).

8. Norman Johnston, *The Human Cage: A Brief History of Prison Architecture* (New York: Walker, 1973).

9. Sommer, *End of Imprisonment*, p. v.

10. Thomas Mathiesen, *The Politics of Abolition* (London: Martin Robertson, 1974).

11. Mathiesen, *Politics of Abolition*, pp. 211-212.

12. American Friends Service Committee, *Struggle for Justice*.

Index

About the Author

John P. Conrad is a project director and a member of the board of directors of the American Justice Institute. Before joining the Institute, he was a Senior Fellow of the Academy for Contemporary Problems of Columbus, Ohio, where he was codirector of the Dangerous Offender Project. He has served as a Senior Fulbright Fellow at the London School of Economics and a Visiting Expert at the U.N. Asia and Far East Institute for the Prevention of Crime and the Treatment of Offenders at Fuchu, Japan.

Mr. Conrad received the bachelor's degree in political science from the University of California and the master's degree in social-service administration from the University of Chicago. He has held teaching appointments at the University of California at Davis, the University of Pennsylvania, and Ohio State University.

Most of Mr. Conrad's career has been spent in correctional services. For twenty years he served in various capacities in the California Department of Corrections. In 1967 he became chief of research of the U.S. Bureau of Prisons. He later served as chief of the Center for Crime Prevention and Rehabilitation of the National Institute for Law Enforcement and Criminal Justice, now the National Institute of Justice. From 1974 to 1976 he was chief editor of *Journal of Research in Crime and Delinquency*. Since 1977 he has conducted a column on criminological research titled "News of the Future" in *Federal Probation*.